CONTENTS

INTRODUCTION: THE BANANA REPUBLIC OF GREAT BRITAIN AND NORTHERN IRELAND

'In a time of universal deceit, telling the truth is a revolutionary act'.

Britain. What does it mean to you? You might be someone reading this from overseas, bewildered at what's become of a country once renowned for stability, moderation and pragmatism. Or you might be someone exhausted by everything surrounding Brexit: the anger, the division, the paralysis, the sheer poison of it all.

Alternatively, you might have long since realised how far this small island's image outstripped the reality. How its international fame and prodigious levels of soft power masked a history hugely dependent on imperial exploitation; a society which has remained extraordinarily class-ridden; a country for haves, not have-nots.

I left Britain in 2012. My reasons were various; but near the top was a belief that the UK had had it for at least the rest of the decade. I could already see what Conservative / Liberal Democrat austerity was doing to the country: ripping its foundations away, leaving its most vulnerable to suffer with no safety net and no hope.

In 2010, under a Labour government, the welfare state protected me. It gave me the chance to choose a new career; I was even fortunate enough to have understanding jobcentre advisors who realised that, with an extremely academic background, there was little point in my applying for things I was chronically over-qualified for. The teacher training course I enrolled in was almost entirely funded by the EU; the housing benefit I received kept a roof over my head and allowed me to move forwards.

The economic insulation I received then is denied so, so many now. The government has deliberately made it as difficult as possible for the disabled or the long-term unwell to receive benefits; many die waiting for appeals to be heard. Meanwhile, those who look for work - even many in work - receive the national disgrace of universal credit: set at a level so miserly, it's close to impossible for them (and literally impossible for many struggling in self-employment) to make ends meet. And which, monstrously, isn't even provided until five weeks after someone applies for it. What they are supposed to do during that time - how they're expected to feed, heat or clothe themselves and their families - has never been explained.

All this has been accompanied by a disgusting narrative which shames the whole country. A narrative which treats the poor and vulnerable as somehow deserving to suffer; entirely ignores the human stories and appalling costs of austerity; and has barely even referred to studies which confirm just how many people have been killed by it.

When an entire country behaves like this; when it forgets the essential ties which bind us all; rewards those born into wealth and privilege if they then walk all over others and lie through their teeth in doing so (Exhibit A: the current prime minister); when it celebrates narcissists while demeaning those who care for others; is completely disinterested in truth or detail; and when its media parrots the falsehoods of the powerful, while itself relentlessly smearing the powerless, Brexit is the sort of thing which results. Yet three-and-a-half years on from that fateful night, nothing appears to have been learned at all. In fact, it's still getting worse.

This book is for anyone, whether within or without the UK, trying to piece together the events of the past decade. Trying to answer the question: 'How did we get here?' Searching for answers, solutions, some sort of hope for the future.

But as you read, I want you to ask yourself a further question. You see, it shouldn't be possible for someone who has lived away from Britain for almost eight years to know more about it than many (perhaps even most) of those there. I live in Uruguay, a small country in the South Atlantic, thousands of miles away from Old Blighty. So I encourage you to keep asking yourself: 'How can someone in Uruguay know so much about the UK which I don't?' The answer, as you'll see, mostly lies with the toxic, compulsively lying British press.

It started with Iraq. The rush to war. Rolling news stations getting the popcorn ready as the UK prepared to rain down bombs, missiles and depleted uranium on an entire people. 'Cheese-eating surrender monkeys'. 'Mission Accomplished'. And through a protracted, almost interminable build-up, with wall-to-wall coverage and conversation, almost no journalist anywhere even bothered to ask themselves: 'Does Iraq still have Weapons of Mass Destruction? Is it really capable of attacking Britain within 45 minutes? Is there any evidence for either proposition?'

It moved on to the deficit. 'Labour has spent us into oblivion! Labour has crashed the economy!' It wasn't just the Tories who chorused this. It was the media. A political party in Western Europe was blamed for an entire global crash... even when its then leader displayed exceptional wisdom and coolness of nerve at a time of real crisis. So much so that by the second quarter of 2010, when according to some, one of the richest countries in the world, with full control over its monetary supply, 'could turn into Greece', the UK grew at a faster pace than at any point since 2001.

On it went, to austerity. 'We have to live within our means!' Any economist who highlighted this utter nonsense - that by cutting, cutting, and cutting some more, we were also cutting our own national income, and placing the economy into deep freeze - was derided as a 'deficit denier'. 'It would be immoral', insisted the government and its many shameless cheerleaders, 'for us to pass our debts onto our children'... all the while those debts grew, grew, and grew some more. Austerity, noted Paul Krugman, was like 'repeatedly hitting yourself in the face for a few minutes'. Krugman was baffled by the British public actively voting for such masochism. I'll tell you why, Paul. It's the media.

What is the role of the political and news media in a modern, democratic country? To report accurately, objectively and fairly; and on behalf of the public, hold truth to power. To give power and a voice to those who have none. Yes, it will always be a conduit between political parties and the populace: but that involves questioning, scrutinising, and supplying critical analysis. For over 15 years now, most of the British media has simply abandoned this. Corporate, vested interests of tax dodging, offshore, billionaire owners rule; journalists go into politics, and vice versa; truth is not told. Propaganda is spread instead. And here's the thing: that propaganda costs lives. Many of them.

According to research, austerity has probably resulted in at least 130,000 more deaths than would otherwise have occurred. 130,000 people (and the real figure is probably much higher), likely dead as a result of national economic illiteracy encouraged by much of the British press. Mortality rates have sharply increased; life expectancy in twenty-first century Britain has begun to fall. In parts of the UK, generally those parts most ravaged by cuts to public services, it has fallen by more than a year.

The Independent, The Guardian and The Mirror cover stories about this sort of thing. Almost nobody else can be bothered. Despite the power which much of the media continues to hold, there is no attempt to educate or inform the British public; no effort to shine a light on hardship and injustice. Instead, when the government parrots tropes such as 'welfare is a lifestyle choice', these are repeated: stigmatising all those who have no voice at all.

After finding that the nature of austerity breached the UK government's obligations to human rights, and therefore contravened international law, the United Nations denounced its failure to reflect the UN Convention on Disabled People's Rights in either policy or law. Instead, its cuts had caused a 'human catastrophe' for disabled people.

In any genuinely civilised country, which hadn't so utterly lost all sense of its decency, morality or heart, this would've represented a national humiliation. It would've demanded profound, serious soul-searching; to heed the UN's findings, and right these appalling wrongs. And it also would've been front page news across not just the left-leaning press... but all the press. Yet how many British people even know about it? How many of them even know about the suffering going on out of sight, out of mind, behind closed doors?

There used to be a criticism, which I still subscribe to in part, that under Ed Miliband's leadership, the Labour Party had failed miserably either to challenge the economic narrative or make its own one. So great was this failure that during the 2015 general election campaign, Miliband's refusal to acknowledge before a live BBC audience that Labour had over-spent during its time in office (but he was right; it hadn't) was greeted with opprobrium, and surely contributed to his party's defeat.

Yet consider. In the last 40 years, only one Labour leader has ever been given anything like a fair hand by the media. The leader who promised to maintain Tory spending plans; whose party had lurched unrecognisably to the right; who knelt at Rupert Murdoch's bootlaces, licking furiously. Tony Blair was only so successful because he pledged so little change. And while New Labour did have a whole host of real achievements, it also lost many millions of voters: who were effectively abandoned by the entire British political process.

Against such a backdrop - a media more concerned with how Miliband looks when eating a bacon sandwich than at least 130,000 people dead as a result of austerity - what chance does any Labour leader have? Their message will always be twisted, manipulated, distorted beyond all recognition. And in this age of social media, up pop so many who read the headlines, hear the soundbites, but aren't interested in the detail, to keep propagating that distortion, and continue spreading the lies.

More than anything else, the 2016 EU referendum revealed just how powerful the right-wing press in Britain have become. A year earlier, David Cameron was granted a pliant media, happy to repeat his disgraceful lie that when he took office, Britain 'had run out of money'; but at the referendum, the shoe was on the other foot. The message of the Remain campaign, however inept it undoubtedly was, was muzzled.

Instead, during a campaign which debased British politics as maybe never before, the 'we can have our cake and eat it' nonsense of Leave held sway. Incomprehensibly, almost nobody among the media bothered to ask themselves: 'What happens if we vote to go?' Specifically: 'How can we have tariff-free trade if we reject freedom of movement? How can we retain a soft border in Ireland if we leave the customs union? How can we export food with a chronic shortage of vets? How in the world will we be able to re-tariff imports to the satisfaction of the entire membership of the WTO in just two years?'

On polling day itself, Britain behaved like a drunk, high on excitement, oblivious to danger. The following morning, it awoke with a hangover unlike any in its modern history... because now, there would be consequences. Colossal ones. First to break this reality to a delirious, very confused nation were Nigel Farage, who abruptly announced that the NHS would not be receiving an extra £350m per week after all; and Faisal Islam, who discovered that the British government, unforgivably, had no actual plan for how to go about leaving the EU at all. And neither, equally unforgivably, did the Leave campaign.

The repercussions of all this are still ongoing even now. All are a result of a public being charged with a decision they weren't qualified to make, by a government and entire political system which had treated most of it with utter contempt for decades. The kicking which resulted was richly deserved... but the lies from the media only intensified even more.

Lies about Parliament: described as the 'enemies of the people' for the crime of desperately trying to protect them from the economic and social catastrophe of No Deal. Lies about the Irish border, with non-existent, pie in the sky 'technological solutions' proposed not only by lunatic right-wing Tory MPs, but their media cheerleaders. And lies, above all, about Jeremy Corbyn: who has been called everything from a Czech spy to Lenin to Stalin to Trotsky to an authoritarian to being too weak to a terrorist sympathiser to an anti-Semite - not to mention quite staggering levels of deliberate misrepresentation of his stance on Brexit.

There has never been a time in modern British history when it's so incumbent on its public to question what it reads and what it hears from politicians and journalists alike. Every day, you are being lied to; every day, you are being played by those whose interests couldn't be further from yours. Those lies are what got the country into this appalling situation; only you, dear reader, can help put it right now.

Can it be put right? Certainly. By kicking the Tories out and voting for something truly different. Which can begin to heal those appallingly deep wounds, bring people together, invest in schools, hospitals, roads, infrastructure, put the country on the path to a truly green, sustainable future… and change the toxic, hostile environment into something warm, open and welcoming. Corbyn and Labour offer that chance. But my great fear is the lies will again triumph: with vastly more devastating consequences than before.

Even from far away, my heart is very much still with the UK. Being British is in my blood. I have friends and loved ones there; I know from them how devastating Tory policies have been to their lives, let alone so many others. To observe Britain from afar isn't merely to watch some sort of cataclysmic post-imperial nervous breakdown. It's to watch in horror as a whole country destroys its international reputation, internal and social cohesion, and sinks beneath the geopolitical waves. Not for nothing have some suggested it's not that far off becoming a failed state; and given everything this book covers, I don't think my reference to it as a Banana Republic is that far off the mark. Though that, of course, is for you to judge.

I also have a particularly personal reason for writing this book. Chapter 6, which covers the single most disgusting campaign of lies, smears, slander and sensationalism I have ever known in any democracy, explains what that is. We also look at Britain's absurd voting system and its many pernicious consequences; the futility of its third party, whose role is frequently cynical, nefarious and to huge numbers of people, causes immense harm; the Brexit referendum, both before and after; the metamorphosis of the Labour Party under Corbyn following Miliband's total failure; and both the media and increasingly dubious world inhabited by opinion pollsters.

We conclude on a (potentially) happier note, as I set out how you can change so much that's wrong with British politics and society; it's in your hands to do so, dear reader. But we begin where the decade began: with the wanton, vicious cruelty of austerity.

1: SOCIAL MURDER: AUSTERITY AND THE POLITICS OF BULLSHIT

'If you want a vision of the future, imagine a boot standing on a human face, forever' - George Orwell

At approximately 00:50 on 14 June 2017, a fridge freezer caught fire in Flat 16, on the fourth floor of Grenfell Tower, North Kensington[1]. Awoken by a smoke alarm, the flat's resident entered the kitchen, discovered the fridge freezer smoking, alerted his friends and neighbours, and called London Fire Brigade at 00:54. The first two fire engines arrived six minutes later, entered Flat 16 at 01:07, and began tackling the fire at 01:14.

Yet six minutes earlier, at 01:08, the fire had breached the window, and begun setting the surrounding cladding panels on fire. So by the time the firefighters started extinguishing the fire in Flat 16, a column of flames was advancing up the column of the building at a terrifying rate: reaching the roof by 01:30, spreading sideways, and bringing fire and smoke into multiple flats.

The fire moved from the east to the north side of the building. Fire doors inside did not close properly, so the smoke spread to the stairwell. Residents became trapped in their flats. Frantically, some switched their lights on and off and waved from windows to attract help. Four people jumped to their deaths; debris began falling off the building, including burning cladding. Frequent explosions were heard from inside. Only 20 people managed to escape between 01:38 and 01:58; more than half of those still in the building after that point would lose their lives.

The fire services were confronted by a challenge whose scale was unprecedented. But inside, their communications equipment did not work properly. The water pressure for the hoses was insufficient; Thames Water had to be contacted in order to increase it. Aerial appliances were not high enough, with a 42m firefighting platform arriving from Surrey only after the fire had been burning for several hours. There was near-zero visibility inside the stairwell. Crew Manager, Aldo Diana, reported: 'Basically you couldn't see your hand in front of your face. It was just thick black smoke. You didn't see anybody else. You literally had to bump into them'.

Like the enormous majority of high-rise buildings in the UK, the Grenfell Tower did not have a sprinkler system. A BBC Breakfast investigation into half the UK's housing association and council-owned tower blocks found that just 2% had sprinklers. England, Wales and Scotland now require such systems to be installed in newly built tall buildings; but there is no such requirement for existing ones.

The Tower had recently been renovated. The Conservative leader of Kensington and Chelsea Council, Nicholas Paget-Brown, said the residents 'did not have a collective view in favour of installing sprinklers'; yet ITV reported that their installation had never been discussed.

The renovation involved the façade of the Tower being fitted with exterior cladding (3mm aluminium sandwich plates with a polyethylene core); a ventilation gap of 50mm between the cladding and the insulation behind it; that insulation being made up of 150mm PIR (polyisocyanurate) foam plates mounted on the existing façade; the existing prefabricated reinforced concrete façade; and new double-glazed windows mounted in the same vertical plane as the foam plates. Both the cladding and insulation plates failed fire safety tests conducted after the disaster.

In 2014, the building inspectors' organisation, Local Authority Building Control (LABC), had stated that the chosen insulation should only be used on tall buildings with fibre cement panels, which do not burn. Yet combustible polyethylene panels were put on top of polyisocyanurate insulation, which burns when heated and gives off toxic cyanide fumes. Despite this, the Royal Borough of Kensington and Chelsea certified the building work as complying with the 'relevant provisions'.

Kooltherm, a phenolic insulation, was also used at Grenfell. According to its own manufacturer, Kingspan, it had never been tested with polyethylene core aluminium panels; and further, Kingspan themselves 'would be very surprised if such a system... would ever pass the appropriate British Standard 8414 large-scale tests'. Kooltherm's LABC certificate states that phenolic products 'do not meet the limited combustibility requirements' of building regulations.

The combustible materials used on the Tower were almost £300,000 cheaper than non-combustible alternatives. These savings were pursued despite Kensington and Chelsea being the richest local authority area in the entire UK: so rich that in 2014, it provided a £100 council tax rebate to all residents. So rich that for many years, it had run consistent underspends in its budgets, which it transferred into capital reserves. Which are so enormous, they could easily pay for sprinkler systems and non-combustible cladding whenever required.

In September 2014, a 'building notice' application for the re-cladding work was submitted to the authority and marked with a status of 'Completed - Not Approved'. Such notices are used to remove the need to submit detailed plans and proposals to a building control inspector in advance. Instead, the works are approved by an inspector during their construction. The building inspector, Geoff Wilkinson, commented that this type of application is 'wholly inappropriate for large complex buildings and should only be used on small, simple domestic buildings'.

Yet despite this cladding being banned on tall buildings in the UK, Grenfell Tower was inspected 16 times... and none of the inspections noted this. The cladding system was reportedly passed by a Kensington and Chelsea building control officer on 15 May 2015.

An estimated 600 high-rise blocks of flats have similar cladding in the UK. By late June 2017, 120 of these buildings in 37 different local authorities had failed fire safety tests: a 100% failure rate. Extraordinarily, despite the police commenting that at Grenfell, the insulation was 'more flammable than the cladding', these tests did not include the insulation. Instead, this was left to councils and landlords.

A year after the disaster, the government acknowledged that a further 156 towers in the private sector had cladding similar to that at Grenfell: a figure expected to rise higher still. At this point, only 19 buildings higher than 18m - including both affordable and private tower blocks - had had their dangerous cladding replaced; only four of 297 private buildings had been fully repaired, and just 17 more had repairs underway. Central government provisions for local councils to take charge of privately-owned buildings in ensuring safe cladding have failed in 90% of cases. Government funds have been withheld for many of these. Tens of thousands of people in the UK are still living in buildings wrapped in flammable cladding; let alone flammable insulation underneath.

And failure of government has been a constant, shameful pattern. As far back as 1986, the Thatcher government abolished a requirement for external walls to have at least an hour's fire resistance to prevent blazes from re-entering buildings and spreading to other flats. Moreover, after the Lakanal House fire of 2009, the coroner had made a series of safety recommendations to improve safety in tower blocks. The report pointed at the flammable panels which covered part of the exterior, lack of sprinklers or safety inspections. In the years following, four different ministers were warned about tower block fire risks highlighted by Lakanal House. Yet they, with Housing Minister, Gavin Barwell, among them, stonewalled requests for meetings and discussions about tightening rules.

On top of this, for years prior to the disaster, Grenfell residents had *themselves* been warning of the potential for catastrophe. In August 2014, the Grenfell Action Group (GAG) wrote the following on their website:

> A number of residents of Grenfell Tower are very concerned at the fact that the new improvement works to Grenfell Tower have turned our building into a fire trap.
>
> There is only one entry and exit to the tower block itself and, in the event of a fire, the LFB could only gain access to the entrance to the building by climbing four flights of narrow stairs.
>
> On top of this the fire escape exit on the walkway level has now been sealed.
>
> **Residents of Grenfell Tower do not have any confidence that our building has been satisfactorily assessed to cope with the new improvement works and we are seeking a meeting with the Chief Fire Officer from Kensington Fire Station so that these concerns can be addressed.**

These warnings proved uncannily prescient. In Germany, as well as laws banning flammable cladding on buildings higher than 22m, segregated fire-stairs and firefighting lifts which can be used by both the fire brigade and injured or disabled people are obligatory. Russ Timpson, of the Tall Buildings Fire Safety Network, commented that 'foreign colleagues are staggered' when learning that UK regulations permit high-rise buildings to only have one staircase.

The coroner for Lakanal House also criticised the Fire Brigade's 'stay put' policy, standard for high-rise buildings across the UK, which advises residents to stay in their flats if a fire breaks out elsewhere in the building. This advice depends on the assumption that construction standards such as concrete and fire-resistant doors will allow firefighters to contain the fire within one flat. Thus Grenfell was not even designed to be fully evacuated: it only had a single narrow staircase, and no centrally activated fire alarm system either.

Quite correctly, the report from the first phase of the public inquiry into the disaster has criticised London Fire Brigade (LFB) for maintaining the stay put policy for over an hour beyond when it should have been changed, as the fire was out of control. There are very serious lessons to be learned on that. But the policy effectively relies on good faith: for building regulations to have been met; local councils or private developers not to cut costs at the expense of safety; and above all, a holistic approach to regulation and building safety which simply does not exist in the UK.

In 2013, GAG published a fire risk assessment from the previous year which recorded safety concerns. Firefighting equipment at the Tower had not been checked for up to four years; onsite fire extinguishers had expired, with some even having the word 'condemned' written on them because they were so old. GAG documented its attempts to contact the management of the Kensington and Chelsea Tenant Management Organisation (KCTMO), responsible for managing the local council's housing stock; yet instead, the council threatened one of the bloggers with legal action, stating their posts amounted to 'defamation and harassment'.

In January 2016, GAG warned that people might be trapped in the building if a fire broke out. As well as only having one entrance and exit, corridors had been allowed to fill with rubbish, including old mattresses. In November, accusing the council of ignoring health and safety laws, the GAG website stated, 'only a catastrophic event will expose the ineptitude and incompetence of [KCTMO]'.

Also in 2016, an independent assessor highlighted no fewer than 40 serious fire safety issues at Grenfell, recommending that action be taken within weeks; yet by October, KCTMO had only acted in 20 of these cases. The following month, the London Fire Emergency and Planning Authority served a fire deficiency notice, which required action by KCTMO by May 2017. These included fire doors, the smoke ventilation system and firefighters' lift controls.

The Grenfell Tower disaster, which claimed 72 lives, and traumatised so many others (including firefighters charged with tackling a fire the like of which they'd never encountered before, despite faulty equipment, low water pressure, ladders which weren't high enough, oxygen which didn't last long enough, near-zero visibility and with the wrong advice provided by their superiors to residents, in a building which contravened safety regulations on every conceivable measure) was a perfect storm in so many ways. A legacy of deregulation of the housing sector, which continues to endanger so many others even now; in which residents had been continually ignored and treated with contempt by the richest local authority in the UK: which, to the disgust of the watching world, even continued in the days after the tragedy. Paget-Brown, tin-eared beyond belief, was eventually forced to resign; but not before his conduct had reminded us all how the poor are routinely disregarded and treated as third-class citizens in Tory Britain.

It is, of course, for the public inquiry to ultimately apportion responsibility and blame. The second phase, which starts next year, will look at the role of the companies involved in the renovation, and deregulation of building standards. But this hasn't stopped much of the right-wing media already misrepresenting Sir Martin Moore-Bick's first phase report, the press embargo surrounding which was broken. Moore-Bick did indeed severely question LFB: that is to say, its managers. Yet his comments were treated by a contemptible Fourth Estate as though they applied to the whole service; in other words, to firefighters who risked their lives to save so many others. As Moore-Bick said, they 'showed courage and devotion to duty'. If only ministers, the local council, KCTMO and those responsible for the renovation could say the same.

◆ ◆ ◆

Those firefighters represent the very best of Britain. Which automatically leads to the question: why, since 2010, have more than 10,000 firefighting jobs been cut, dozens of fire stations closed (including ten in London), fire engines scrapped and even the emergency rescue equipment slashed? Why, indeed, did Boris Johnson, then Mayor of London, respond to a question highlighting all these disastrous cuts with 'get stuffed'? The answer, of course, lies with austerity: accepted as necessary over the last decade thanks to the lies of the Conservatives and Liberal Democrats, which has deliberately targeted public services and the poor, while allowing the rich to get richer than ever.

It never ceases to amaze me just how many people cannot make the connection between massive cuts in budgets and jobs and much greater risks to everybody's safety. Johnson's successor, Sadiq Khan, is routinely held personally responsible for rising knife crime; but his authority is dependent on resources from central government. Since 2011, a billion pounds have been lost from the Metropolitan Police budget; and while London's population has grown by more than 1.5m since 2003, it has fewer police officers than at any point since. In fact, over the last decade, the number of police across the 43 forces in England and Wales has fallen by over 20,000. Absurdly, Theresa May denied any link between this fall and 'certain crimes'.

Austerity cuts across all aspects of society in all sorts of devastating ways.

As many as 1,000 Sure Start centres may have closed in England since 2010, with the poorest areas of the country worst hit. Thousands of children have ended up in hospital as a result. By 2015, nearly half of Rape Crisis organisations in England and Wales were facing closure due to lack of funding. Council support for women's refuges has been cut by nearly £7m.

Moreover, the local community provided five separate warnings about Salman Abedi, the Manchester suicide bomber: who killed 23 and wounded 139, more than half of them children. But of course, when police budgets are cut, so are community outreach services. And as we saw several times during the 2017 general election campaign, and again during this one too, in any society threatened by terrorism, cutting police numbers by such absurd amounts is a recipe for disaster.

All this is without even mentioning the minimum 130,000 unnecessary deaths caused by austerity (a figure which likely greatly underestimates the actual total); the doubling of the number of people claiming disability benefit attempting suicide; fully 74% of those denied Personal Independence Payments (PIP) by the Department of Work and Pensions (DWP) winning their appeals (because the private companies undertaking risible 'health assessments' do so for profit, and are incentivised to reject claimants): appeals which are often heard many months or even up to 17 months later. So what are claimants supposed to do in the meantime? How do they even survive? Hardly surprisingly, complaints about this disgustingly cynical process have risen by over 6,000% in just 3 years; while the DWP has wasted £200m in defending appeals and spent over £600m on extending the contracts of the disgusting companies responsible.

The policy of the government is easy to explain. The entire, monstrous idea has been to terrify the poor, the sick, the disabled into *not even trying to claim*. Because if they don't claim, it can make savings. Such an approach has also stigmatised these poor people in public opinion; so hate crime against disabled people is also rising alarmingly.

More than a million benefit sanctions have been imposed on disabled people alone since 2010. As for their able-bodied counterparts: in 2013, Manchester Citizens Advice Bureau compiled a comprehensive report on benefit sanctions. Its findings included:

40% of respondents not having received a letter from the jobcentre informing them of the sanction

Almost a quarter not knowing why they had been sanctioned
More than half receiving no information on how to appeal
Almost a third being sanctioned for 10 weeks or more
71% being left with no income whatsoever
71% being forced to cut down on food; 49% on heating
More than 80% going into debt as a result
Mental health conditions being severely exacerbated

Individual cases, meanwhile, were like something out of Kafka:

Someone being sanctioned for applying for 10 jobs in one week, five jobs in the next; because they were required to apply for seven jobs per week
Someone being sanctioned for arriving 15 minutes late for their appointment due to an earlier job interview
Someone not carrying on looking for work after securing a paid job
Someone sanctioned for attending a job interview over a benefits appointment
Someone sanctioned for not attending a benefits appointment on a day the office was closed

These were no rarities. Other cases of sanctioning, uncovered by the Trussell Trust in 2015, included:

A claimant who carried out 60 job searches, but was sanctioned for missing one that matched his profile
Missing an appointment because he was in hospital with his partner, who had just given birth to a stillborn child
Missing an appointment because his brother had died that day. He tried to ring the jobcentre and explain, but could not get through; so left a message which was not passed on
Missing an appointment because he had been hospitalised that day with a suspected heart attack
Missing an appointment because, although he had turned up in good time, *the length of the queue in the jobcentre* meant he couldn't keep it

There are many similar stories across the country. In 2012, Catherine Hale, who has suffered for many years with severe ME, was placed in the work-related activity group of those claiming Employment and Support Allowance (ESA) and referred to the jobcentre. She brought a copy of her work capability assessment (WCA) to show her jobcentre advisor. To which the response was: 'Oh, I can't look at that dear, I'm not even qualified to put on a sticky plaster'.

Six months later, letters began to arrive inviting Hale to attend an interview at a Work Programme provider and discuss what employment may be suitable. As Hale explained to The Guardian:

> Each letter came with a threat attached that if you do not turn up your benefit will be affected. The first time I was supposed to go I was really poorly and could barely get out of bed. I was aware I had to phone them up. They were all really rude and didn't pass on your messages. There was no compassionate human being in the system at all. I had a kind of breakdown from the anxiety. There was something about being framed as a worthless, feckless, good-for-nothing that left me feeling persecuted and empty of self-belief.

Then Seetec, the provider, informed her that the centre she was required to attend had moved to Woolwich, south London.

> I looked it up and it involved taking two trains and walking almost a mile. I advised them my WCA said I can't walk more than 200 metres and requested adjustments. I never got any reply to that letter or any other letter I've ever written to Seetec. Then I started getting letters mandating me to four-hour workshops three days a week for four weeks in a row. My WCA report says I can't sit for more than an hour without pain or discomfort so I wrote and pointed this out.

Yet she was nonetheless sanctioned by £71.20 per week and didn't even receive a letter to tell her. It's hard to imagine a more open and shut case of discrimination under the Equality Act 2010.

Jobcentre advisors were actually being incentivised by the DWP to administer sanctions. As Angela Neville, a former special advisor in a jobcentre, revealed: 'We were given lists of customers to call immediately and get them on to the Work Programme. I said, "I'm sorry this can't happen, this man is in hospital". I was told [by my boss]: "No, you've got to phone him and you've got to put this to him and he may be sanctioned"'. This, though, was merely the tip of a perniciously cruel iceberg:

> Staff are subjected to constant and aggressive pressure to meet and exceed targets. Colleagues would leave team meetings crying… the pressure was incredible. Advisers were actively encouraged to impose sanctions (along the lines of 'sanction of the month') to contribute to the points system that ranks jobcentre offices…
>
> And it was happening all the time. A customer maybe would be a little bit late or would phone in and the message wasn't passed on. It was very distressing to have customers literally without food, without heat, without resources and these are unwell [and] disabled customers.

Imagine for a moment that you were left entirely without income for eight weeks, ten weeks, even up to a year. What would you do? Hopefully you're fortunate enough to have friends or family who you could stay with, maybe even lend you money... but what if you didn't? What if you were completely on your own, without any income at all?

The answer is that unless you were lucky enough to find work very fast (an impossibility in the case of many disabled or long-term unwell people; a near-impossibility for homeless people), you'd very likely die. You'd die, like David Clapson: whose benefits were stopped after he missed one meeting at the job centre. Clapson was diabetic; and without his jobseekers' allowance, he couldn't afford to eat or put credit on his electricity card to keep the fridge where he kept his insulin working. When he died, Clapson had no food in his stomach. Yet the coroner refused to hold an inquest.

You'd die, like Stephen Smith: who had chronic obstructive pulmonary disease, osteoarthritis and an enlarged prostate which left him in chronic pain; yet was denied benefits and deemed fit to work. His weight dropped to six stone; shocking pictures from hospital made headline news around the UK. Tellingly, a review found that the DWP had 'followed policy'; in other words, *this is the policy.*

You'd die, like Jodey Whiting: who suffered multiple health issues, including curvature of the spine and a brain cyst, and took 23 tablets each day. She missed a work capability assessment because of being hospitalised with pneumonia, had her benefits stopped, and committed suicide two weeks later. The DWP has refused to allow Whiting's own mother, Joy Dove, to see the report into her daughter's death.

In August 2018, under a Freedom of Information request, the DWP was forced to release statistics which showed that 111,450 claims for ESA were closed following the deaths of claimants between March 2014 and February 2017. So are these among the people often headlined as having been killed by austerity?

No, they're not. The report which found that over 130,000 had died thanks to government policy only looked at preventable diseases or disorders such as heart disease, lung cancer or liver problems. It didn't look at those who died as a result of their benefits being stopped or denied at all. In other words, the real figure for austerity's death toll is *far, far higher* than 130,000: very likely, it's over 300,000.

I haven't even mentioned PIP claimants in the above. Of these, between April 2013 and April 2018, 73,800 died within six months of their claims being registered; 17,070 died after registering but before the DWP making a decision; 4,760 died between their case being referred to and returned from an assessment provider.

Of course, at least some of these people will have died naturally. But in a supposedly First World, fully developed country, hardly all or even most of them. Which is probably why the DWP doesn't keep records on cause of death: because it knows that if it does, it would be criminally liable. It even failed to send its own independent reviewer documents which linked the government's fitness for work test with the deaths of disabled benefit claimants. 'Peer reviews' into the deaths of such claimants are instead conducted in secret.

Where they should be conducted instead is in public: at a fully independent public inquiry. That is what any halfway civilised country would do. And it would also prosecute and imprison the ministers responsible. But this is Britain in 2019; so naturally, there's no chance of that.

So much so that when the United Nations' rapporteur on extreme poverty and human rights, Philip Alston, condemned the UK for austerity, describing child poverty levels as 'not just a disgrace, but an economic and social disaster'; said he had met people who sold sex for money and had joined gangs to avoid destitution; and compared the DWP's policies to those of nineteenth century workhouses - and when Theresia Degener, head of the UN Committee of the Rights of Persons with Disabilities, described welfare cuts as a 'human catastrophe', resulting in 'grave and systematic violations of the rights of disabled people', the response from the government was total, blanket denial; and from much of the media, it was... crickets. Nothing at all.

Which was a particular disgrace given the Orwellian gagging clauses which charities, voluntary sector organisations, social enterprises and other companies have been forced to sign in order to receive government funding. The clauses have been inserted into contracts by the DWP since 2015, and include such terminology as contractors 'must pay the utmost regard to the standing and reputation' of the DWP; and do nothing which either brings the DWP into disrepute or 'damages the reputation of the [DWP] or harms the confidence of the public in the [DWP]'. The UN reports provided the chance to finally get the government's disgusting policies discussed, and their hideous cruelty examined. But most of the media, whose job it is to hold a glaring flashlight to power, and what it is doing to the most powerless of all, could not have cared less.

As if all this wasn't enough already, I've yet to even touch upon universal credit: the rollout of which has been a disaster, is absurdly derisory and pushing families into destitution. There is a five-week wait before anyone receives anything (a wait which will inevitably have killed some claimants); and what's provided often barely even covers someone's rent, let alone their maintenance costs. In the case of self-employed people, many of whom are pushed into this by jobcentres desperate to get them off their books, (while the government crows about falling unemployment figures), yet don't have the skills required, if they earn *below* a certain threshold, they receive... no universal credit whatsoever. Yes, you read that correctly. Here's an illustrative example from the Citizens Advice Bureau:

Nadia is 22, single and works as a self-employed painter. She's expected to work 35 hours a week. This is used to calculate Nadia's expected monthly income, using the minimum wage for her age group of £7.70:

35 hours x £7.70 = £269.50 per week
£269.50 x 52 weeks = £14,014 per year
£14,014 ÷ 12 months = £1167.83 per month

The DWP take off £92.95 for tax and National Insurance.
This would make Nadia's expected monthly income, after deductions, £1,074.88 per month - this is her minimum income floor.

During January, Nadia earns £200.
Her Universal Credit payment is worked out using her minimum income floor of £1,074.88 per month.
This means her Universal Credit payment is lower than what she needs to cover her costs.

This is what the likes of David Cameron and Iain Duncan Smith meant with phrases such as 'we must make work pay'. It didn't mean pushing wages up to something dignified and reasonable. It meant cutting benefits below even subsistence levels; in some cases, to nothing at all.

Yet absolutely none of this - zero - has been necessary. Austerity carried out in this way, punishing the poor, the weak, the disabled, the infirm, the powerless, the voiceless, is and has always been a deliberate political choice. How do I know this? Because its entire foundation is based on not one, not two... but three separate lies.

The first lie was that 'Labour caused the 2008 crash'. It did not. A political party in Western Europe cannot cause a global financial crash, the origins of which lay in toxic sub-prime mortgages: which the Clinton administration began encouraging in the mid-1990s and were not regulated at all. And when the US sneezes, the rest of us catch a cold.

My source that Labour didn't cause the crash? Only George Osborne himself. Listen to this interview and ask yourself: what kind of country permits such a grotesque lie to become accepted as fact, and the man responsible to laugh it off and prosper from it?

The second lie: 'We'd run out of money / we could've become Greece!' A great deal of this owes to the cynical beyond belief manipulation and exploitation of a note which Liam Byrne, Chief Secretary to the Treasury, left his successor, David Laws. It read as follows:

> Dear Chief Secretary,
> I'm afraid there is no money. Kind regards - and good luck!
> Liam

In 1964, the outgoing Chancellor of the Exchequer, Reginald Maudling, left a near identical note to the incoming James Callaghan. 'Good luck, old cock... Sorry to leave it in such a mess'. Maudling wrote that at a time there was still common decency, even fraternity and respect, between politicians from different parties. Byrne, whose tone was the same, could not have appreciated that Cameron's Tories and his Liberal Democrat coalition partners would instead bring themselves and politics into total disrepute.

The Lib Dems spent summer 2010 constantly parroting the note as though it had been serious. In the 2015 election campaign, Cameron paraded around the country, waving the note everywhere he went. It was the absolute debasement of serious debate on something, government economic policy, which impacts hugely on every man, woman and child in the country. It was used to justify cuts so swingeing, they killed horrific numbers of people, as we have seen. The politics of bullshit.

The reality? It was rather different. Countries which control their own monetary supply (unlike Greece, or any euro member) cannot, by definition, 'run out of money'. And in the second quarter of 2010, at a time we were supposedly on the verge of 'turning into Greece', the economy grew more quickly than at any time since 2001. Its subsequent decade-long sluggishness has been a direct result of austerity: which never mind the moral objections to it, hasn't worked at all.

The Tories and the media used the preposterous Greek analogy to pile the pressure onto the Lib Dems to get the coalition negotiations over quickly. In other, grown-up countries, such negotiations take weeks, even months. In the meantime, life goes on as normal. But not in Britain: which in May 2010, was governed not by the people, not even by elected representatives, but by a combination of the right-wing press and financial speculators. Criminal ones.

Britain went to the polls on 6 May. In the early evening, UK time, a flash crash occurred on the US stock market: wiping a trillion dollars off stocks and shares. The Dow Jones plunged almost 1,000 points (9%); but had recovered considerably by the close. Five years later, the US Department of Justice laid 22 criminal counts, including fraud and market manipulation, against Navinder Singh Sarao, a trader. Among the charges were the use of spoofing algorithms: just prior to the crash, he placed thousands of E-mini S&P 500 stock index futures contracts, which he planned to cancel later. These orders amounted to 'about $200m worth of bets that the market would fall'... yet were 'replaced or modified 19,000 times' before being cancelled. Sarao did all this from his parents' house in Hounslow, west London.

This extraordinary event helped contribute to the media narrative during the days following the election. 'The markets are jittery... we need stability and certainty!' But that is the reality of a world based on financialisation and monetarism; whole countries' futures are in the hands of individuals whose interests are, to put it mildly, not yours and certainly not mine either.

The third lie, though, was much greater than even the other two. In 2010, Carmen Reinhart and Kenneth Rogoff wrote an enormously influential, widely cited paper: which concluded that in countries with a public debt of over 90% of GDP, this slows down growth. In February of that year, in his speech at the Mais lecture, Osborne, who would become Chancellor three months later, said the following:

> Perhaps the most significant contribution to our understanding of the origins of the crisis has been made by Professor Ken Rogoff, former chief economist at the IMF, and his co-author, Carmen Reinhart... The latest research suggests that once debt reaches more than about 90% of GDP, the risks of a large negative impact on long-term growth become highly significant.

Yet the entire thing was based on an error in a spreadsheet. A few rows left out of an equation to average the values in a column turned a conclusion which should've read that countries with 90% public debt ratios see their economies *grow by an average 2.2%* into one which stated, completely erroneously, that they fall by 0.1%. And an average 2.2% growth is far in excess of what Osborne delivered. Instead, by taking an axe to the state and social security, Slasher Osborne presided over the slowest recovery since the South Sea Bubble.

In 2009, Barack Obama, whose fiscal stimulus package took the US out of its worst economic predicament since the 1930s, explained the problem with austerity very simply.

> Economists on both the left and right agree that the last thing a government should do in the middle of a recession is to cut back on spending. You see, when this recession began, many families sat around their kitchen table and tried to figure out where they could cut back.
>
> That is a completely responsible and understandable reaction. But if every family in America cuts back, then no one is spending any money, which means there are more layoffs, and the economy gets even worse. That's why the government has to step in and temporarily boost spending in order to stimulate demand.

None of the above is rocket science. It's basic macro-economics. Countries are not run like household budgets. Instead, they're a lot more like enormous businesses, with the prime minister the CEO. Enormous businesses borrow to invest in state-of-the-art technology: investment which pays off hugely in the medium and longer term. You might be reading this as a small or medium-sized business owner; have you never borrowed to invest? You might also be reading this as a mortgage owner: borrowing massively in excess of your income enabled you to buy a home, which will since have turned into a hugely valuable asset, giving you and your family long-term security.

Yet when borrowing and investment are instead disincentivised, companies can't invest in technology, so productivity falls. And when a country cuts its expenditure, its income will fall in tandem. New businesses can't start up; people have less and less disposable income to put into the economy (a situation made far worse by social security cuts); all sorts of employers, public and private, lay people off: increasing the benefit bill at the same time as their turnover continues to fall. Watch this video here; it explains it all clearly and simply.

Have you ever seen the timeless *Ferris Bueller's Day Off*? Remember the hapless teacher trying to explain voodoo economics to a class of yawning teenagers? What Osborne and Cameron did wasn't that far off voodoo economics; it really wasn't far off the nonsense of the Laffer Curve.

In 1974, the economist, Arthur Laffer, literally invented an economic theory on the back of a napkin. Laffer claimed that cutting taxes on the rich was always right: because this would give them extra incentives, so they would work harder and pay the money back (and more besides) in extra revenue. This entire theory is essentially the basis of neoliberalism, so-called 'trickle-down economics', Reaganomics and Thatcherism.

As Jonathan Chait[2] explains in *The Big Con*, Laffer:

Pulled out a cocktail napkin and drew a parabola-shaped curve on it. The premise of the curve was simple. If the government sets a tax rate of zero, it will receive no revenue. And if the government sets a tax rate of 100 per cent, the government will also receive zero tax revenue, because nobody will have any incentives. Between these two points - zero taxes and zero revenue - Laffer's curve drew an arc. The arc suggested that at higher levels of taxation, reducing the tax rate would actually produce more revenue for the government.

But there was a problem. A rather large one. Laffer's analysis was completely at odds with reality in his own country, let alone anywhere else. From 1947 to 1964, the top rate of tax in the US was 91%. According to the Laffer Curve, the economy should have tanked throughout; but instead enjoyed the longest sustained boom of the twentieth century. In the 1980s, Reagan slashed the top rate; but there was a severe recession in 1982, and the growth that followed was merely an average recovery. Both Reagan and Thatcher's policies didn't so much result in 'economic miracles' as their nations moving from one slump to the next. In 1993, Clinton increased the top rate of tax from 31% to 39.6%, and Laffer predicted an economic collapse. In fact, the next long boom immediately followed: including in the UK.

All the evidence, all of it, is on the side of conventional Keynesian macro-economists. Countries in trouble spend themselves back out of it; cutting simply leads to more trouble. And more trouble. And even more trouble. Right now, in late 2019, global economic signs are increasingly ominous; yet instead of getting itself shipshape, Britain has doubled its national debt in a decade. All thanks to a policy built on at least three outright lies, if not more.

The brilliant economist, commentator and writer, Grace Blakeley[3], who in my view, is a future Labour Chancellor (and that's the bare minimum of what she's capable of), explained why austerity doesn't work on the BBC last year.

We've taken money out of the productive base of the economy. It would be like a business - a bar - saying 'I'm going through hard times, so I'm selling all my bar stools; I'm gonna close an extra day a week; and I'm gonna stop selling more expensive beer. And ultimately you get to a point where that reduces your revenues, and then the business fails even more, and then you have to cut even more.

When Michael Portillo responded by referring to the family budget analogy, displaying his total economic illiteracy for the whole country to observe, Blakeley administered a searing putdown. Probably the best explanation of the nonsense of austerity economics that I've ever heard.

We're in this family. We're spending more than we're earning. What are we gonna do? OK, we're gonna stop feeding our children and we're gonna stop paying our rent. 8 years down the line, the kids are dead and we've been kicked out of our house, but hey! At least we're not spending more than we're earning any more.

Alan Johnson then reminded viewers that since the eighteenth century, almost all countries - especially the advanced ones now - have lived 'outside their means'. What happened to those countries? Other than progress, development, innovation, better life chances for everyone, lower mortality rates and greater life expectancy, the answer is nothing. The completely blank look on Portillo's face told its own story.

In any developed country which controls its own monetary supply, the idea of 'sound money', at the heart of Tory economic discourse since Thatcher's time, isn't that far off being complete nonsense. Not quite total nonsense: mostly thanks to the absurd power of entirely unaccountable credit agencies, and the impact of their forecasts (however wrong they frequently are) on a government's ability to borrow.

Yet for a decade now, through Quantitative Easing, the Bank of England has been deliberately printing far more money than normal, while keeping interest rates close to zero. This has benefited banks and the very rich, while - contrary to the warnings of the right whenever Labour talks about investment - inflation has remained pretty low. So it's alright to do this for the banks, but it's not alright to do this for ordinary people?

Not only that, but the way to reduce the deficit and debt is the opposite of what the UK has done. If a country spends and invests in the future, the economy grows. The tax take rises. The deficit falls. Rinse and repeat. By and large, with periodic adjustments and rebalancing of course, it's always been that simple.

Portillo also repeated the quite risible mantra that it would be 'immoral' to pass our debts on down to future generations. Yet that is exactly what austerity has achieved. Wages are still at pre-2008 levels; a whole generation of young people have been as good as written off; rent prices are ludicrous; more and more people face a lifetime of never owning a home; while the Tories' so-called 'jobs miracle' is based on false figures which don't count anyone who doesn't claim unemployment benefit, and - get this - treat someone who works for one hour a week as 'employed'. Take one person who used to work a standard, dignified 40-hour-a-week job; give 40 people a one-hour-a-week job instead, and presto! There's your 'jobs miracle'... along with destitution and despair for anyone affected.

In England and Wales, life expectancy has even gone into reverse. And with the poor suffering so much, they find themselves forced into completely substandard accommodation which often looks like this, seriously endangering their health. In 2015, the Labour MP, Karen Buck, introduced the Homes (Fitness for Human Habitation) Bill. Its purpose was to 'require that residential rented accommodation is provided and maintained in a state of fitness for human habitation. The Bill was filibustered, so ran out of time. The proposals were reintroduced in 2016: whereupon 312 MPs voted against it, 309 of whom were Tory MPs. Most of those opposed were landlords. In a so-called advanced, First World country, it took until 20 March of this year for it finally to become law that homes are required to be fit for human habitation.

Tenants also face ridiculous rent prices which rise all the time; and if they complain to their landlord about the conditions, something being faulty or needing to be repaired, they are kicked out. Huge numbers of people receiving housing benefit are discriminated against by landlords; while those who don't discriminate receive a total of £9.3bn (not a misprint, however much I wish it was) from the taxpayer, nearly double the amount from a decade ago.

Death, devastation (of families and communities across the country), debt (both national and personal). That is the impact of austerity: a policy based on lies, parroted by politicians and the press with further lies. Which proved so effective that in August 2010, even my best friend, who I love to bits, is extremely well-informed, super-intelligent and very analytical, said to me over lunch with a look of pure, innocent shock: 'Shaun, they spent *all the money*!' That is how this works; and as we'll see, it was only the start of a decade of fake news, post-truth and the politics of bullshit. All of which has persuaded tens of millions of Britons to continually vote against their own interests.

Instead, they've voted for people who do not care about them and don't have the first thing in common with them. People like Cameron and Osborne. When Lord Ashcroft and Isabel Oakeshott released their salacious unauthorised biography of the former, while the media obsessed with whether or not the then prime minister had indeed had carnal relations with a dead pig's head, my focus was elsewhere: on what the book revealed about who he truly was. Specifically: how could someone who continually moved in such high company, was so at ease amid the wealth and excess of his friends, possibly have the remotest sense of the impact of his government not just on the poorest, the weakest… but merely on the common man?

The book movingly outlined the torment and heartbreak which Cameron and his wife, Samantha, experienced over the death of their son, Ivan. Samantha spoke at length to the Mail on Sunday about that awful time, revealing how hard they had fought to get Ivan into the special needs day care centre he desperately needed; and were able to afford night care, which eased the horrendous strain on their marriage. 'Looking after a disabled child pushes you to the limits of what you can cope with… physically, emotionally… By the end of the first year we'd both been working and Ivan needed 24-hour care. We were totally shattered and pretty much at breaking point'.

Cameron frequently referenced this tragedy in his speeches, often to reassure the public of his commitment to the NHS. Yet in light of his family's experience, it is extraordinary how savagely carers were hit by austerity; and that the very respite care which the Camerons depended upon was cut by local authorities. Changes were made to the Disability Living Allowance under the coalition; and catastrophically, the Independent Living Fund was axed, removing at a stroke the chance for severely disabled people to lead more independent lives and live with dignity.

Ask yourself: how can someone who *knows* how demanding it is to raise a disabled child, who *knows* how incredibly important high-quality care for that child was, possibly have overseen such abhorrent cuts? The answer is that Cameron never understood for a single moment what life is like for those without the wealth he and his family enjoy; nor did he care.

So much so that the man who plunged the country into disaster through a referendum he treated with all the care and preparation of a student in a last-minute essay crisis, then did an instant runner from the gigantic mess he created, said recently that his government 'should have cut public services deeper and earlier'. Level of self-reflectiveness on the colossal human misery he caused? Zero. In fact, he thinks that human misery should've been even worse.

As for his Chancellor: as the Grenfell fire raged in the distance, Osborne tweeted out his shock. If irony wasn't already dead, it perished at that moment along with 72 others. Osborne's cuts and encouragement of deregulation had done so much to cause this disaster; while his coalition government devastated access to legal aid. The Lib Dems especially should never be allowed to forget this; this national disgrace left the residents with no redress whatever as they battled the council, KCTMO, and were threatened in response.

If you ever wanted to know just how mindbogglingly out of touch the Tories truly are, here's two examples. At the end of last year, after spending his life savings defending himself in the courts, the Tory MP, Nigel Evans, complained bitterly about the savage cuts to legal aid; cuts which *he had voted for*. And in 2015, Cameron himself wrote to his local council to complain about cuts to frontline services which his *own government*'s slashing of the budget had caused. Truly, stranger than fiction.

◆ ◆ ◆

And then, there was the ending of tax credits. These were utterly critical to so many in work: enabling them to make ends meet, however narrowly. The lifeline separating them from poverty and even destitution. With no regard whatever for the human consequences, Osborne removed them. Everyone knew what this would do; the Institute for Fiscal Studies set it out in stark terms. But the government went ahead with it regardless.

Here's a section from the maiden speech of Mhairi Black, the brilliant former SNP MP:

> Before I was elected, I volunteered for a charitable organisation. And there was a gentleman who I grew very fond of. He was one of these guys who has been battered by life in every way imaginable. You name it, he's been through it. And he used to come in to get food from this charity. And was the only food he had access to and it was the only meal he would get.
>
> And I sat with him and he told me about his fear of going to the job centre. He said, 'I've heard the stories, Mhairi. They try and trick you out; they'll tell you you're a liar. I'm not a liar, Mhairi, I'm not!' And I told him 'it's OK, calm down. Go, be honest, it'll be fine'.
>
> I then didn't see him for about two or three weeks. I did get very worried. And when he finally did come back, I said to him, 'how did you get on?' And without saying a word, he burst into tears. That grown man standing in front of a 20-year-old, crying his eyes out.
>
> Because what had happened to him was that the money he would normally use to pay for his travel to come to the charity to get his food… he decided that in order to afford to get to the job centre, he would save that money. Because of this, he didn't eat for five days. He didn't drink. When he was on the bus on the way to the job centre, he fainted due to exhaustion and dehydration. He was 15 minutes late for the job centre and he was sanctioned for 13 weeks.

And here, too, is a speech by Frank Field, then still a Labour MP, given to Parliament in December 2017.

> I've done surgeries for 38 years. On my last surgery, Friday, for the first time ever, a gentleman rose after we'd spoken and I tried to persuade him not to commit suicide. Such was the desperateness that he saw the future for himself. And I realised that the hand that shook my hand was wet. He'd been crying. And the hand that shook my hand was the hand that wiped away those tears.

On Friday, Feeding Birkenhead, which is the most brilliant, but ought to be unnecessary organisation, reported a family coming in. Of husband, wife and young child. The child was crying with hunger. The family was fed. The father said it'd been a lucky week for him - because neighbours had taken pity and invited him to a funeral so that they could finish off the food after the other funeral guests had been fed.

When the little boy was shown the shelf where toys were, but also on that shelf were lunch packs, he chose the lunch pack.

That is the reality of the country the Tories (including Heidi Allen, moved to tears by Field's speech, yet who herself voted for cut after cut) have created. A country which devastates the lives and dreams even of young children. And which is still destroying people's lives the length and breadth of the UK even as I type. People like David Bevan, a diabetic declared 'fit to work' by the DWP earlier this year, who dropped dead while waiting for an appointment at Llanelli jobcentre. People like Kevin Barnes, who served in the Royal Navy for 17 years, but whose leg was amputated a month ago; and has been provided just £16 a month universal credit and told to find a job.

People like this man, with a disabled wife and disabled child: who along with his partner, had paid into the system all their lives, then found themselves unable to afford even 70% of their basic bills. They lived off their savings, then sold their home, all their belongings, everything they had ever worked for… and ended up renting and in ever-spiralling debt, with no chance of ever escaping it.

In the end, austerity isn't about statistics. It's about people. People just like you or me. And to those reading this who consider themselves fine right now: the chances are, you're probably only one life-changing event or even one redundancy from experiencing what so many of those I've mentioned in this chapter have. That is why civilised societies have genuine safety nets: to take care of each other, not just ourselves. But Britain ceased to be a civilised society long ago.

As Aditya Chakrabortty, far and away the outstanding journalist of the decade, and one of the British media's few true heroes, put it six days after Grenfell:

In Victorian Manchester, Friedrich Engels struggled to name the crime visited on children whose legs were mangled by factory machines, or whose parents were killed in unsafe homes. Murder and manslaughter were committed by individuals, but these atrocities were something else: what he called social murder. 'When society places hundreds of proletarians in such a position that they inevitably meet a too early and an unnatural death, one which is quite as much a death by violence as that by the sword or bullet; its deed is murder just as surely as the deed of the single individual'.

Over 175 years later, Britain is still a country that murders its poor. And if it votes Conservative again at this election, the death toll will inevitably grow even further.

2: VICTIMS AND PERPETRATORS: THE LIBERAL DEMOCRATS

'I think I've just destroyed the Liberals' - William Hague

'The Lib Dems must be <u>condemned</u> to being treated with maximum contempt. Forever' - Yanis Varoufakis

Imagine a country where the views of well over half of the electorate are discounted and treated as an irrelevance. Imagine a parliament in which well over half of the MPs are locked into place for life, depending entirely on where their constituency happens to be. Imagine a political system in which alternative parties have no chance of making any serious impact, despite obtaining the support of more and more people and the two major parties being in deepening decline. And imagine a so-called democracy where, despite a demonstrable majority against right-wing neoliberalism having been in place for decades, that very thing has been implemented by, at different times, both its major parties, with disastrous consequences for the country and public policy. That so-called democracy is in Britain.

At general election after general election going back many decades, the Conservatives and, until only recent years, Labour have focused almost all their resources, almost all their policies, on little more than 100,000 voters out of an electorate which now numbers around 46 million. In 2015, Ed Miliband's aim in this wasn't to win some grand parliamentary majority with which to implement radical change. Instead, it was to secure about 35% of the vote; the famous, miserably ill-conceived '35% strategy'. Yet this year, electors are still being told that if they vote for their first choice, they might well end up with the option they least want, so should vote for their second choice instead. Even, in some parts of the UK, the second worst choice. They must vote not for what they want, but against what they don't want; despite the latter option having failed to protect the interests of the majority for four decades... and counting.

Over the last 20 years in particular, as election results and turnouts have come in, politicians of all hues have uttered meaningless platitudes about how they must re-engage the electorate with the political process and regain trust in politics: which has never been more fragile than now. Then most have instantly gone straight back to doing the same old wilfully self-interested things and continued to uphold a medieval system designed to lock in the status quo forever. This is a system that disenfranchises the public from their supposed representatives, with consequences far, far beyond the ballot box. Yet which, incomprehensibly, very few people ever even talk about.

Democracy is supposed to protect the interests of the people. In Britain, for 40 years now, it has done the exact opposite: routinely working against the interests of the many, in favour of the few. First Past the Post (FPTP) doesn't merely lock the public out of democracy. It has resulted in policy after policy from both major parties which have done the country enormous, ongoing harm: dividing it not so much down the middle, as between the wealthiest and everyone else.

Consider this. Since 1979, the Thatcherite neoliberal consensus has been implemented, consolidated, and until Jeremy Corbyn's sudden rise in 2015, was accepted by all three major UK-wide parties: despite there being no evidence that the majority of the British public actually supports it. Over the same timeframe, economic discourse and analysis in Britain has constantly favoured Tory trickle-down economics, monetarism, and more latterly, austerity; despite inequality having increased massively; despite social mobility having remained so static that it has long been the worst in the Western world; despite this very policy having ground the economy to a halt and doubled the national debt; despite each new intake of MPs coming from narrower degrees in class than their predecessors; despite a whole generation being increasingly unlikely to own their own homes: the first generation in modern history to be less well-off than their parents; despite even the Union itself now being in clear and present danger.

How has this happened? It's not that the British public has shifted dramatically to the right. It's that its electoral system has. In any genuine democracy, not only would the split of the left in the early 1980s (formalising a grim process that began at the extraordinary general election of February 1974, when Labour lost 6% of support and the Tories lost 8.5%) have been of no major consequence; it would have been a demonstrably good thing, allowing electors more real choice.

But under FPTP, its consequences were a disaster. With, in effect, two parties now competing on the left, and only one on the right, it enabled the Conservatives to gain huge majorities on only around 42% of the vote, and forced Labour to move ever further rightwards to have any hope of winning, turning it into something almost unrecognisable. Especially in Scotland, so many protest that 'I didn't leave Labour. Labour left me'; but what they don't understand is why.

FPTP is so disproportionate, so wildly unrepresentative, that general election after general election come down to no more than 100 marginal seats. Swing voters in these constituencies aren't in the centre; they're not the median of the entire electorate. By and large, they're on the centre-right or further right: middle-aged or older homeowners with concerns over issues like crime, pensions and immigration. So what, for so long, did both major parties do? They designed almost their entire agenda around the wishes of this small group.

That's why neither party will ever seriously touch pensioners, the most influential voting demographic in the UK by a long way (and when they do, as with Theresa May's abortive 'dementia tax' in 2017, embarrassing U-turns have followed immediately). Worse: for much of the decade, benefit sanctions have been vote-winners in swing constituencies; even when the consequences for the poor, the sick, the disabled and mentally ill should shame any so-called civilised society.

The poor? They haven't counted in Britain's electoral system; they've been treated as an irrelevance. Instead, until Corbyn's emergence (and now, under Jo Swinson, through the Liberal Democrats as well), all major parties have waxed lyrical about 'Britain's hard-working families', because of their need to be seen as siding with these middle or higher-income earners. Those who can't find work or are too ill to do so? Until Labour's great shift since 2015, nobody spoke or cared about them. They don't make the difference under FPTP, so they may as well not exist as far as public policy and discourse are concerned.

The obsession with keeping homeowners happy is what leads to Conservative pledges on inheritance tax (which panicked Gordon Brown into failing to call an early general election in 2007, and were successfully repeated by David Cameron in 2015); and grotesquely, to the extraordinary, ongoing failure to build desperately needed housing over the last 40 years, or take any real action on maximum rents, buy-to-let landlords, or a land value tax. Why? If demand overwhelms supply, the demographic that decides British general elections benefits, while the majority are impoverished by extortionate, ludicrous rent and house prices. In any democracy, the interests of that majority would be protected. Under FPTP, those of profiteers are instead.

All this, of course, is also why Cameron unbelievably announced not a desperately needed mass build of new homes; but the forced sale of social housing. This killed two birds with one stone: inflating the property bubble even further, while reaching out to younger, aspirational swing voters. The 'right to buy' sounds wonderful... until you realise that under a mountain of mortgage-related debt, what goes up must inevitably come crashing down, to say nothing of the crisis levels of housing shortages which the Tories have encouraged for decades.

Quite what any government is going to do when, 30 years or so from now, it is faced with a whole generation of pensioners who need housing benefit just to survive, heaven only knows. But that's what happens when the common good is ignored; and FPTP has forced it to be so. With absurdly unrepresentative outcomes only compounding things still further.

First, despite 64% of voters (and close to 80% of the entire electorate) not voting Conservative in 2010, a nine-tenths Tory government resulted. Then, courtesy of the most disproportionate election result in modern times, where the Tories received just 2% more of the total electorate than at their annihilation in 1997, FPTP delivered an outright majority for Cameron. Throughout the whole decade, this has facilitated a government which has waged disproportionate war on the poor: with the most grievous, frequently lethal consequences for social structures, communities and an alleged safety net which has been as good as removed, while the rich have grown even richer.

Proponents of FPTP might interject here with: 'But the Tory/Lib Dem coalition was a disaster! And in proportional systems, coalitions formed through backroom deals which reward small parties would be the norm!' Except that:

(1) In countries with proportional voting systems, alliances are formed before, not after elections. The profound illegitimacy of the 2010-2015 coalition lay in so many having voted Lib Dem to keep the Tories out, not let them in.

(2) The Lib Dems, so used to Britain's endemically tribal, adversarial system, simply didn't understand coalitions. In any coalition, the smaller party holds all the cards; they can walk away at any time. In the absence of large concessions in their direction, they simply should not have joined.

(3) Vastly more proportional systems already exist in Scotland, Wales and Northern Ireland, the result of which has been a vastly more consensual,

grown-up approach to politics in the first two; and even power-sharing for a very considerable period in the latter. If Northern Ireland - with all its ancient sectarian enmities - could do this, why can't the rest of the UK?

At Prime Minister's Questions every Wednesday, two baying mobs hurl abuse at each other and behave like a pack of hyenas. The Labour MP, Stella Creasy, refers to Westminster as 'Hogwarts gone wrong': a legislature entirely disconnected from the general public. Yet parliaments in other countries are open and accessible to the people. At Holyrood, First Minister's Questions take place in an atmosphere unrecognisable from the House of Commons, despite all the competing passions which the Scottish referendum and its ongoing aftermath have generated.

Scottish politics are now more representative of the people than ever before; while Westminster's adversarial nature turns millions off. It is filled with career politicians who look the same, sound the same, whose families supported them through university degrees and unpaid internships, went on to work for think tanks, NGOs or MPs, and who - reared under the Thatcherite consensus enforced by FPTP - have little or no conception of the reality of life for tens of millions of Britons.

Not only that, but if someone from outside that privileged, professional politician's background wants to stand for election, it almost solely depends not on what they stand for, but where they live. Marginal constituencies are the exception, not the rule; the bulk of MPs are beneficiaries of lifelong sinecures if they happen to live in not so much safe seats as rotten boroughs, where it doesn't matter how little or how much campaigning they do, how little or how much work they perform for those they are supposed to represent. The expenses scandal, hardly surprisingly, was the result of this; the almost total failure to do anything much about it, likewise.

Goodness knows how many talented people are lost entirely to political life thanks to such an antiquated system. They find themselves with no chance of ever changing anything. Is it any wonder so many MPs are so astoundingly mediocre, and have so little idea about what life for ordinary Britons is really like?

In the late 1990s, Blair had the chance to implement the findings of the Jenkins Commission on electoral reform. Thanks to the blockheadedness of Brown and John Prescott, but also to his own narrow-minded short-termism, he failed to do so. To them, Labour's party interest was vastly more important than the public interest; something which would actually represent the will of the people. A move to proportional representation could have locked the Tories out forever and guaranteed New Labour's legacy. But under FPTP and neoliberalism itself, thinking of the longer term just never happens.

Consider: at every election since 1979, had PR been in place, not only would every single share of the vote have been very different, but other genuinely representative parties would've emerged too. And without tactical voting - without electors throughout the country forced into voting against something, rather than for something - again, the results would've changed dramatically. Both major parties only continue to dominate the landscape because of a wholly iniquitous system.

Most importantly of all: proportional systems don't just prevent unrepresentative, bordering upon illegitimate outcomes. They also ameliorate divisive, tyrannical policy. In 1987, despite 58% of voters, and almost 70% of the total electorate, failing to vote Tory, the poll tax was the result. Had PR been in place in 2001, Blair would surely have been prevented from taking Britain to war in Iraq. No decision other than Brexit did more to damage Britain's reputation abroad or disenchant the public at home. Under PR, the strength of the Lib Dems would've meant that the split in the Labour party would've proven decisive. It's hard to imagine Blair would've even considered war had the parliamentary arithmetic been against him.

Compare this with Germany, whose electoral system was actually designed by the British in the late 1940s, and has helped build by far the strongest, most politically stable country in Europe. Even if its constitution didn't prevent it from going to war, the presence of the Greens in coalition with Gerhard Schroeder's Social Democrats certainly would have. German politics are mostly so non-tribal and mature that Angela Merkel even formed a Grand Coalition with the SDP in 2005: unthinkable in Britain, yet which succeeded and got things done for the benefit of the whole country.

Or Uruguay: where the *Frente Amplio* (FA) (Broad Front), in place since 2004, slashed poverty and inequality and maintained constant, at times dramatic, economic growth. Again, its proportional system protects against bad policy. The essentially social democratic FA only remained in power by pursuing a centrist economic approach, encouraging foreign investment and controlling inflation. Had it moved too far to the left, its two rivals on the centre and centre-right would have combined at presidential run-offs to keep it out of office. Only now, exhausted after fully 15 years in power, has it finally been defeated; and only by a hair's breadth at that.

By contrast, so appalling is Britain's absurd electoral system, it's done more to precipitate the prospect of Scottish independence - the break-up of the nation state itself - than anything else. Scotland voted heavily Labour at every election between 1979 and 2010; the Tories were wiped out after 1997. Yet thanks to FPTP, it was rewarded with the Tories after five of those elections; Tory lite after the other three. Entirely understandably, the Scottish electorate has had enough. The Scottish National Party (SNP) has taken full advantage; independence may well be the ultimate result.

Given all this, you might imagine that I sympathise with the Lib Dems. No party has been more consistently squeezed and punished by FPTP, after all. Until 2010, they, not Labour, were my natural home: and had been ever since the first election I voted at, in 1997. Not that I actually voted for them that year: FPTP and the need to vote tactically in Harrow West saw to that. My vote at every election has always been anti-Tory depending on where I lived; but at my first five general elections, this meant I could only support the party most in tune with me twice. A farcical situation in Britain's so-called 'democracy'.

Why did I consider myself a natural Lib Dem? From late 1997 onwards (specifically, when Labour introduced university tuition fees), it was plain they were now to the left of Labour: marrying social democracy with social liberalism in a manner too often absent from the Blair government. On the electoral system, on drugs, even on their famous 'penny on income tax', the Lib Dems offered new ideas and engaged not with symptoms, but causes; while Labour's promise to be 'tough on crime, tough on the causes of crime' proved so much hot air as government by Daily Mail took over: Iraq, 90 days for terrorism suspects, ID cards, detention of children.

Like any Lib Dem, I was always conscious of what separated me from Labour; but this difference never even resembled the chasm separating me from the Tories. I never forgot which side my bread was buttered on; who, to put it in the always tribal parlance of British politics, the true enemy was.

Under first Paddy Ashdown, then Charles Kennedy, the party gained ground, but only because its rise was tied to Blair's transformation of the political background. Labour's dominance couldn't last forever: electorally speaking, Blair was always a complete one-off. But under Kennedy, it became horribly apparent that the party had no long-term strategy: what would it do when the Tories recovered, as they inevitably would?

It's no coincidence that the internal coup against Kennedy of January 2006 occurred only weeks after Cameron had become Tory leader. An old-fashioned liberal, One Nation Tory (at least, so he attempted to portray himself), Cameron immediately set his sights on peeling off 'soft Tory' Lib Dem voters: social liberals and small 'c' conservatives who would happily have voted Tory under John Major or Edward Heath, but loathed how reactionary and plain nasty the party became under William Hague or Michael Howard (and would do so again under May).

Rapidly transforming public perceptions of his party, Cameron had a dramatic initial impact; while the Lib Dems began to panic. First, Sir Menzies Campbell, such an impressive spokesman on world issues hitherto, proved a disaster as leader... then Clegg began to chart a rather different course.

Along with David Laws, Danny Alexander and others, Clegg led the so-called 'Orange Book' liberals: who believed that government should keep out of people's lives not just socially, but wherever possible, economically too. Their thinking was much more in line with the old Liberal Party; they believed the future lay in gradual realignment right in the very centre.

That Clegg was so centrist is surely why both Cameron and Brown sought any opportunity to 'agree with Nick' at the famous first TV debate in 2010: following which, the party briefly catapulted into public consciousness in a manner never seen before. The Lib Dems even led several opinion polls; a dramatic electoral breakthrough beckoned. But both the chronic iniquities of FPTP and a late squeeze ahead of a probable hung Parliament foiled them. Against all expectations, the party actually lost 4 seats; and now, a horrible decision lay ahead.

For so long, the Lib Dems had held together a loose coalition of social democrats and liberals. To make matters more complicated, while their members leaned left, most of their voters leaned right: their heartlands, such as south-west England, south-west London, and parts of Scotland, were all soft Tory. And in 2010, while the party proved able to resist the Tories in such areas, wherever it was up against Labour in a marginal seat, it almost always lost: frequently much more heavily than had been thought possible.

In Islington South and Finsbury and Oxford East, both held by Labour by tiny, three figure margins, I watched thunderstruck as pledges of absolute support from mainly younger voters following the first TV debate turned into apathy; even, by the end, fear. With Brown heading for certain defeat, Labour threw all its resources into getting out its core vote: at which it was astonishingly adept. This traditional support has been built up over many generations, family members passing it down to their children and grandchildren: how could the Lib Dems, continually forced to look in two directions at once by the electoral system, possibly compete?

Answer: they could not. I've no doubt that this obvious inability to challenge Labour in its heartlands was part of what informed Clegg's momentous decision to join the Tories in coalition; a decision greeted by vast amounts of Lib Dem activists with dismay. The morning after the 2010 election, every Lib Dem everywhere knew what the numbers meant. We knew a rainbow alliance of progressive parties was not viable, propping up Brown would appear very illegitimate, and most Labour MPs could see that and were not interested; and that the panicky markets and right-wing press would demand stable government, with cuts having been promised by all three major parties.

Yet I hadn't campaigned for the Lib Dems in order to prop up the Tories; nor had most activists and members. In Islington, people had worked 16 or even 18-hour days for miserable remuneration only to receive this almighty slap in the face. 'I'm a Lib Dem because I want reform, not power', I said to my best friend; but her response was simple. 'How will you get reform without power?'

That, in the end, was the key. What was the point of the Liberal Democrats if not to implement our policies when we had the chance? What was the point of us existing as a separate party if we were merely some adjunct to Labour? And if we didn't join a coalition to temper the Tories' most gratuitous excesses, who else would?

That chance to implement some of our ideas was why the infinitely more electorally sensible option of confidence and supply was ruled out. Plus, Clegg argued, if we could make a coalition work, Britain's age-old adversarial system could finally begin to recede; and maybe even join the civilised world at last.

To do this, the Lib Dems had to demonstrate that they understood how coalitions are supposed to work; but Laws' negotiating team simply did not. The Tories needed us; we did not need them. Every Lib Dem knew that joining Cameron in coalition would be electorally lethal; in all likelihood, it would destroy the party. Doing so therefore required vastly more than the miserably few concessions extracted: above all, on electoral reform.

During the 1992 election campaign, thought quite likely to result in a hung Parliament, Ashdown repeatedly stated that in any negotiations, PR would be the red line. John Major derisively referred to this as 'Paddy's Roundabout': presaging Cameron's approach in 2015, when he warned the electorate that to avoid 'shabby backroom deals', they should vote Conservative.

PR remained the Lib Dem *cause célèbre* throughout the next 18 years - and given how much they (along with millions upon millions of voters) suffered and were disenfranchised by FPTP, if they didn't demand it when a hung Parliament finally came along, when would they? But Clegg didn't. Disgracefully, despite having correctly dismissed it as a 'miserable little compromise', Clegg allowed himself to be bought off completely by William Hague's nefarious 'extra mile' of a referendum on the Alternative Vote (AV).

AV is the only electoral system anywhere which is frequently even more unrepresentative than FPTP. It often produces bizarre outcomes in Australia; not to mention the 2010 Labour leadership election, which Ed Miliband 'won' despite his brother receiving more first preference votes. Even now, remarkable numbers of people believe Britain rejected 'proportional representation' at the 2011 referendum; yet AV is about as far removed from PR as it's possible to conceive.

In committing this appalling volte-face over his party's most cherished aspiration - a desire to turn Britain into a genuine democracy at last - Clegg set the cause of electoral reform back decades. Now, no party wants anything to do with it; yet what could be more important than democracy? Especially when FPTP has resulted not in 'strong, stable government', but two hung Parliaments out of the last three; and bad, divisive, unpopular, unrepresentative governance, against the backdrop of an angry, anti-political, even apolitical climate, in which the will of the majority has been ignored for so long. Now are you beginning to understand the Brexit vote?

Hague, though, was delighted. He knew his party would mobilise all their heavy weaponry in a referendum; that Clegg would suffer huge blowback from voters furious that he'd joined the Tories; and if the plebiscite was lost, he could then claim that Britain had decisively rejected voting reform. Upon completion of the coalition negotiations, Hague told his wife, Ffion: 'I think I've just destroyed the Liberals'.

As well as the AV debacle, there was the great betrayal on tuition fees:

which the Lib Dems had pledged to stop, then voted through. There was no reason for them to do this; that they didn't simply sit on their hands and abstain was inexplicable. Even George Osborne advised his coalition partners not to support it! Nothing turned younger voters away from politics more than this.

Their support for the bedroom tax, huge cuts to legal aid, and even the imperilling of judicial review cast them in a dreadful light; as did their propping up of a government which had begun waging ideological war on the most vulnerable. When a smaller party is in coalition with a larger one, it can veto anything it wishes; why did Clegg's party not do so?

To subsequently present itself, as it tried to during the 2015 election campaign, as having 'moderated' the evil Tories bore no resemblance to public perceptions; and in politics, perceptions are everything. To so much of the public, the government had been nine-tenths Tory, and Clegg had enabled something they had not voted for. When his party claimed it had implemented 75% of their manifesto, the only reasonable conclusion could be: that manifesto must have been horrendous.

Appalled by the rank incompetence of the coalition negotiations, and especially by AV, I left the party in 2011: joining many others in moving into Labour's ranks. The Lib Dems were now not so much centrist as centre-right; only Labour seemed to offer a progressive alternative. Ed Miliband gradually began to appeal; Clegg seemed increasingly repellent.

As for his strategy: the failure to present the Lib Dems in coalition as anything other than a right-wing party would mean, surely, that when up against the Tories in their heartlands, their MPs would be hobbled. Why would swing voters choose hamburger - the coalition - rather than the raw red meat of pure Tory steak? Which is precisely what materialised.

Their electoral meltdown in 2015 was followed by barely any recovery at all, and an even lower share of the vote, in 2017. So what is the point of them? It's a question which Lib Dem devotees fail to ever answer honestly.

In practice, the way FPTP operates, their party so often takes crucial votes away from Labour: enabling the Tories to win. If the only purpose of the Lib Dems is to help the Conservatives continue their carve-up of the UK into a nation of a few haves, many have-nots, frankly, they shouldn't exist at all.

And while it's certainly disappointing that electoral reform doesn't seem to have occurred to Corbyn (albeit, Labour's proposed constitutional convention might well point to exactly that), the reason that ship has sailed has far less to do with him, much more to do with Jo Swinson. Whose leadership of her party is increasingly bizarre; and frankly, bordering on the nefarious.

◆ ◆ ◆

After the coalition resulted in the Lib Dems meeting such a grisly fate, the idea of an arrangement, however loose, between Johnson's Hard or No Deal Brexiteers and Swinson's group of at-all-cost Remainers would seem absurd… which is why the media, miles behind the zeitgeist as usual, haven't even acknowledged the possibility. But after the madness of the last four-and-a-half years, nothing about British politics should be considered unthinkable or impossible. This is a world where satirists have been rendered redundant; where truth has been stranger than fiction for a long, long time now. And during this election campaign, very strange things have been happening.

Swinson seems to be running a borderline presidential campaign. The Lib Dem bus is decked out with her image, and emblazoned with 'Jo Swinson's Liberal Democrats'. One wonders how that bus manages to stay up given how much her ego clearly weighs. Two years ago, May comically attempted a similar cult of personality (in her case, the only one in human history around someone who didn't have a personality): which did not exactly work out to her advantage.

But in Swinson's, it comes across almost as a female version of something Johnson might do. Never mind the policies; just look at me! That the Lib Dems clearly believe she's such a powerful electoral asset is bewildering enough… but that they've taken a leaf out of the Tory playbook and indulged in fake news across a variety of seats, even more so. Fake news which deliberately, wilfully misrepresents the chances of their candidates, invariably at Labour's expense. They even appear to be in the business of forging emails.

Swinson has been lying relentlessly about Jeremy Corbyn and Labour ever since she became leader. Even when called out on her lies, she treated it as a laugh. The last decade in politics appears to have taught her: nothing matters. There are no consequences to lies, betrayal, or leading the public up the garden path. The only thing which matters to the media is gossip, tittle tattle, personality, and pigeonholing.

Most of that pigeonholing - that narrative - has been parroted by Swinson for all she's worth: not about Johnson, but about Corbyn. She lies about his position on Brexit, which has continued to follow the path set out in both the 2017 Labour manifesto and at the 2018 Labour Party Conference. She apes Tory jibes about him being 'a threat to national security' because he'd rather not annihilate hundreds of millions of people and precipitate nuclear apocalypse.

She insists she would never do any kind of deal with him. And while in theory, that's her position regarding Johnson too, an analysis of how often she refers to Corbyn in speeches, interviews and at press conferences, and how rarely she refers to Johnson in similarly disparaging terms, would be horribly revealing.

Consider this. Such are the grotesque iniquities and anomalies of the UK's ludicrous electoral system, if two Remain or soft Remain (in the sense that Labour have guaranteed a second referendum) parties run in the same seat, they risk (in some cases, guarantee) handing it to the hard Brexit-backing Tories. In 2017, Labour extraordinarily won Canterbury with a majority of just 187. Rosie Duffield is strongly pro-Remain. So what in the world did the Lib Dems think they were doing by parachuting the former Telegraph journalist Tim Walker, who once worked alongside Johnson, in to contest the seat?

To his credit, heeding the concerns of so many, Walker stepped down... whereupon Swinson immediately announced a new candidate would be chosen instead. It's a kamikaze mission intended to blow both Remain candidatures to smithereens, isn't it? Just as in Finchley and Golders Green: which Luciana Berger has chosen to fight despite the incumbent Brexit-backing Tory defending a lead of just 1,657 over Labour from 2017, when the Lib Dems finished over 21,000 votes adrift.

Reports I've been hearing from the doorsteps suggest Remain-supporting locals are none too impressed with Berger's conduct. Quite right too. Yet the same applies in many constituencies across the country. Just what are the Lib Dems playing at here?

In fact, the very reason this election is happening at all - in deep mid-winter, when it gets dark early, when some students may already have returned home and not be registered to vote there, when it's all the more difficult to whip up enthusiasm - is... the Lib Dems. Who never had any desire to bypass the Fixed Term Parliaments Act while Corbyn was doing better in the opinion polls... but smilingly acquiesced when (1) It was known that Labour didn't want a general election and (2) Johnson greatly desired one.

Something else too. On 23 October, Labour put forward an amendment to the Queen's Speech, which:

Respectfully regrets that the Gracious Speech does not repeal the Health and Social Care Act 2012 to restore a publicly provided and administered National Health Service and protect it from future trade agreements that would allow private companies competing for services who put profit before public health and that could restrict policy decisions taken in the public interest.

It's vital to clarify that this was symbolic. Nothing in this motion would have required the government to do anything. Yet incomprehensibly, on a motion which opposed privatising the NHS, which would have passed with Liberal Democrat support, 19 of their MPs... abstained?!

In 2017, just 12 Lib Dem MPs were elected. Since then, the party has picked up nine more. Jane Dodds, who won the Brecon and Radnor by-election; Berger, Chuka Umunna and Angela Smith from Labour, via the failed vanity project of Change UK; Heidi Allen (who isn't standing at this election) and Sarah Wollaston, from the Tories via Change UK; Sam Gyimah, Philip Lee and Antoinette Sandbach: all direct from the Tories. Gyimah, Allen and Sandbach were the most recent to join.

In fairness, all the ex-Conservatives I've mentioned here were infuriated by their party's direction of travel and both May and Johnson's appalling leadership. Yet when a Lib Dem leader stands up and says she couldn't work with Corbyn because of his reluctance to press the nuclear button, something is up. Everything about Swinson's electoral strategy is geared towards winning over liberal and moderate Tory voters; there is nothing on offer for Labour voters at all.

What Swinson appears to be doing is creating some new-fangled, glossy, modern Conservative Party, to attract all those alienated by an ever further right actual Conservative Party: which can no longer be remotely trusted with the economy, basic governance, or even not wrecking the UK altogether. And whose membership is breathtakingly racist, Islamophobic, even nihilistic.

But the question is: why is she doing this? Is it just for reasons of electoral expediency, i.e. how many seats in southern England are Tory-Lib Dem marginals? Or does she have more than an eye on something longer term? If not a formal arrangement with Johnson, an informal one which keeps Corbyn out of Downing Street?

'Impossible!', I hear you cry. 'How could a party of ultra-Remainers possibly join forces with a party of ultra-Brexiteers?' But it's not impossible. Not in any way. Across the world, in places as far flung as the US, Spain and Uruguay, so-called centrist, 'liberal' parties have proven alarmingly eager to throw their lot in with the right or far right.

Remarkable numbers of establishment Democrats deride Bernie Sanders: who represents not corporations and lobbyists, but the people. Sanders' policies are nothing more than mainstream European social democratic ones; yet some reserve a level of scorn for him which they barely even have towards Donald Trump.

Spanish politics has been brought to its knees by the unwillingness of *Ciudadanos* to work with the Socialists, while jumping at the chance of a coalition with the Franco-ist, rabidly nationalist, xenophobic, chauvinistic, misogynistic, far-right VOX. This has destroyed *Ciudadanos* electorally: it has lost more than half its support in a matter of months, but this didn't stop it careering down a political suicide mission. VOX, meanwhile, have grown in support alarmingly, and hit 15% at the recent Spanish election.

Even in Uruguay, where moderation and good sense have underpinned everything about the political system since the mid-1980s, the supposedly liberal *Colorados* spurned the left, and joined up with a party led by a former Commander-in-Chief of the Army, who wants to militarise the police.

This, ultimately, is what liberals always do. They will always choose capital over labour; even if it leads to something approaching fascism. They define themselves first and foremost by not being of the left; hence their continued willingness to abandon the poor and vulnerable; their constantly punching left, not right; and the nauseating peak Lib Dem moment of 5p plastic bags being exchanged for even tougher benefit sanctions. Yes, you read that right. Even worse: they thought it was an achievement.

'But how on Earth would it happen? How could it possibly be sold to the public?' Here's how. Imagine, the morning after the election, the Tories are the largest party but unable to govern by themselves. Imagine the media assume that Johnson would emulate May and reach out to the Democratic Unionist Party. But he can't do that, because the DUP will never back his Brexit deal.

What would he do instead? Govern in a minority? Resign? Not a bit of it. In the spirit of 'openness' and 'national unity', he'd make the 'astonishing gesture' (all quotes the media would use) of a 'broad, bold, comprehensive offer to the Liberal Democrats'. Who would suddenly be placed under enormous pressure by our beloved right-wing press to accept: because 'the markets need certainty! We cannot have more instability at this of all times!'

All this would be done to 'keep the dangerous Jeremy Corbyn out of Downing Street', with Swinson painting herself as the conquering heroine: the leader who'd secured a second referendum, put the ever-fearful minds of the rich and super-rich at rest, and enabled a 'strong, stable government in the national interest'. If a Tory/Lib Dem coalition were agreed, Corbyn would probably resign; his most fervent supporters might well leave with him.

Would it work? In how our pathetic media - entirely uninterested in the appalling, often lethal consequences of the last decade for ordinary people, trapped in a hermetically sealed, self-regarding, incapable of self-reflection bubble - would treat it initially, yes. It would be hailed as an outbreak of sanity: something on the table for Leavers and Remainers alike. The referendum, it would be argued, would then finally lance a 4-year-old boil.

Yet the truth is that after campaigning as the only 100%, unequivocally Remain party in England, any kind of arrangement between Swinson and Johnson would be the ultimate betrayal. If the referendum was lost - as, with the Tories ploughing resources and dark money in, not to mention the backing of their media pals, it surely would be - it'd actually usher Britain towards No Deal. Which is why the hilariously named European Research Group (they hate all things European, they do no research at all, but at least they're a group) were suddenly so eager to back the deal: which stipulates that if no free trade agreement is reached by December 2020 (and it's impossible for one to be realised by then), the UK can walk away on WTO terms.

Such an outcome would break Britain altogether. No Deal would have economic and social consequences which are so catastrophic, they'd make austerity look like a tea party. All sorts of environmental and food regulations would disappear; Britain's farming and fishing industries would collapse; the NHS will be carved up and sold off to US pharmaceutical companies. And that's without even considering the short and medium-term impact to food and medical supplies.

Then imagine how Remainers would feel. Having voted in their droves for the Lib Dems, and a 'brighter future', they'd be rewarded with the most right-wing government Britain would have ever known. Think back to the betrayal of all those young people in 2010; then think of how they, and today's young, would all be sacrificed on the altar of this too. Imagine the fury that would generate and the horrendous harm it would do to Britain's already tattered, broken almost beyond repair body politic. All so Swinson and her colleagues could have ministerial patronage and Jags.

If you think I'm being hysterical here, it's incumbent on you (though really, Swinson herself) to answer the following:

Why are the Lib Dems campaigning heavily in Labour-Tory marginals where they have no chance of winning, but will inevitably hand them to pro-Brexit Tories?

Why are the Lib Dems using phony, fake campaign material to convince people to vote for them in places they have no chance of winning, handing these seats to the pro-Brexit Tories as well?

Why has Swinson repeatedly lied about Labour's position on Brexit, despite it having guaranteed a second referendum (with the alternative being its own, much softer deal)?

Why did the Lib Dems abstain en masse on NHS privatisation?

Why did the Lib Dems enable Johnson's desire for an election, when they knew Labour wanted to wait?

Why, unlike Labour, hasn't Swinson highlighted that Johnson's deal will almost certainly result in No Deal?

When before now has any Lib Dem leader ever focused a campaign around willingness to press the nuclear button?

Why are so many who've joined Swinson's party dyed in the wool One Nation Tories: which Johnson, the chameleon extraordinaire, already has considerable experience of portraying himself as when Mayor of London?

Why has Swinson obsessed in her public comments with misrepresenting and denouncing Corbyn, while rarely doing the same thing with Johnson?

Why did Swinson back austerity so eagerly and accept donations from fracking companies? Take a look at her record here. Bedroom tax, even lower benefits and even less support for councils? 'Yes please!' Higher sickness or disabled benefits, guaranteed jobs for the long term unemployed or merely raising benefits in line with inflation? 'No, thanks, down with that sort of thing'. Truly, more Tory than the Tories.

If you can answer all the above in ways which don't completely incriminate her and her party, you have my undying admiration. But I know what it looks like. Ahead of 12 December, the only advice I can give you is to let everyone in the UK know what's on the cards here. If they vote Lib

Dem, they're about to be sold down the river in a manner unprecedented even by Britain's non-existent contemporary standards. Spread the message, campaign for all you're worth, go door to door. Don't let anyone be taken in by yet another disgusting bout of politics treated as a game, when for so many, it's actually a matter of life and death.

Fool me once, shame on you. Fool me twice, shame on me. Want to know the dictionary definition of a country which has lost the plot? It's one which, with the patient in critical condition but a life-saving solution in the offing, immediately begins re-administering the poison. The Lib Dems' betrayal of so many voters, and especially their facilitating Tory austerity, played an enormous role in causing Brexit. At this election, whatever you do, don't let them do it again.

3: THE TROUBLE WITH POLLS: ED MILIBAND AND THE 2015 GENERAL ELECTION

'Opinion polls are a device for influencing public opinion, not a device for measuring it. Crack that, and it all makes sense' - Peter Hitchens

In the annals of modern British political history, the 1992 general election was the ultimate watershed. Defeat at a fourth consecutive election represented - under FPTP, at least - a repudiation of socialism which would last a quarter of a century: from whence, the Labour Party's transformation into something almost unrecognisable was triggered. As the Conservatives fell apart over Europe, the Blairite consensus would, following John Smith's tragic death, go on to hold sway, storing up huge future trouble for Labour amongst its traditional support: above all in Scotland.

Meanwhile, much as the US Republicans have only won one presidential share of the vote since 1988, heading into the 2015 general election, the Tories - once the most successful electoral force in the Western world - hadn't won a single parliamentary majority since 1992: when John Major's victory came as a huge surprise. Not only to his party, but to the pollsters.

Throughout the campaign, Labour were believed by almost everyone to be ahead: on course for a small majority, and with a worst-case scenario of being the largest party in a hung Parliament. Britain was in recession; memories of the poll tax were still fresh; Neil Kinnock, Labour leader, had done a huge amount to drag his party away from the militant tendency. But something about Kinnock never convinced; somehow, despite continual boom and bust under the Tories, more than enough of the public remained fearful of a return to the union-dominated ungovernability of the 1970s. Smith's Budget plans, announced early in the election campaign, were leapt upon by his opponents and only exacerbated public fears of heavy tax rises and economic meltdown.

History records that meltdown occurred only five months after the election: Black/White Wednesday, 16 September 1992, when Britain was forced out of the Exchange Rate Mechanism (ERM), and the Tories' reputation for economic competence was shredded for a generation. Given

Labour had become considerably more pro-European than the Tories, it's actually a very good job for them that the 1992 election was lost; to have suffered such a humiliation less than six months after regaining power for the first time since 1979 would have been ruinous. Perhaps even, fatal. But why was it lost?

Famously, the pollsters had failed to take into account potential 'shy Tories': those embarrassed or unprepared to admit they were intending to vote for Major's party, whose brand had already become toxic across huge swathes of the UK thanks to Margaret Thatcher. Pollsters did at least detect something of a narrowing in the race - some sort of movement towards the incumbency – with exit polls on election day predicting a hung Parliament, with the Conservatives (just) as the largest party. But ultimately, this was well out: as the night wore on, and especially after David Amess held on in the bellwether marginal of Basildon, it became clear that not only were the Tories still the largest party, but they'd actually won a majority: via the greatest amount of votes ever cast for any political party in Britain. Their lead over Labour was almost eight per cent.

For 23 years, 1992 would remain both Labour and the pollsters' *Goetterdaemmerung*. Both would change their approach hugely in the years ahead: the latter resolving never to make such a mistake again, building all sorts of adjustments into their methodology to ensure this. By and large, these worked: Labour's majority of 66 was being correctly predicted even as the 2005 campaign got underway; exit polls on election night in 2010, dismissed by many because of how much they were assumed to understate Liberal Democrat support, actually proved pretty much bang on the money.

But 2015 posed entirely new challenges: multi-party politics conducted within an outmoded electoral system which cannot cope; post-referendum transformation in Scotland which threatened Labour's complete destruction; UKIP peeling off support from both major parties; and in England, a series of desperately tight Tory-Labour marginals which were almost impossible to call, but would decide the outcome.

Hot off the heels of Nate Silver's extraordinary accuracy in predicting the 2012 and 2008 US election, a series of forecasting and 'nowcasting' websites sprung up: Election Forecast, with which Silver and fivethirtyeight.com had a tie-in; Elections Etc; the New Statesman's May 2015; even one hosted by The Guardian. The latter two were 'nowcasting' sites: extrapolating the outcome from the polls as they stood. The former two were forecasts, with inbuilt swings back to the incumbency: in this case, the Tories and Lib Dems.

For several weeks, all but one had predicted that combined, Labour, the SNP and smaller parties such as Plaid Cymru, the Social Democratic and Labour Party (SDLP), and the Greens, would hold an anti-Tory majority in the House of Commons. Indeed, until a matter of days before the election, May 2015 thought merely the combined Labour-SNP seat total would be enough; The Guardian still did on 5 May, just two days before the contest.

May 2015 was confident enough to splash a detailed, convincing piece explaining why Ed Miliband held many more routes to 10 Downing Street than David Cameron; but three days before the election, suddenly began to have second thoughts. Now, it highlighted the possibility of a late movement back towards the Tories, very much like the unexpected swing to Likud in the final hours of the Israeli elections in March of that year. It noted the mounting prospect of any Labour-led minority administration being deemed illegitimate by public (if certainly not constitutional) opinion should Labour finish second on votes and seats, especially should it be dependent on SNP MPs to carry legislation… and also pointed towards something else. One of two things which were surely giving polling companies and forecasting websites sleepless, cold-sweated nights.

Throughout the period leading up to the final dash for votes, opinion polls had been deadlocked: perhaps with the Tories a fraction ahead, but no more than that. But most of these polls were internet-based; and given how the Scottish referendum polls over-estimated support for the 'Yes' campaign, and their tendency to attract responses via one click from some who don't carry through their opinion on polling day, I was convinced they were wrong.

Conversely, in telephone polls, the Tories held a consistent three-point lead. This fit in with the idea that older voters were less likely to be part of internet-based surveys; younger voters less likely to have landlines; and over the phone, questioned one-to-one, voters are more likely to be honest. But at general elections, older people vote far more than their younger counterparts. Simplistic though this must sound, while internet polls should be expected to lean towards leftist, progressive parties, phone-based ones are likely to do the opposite: but the latter are considerably more likely to represent the true picture.

As May 2015 noted, a slightly more than three-point lead for Cameron would put him in a strong, though not impregnable position: with a combined

Tory-Lib Dem-Democratic Unionist Party (DUP) bloc close to the de facto winning line of 323 seats. Yet even this underestimated the likely outcome.

Despite all their changes to make allowances for shy Tories and late moves towards the incumbency, the polling companies continued to underestimate Tory and Lib Dem support in 2001, 2005 and 2010; and overstate Labour support. This went largely unnoticed because the Labour landslide in 2001, heavily reduced majority in 2005, and - after the first televised debate and accompanying 'Clegg bounce' changed the picture completely - hung Parliament in 2010 were all so predictable. The pollsters got the bigger picture right; but the detail was still awry in very consistent areas.

But the real bombshell for psephologists - and just as much, for Miliband - landed on 4 May: when a Guardian/ICM poll found a huge difference in Sheffield Hallam when electors were asked first, to put the local context and candidates to one side, and name their nationwide preference; but second, the candidates' names were included as part of the question. Names, of course, which included that of Nick Clegg, Lib Dem leader and deputy prime minister.

On the nationwide question, Labour emerged with a 34-32 lead: in line with the recent constituency polling of Lord Ashcroft, who we'll come to in a moment. But on the second question, Clegg shot seven points ahead of Labour challenger, Oliver Coppard, thanks to huge tactical voting from Conservatives determined to help ensure a continuation of the coalition. Clegg ultimately held on fairly comfortably.

The implications, though, were much broader. With uniform swings (which saw Amess' victory in Basildon translate remarkably seamlessly into a Tory majority in 1992) very much a thing of a past, and British politics in uncharted, multi-party territory, Ashcroft conducted a whole series of individual constituency polls throughout the run-up to and during the election campaign. His work was greatly appreciated by forecasters and psephologists. But it was also flawed.

The problem was as follows. When asking electors their voting intentions, Ashcroft did not name the candidates; but on polling day, of course, all are listed. And with no other local data to go on, both May 2015 and Election Forecast used Ashcroft's findings to help predict the outcome.

Even against that backdrop, Ashcroft found the Tories had opened a surprising, almost inexplicable four-point lead in Croydon Central: where according to his snapshots, an eight-point swing had occurred over a single month, despite Labour having been assumed by almost all observers to have had the better national campaign, and their having closed up and tied the national opinion polls. He also found that in Wirral West, a seat long considered highly likely to fall to Labour, held by the divisive figure of Esther McVey, Minister for Employment (and before that, Parliamentary Under-Secretary for Work and Pensions), the gap had been reduced from five to three points. McVey ultimately lost, by a whisker; Gavin Barwell squeaked home in Croydon Central by an even narrower margin.

In their updated position, May 2015 highlighted 27 seats in which, according to Ashcroft, Labour were at least four points ahead. But while that might sound comfortable, it was actually within the margin of error, and based on data which did not name individual candidates. According to Election Forecast (also dependent on Ashcroft's data), McVey had an 85% chance of losing; she ultimately fell short by just 0.9%. The data was wrong. Very wrong. Just as in Sheffield Hallam, where May 2015 had been so dependent on Ashcroft that until The Guardian's bombshell poll, the deputy prime minister's constituency, quite remarkably, had sat in the Labour column.

To put that 85% probability in Wirral West into perspective, it coexisted alongside Election Forecast putting McVey's opponent, Margaret Greenwood, just four points up. Huge numbers of similarly high probabilities were given by the website for seats so close, they were practically on a knife-edge; and based on data which was (a) very flawed; b) collected before the late incumbency swing which happens at so many elections all over the world. Election Forecast insisted they'd accounted for this: but given their reliance on Ashcroft's information, and national opinion polls which told a different picture depending on whether they were conducted over the internet or telephone, their numbers were wrong to begin with.

In Israel in 2015, at the Scottish referendum, and at both the 2014 and 2019 Uruguayan elections, the status quo out-performed forecasts. In the former case, the race was believed to be extremely close throughout much of the year: for substantial chunks of which, it seemed that Luis Lacalle Pou's centre-right *Partido Nacional* and Pedro Bordaberry's further right *Partido Colorado* would combine in a second round run-off to defeat the governing leftist *Frente Amplio* (FA) (Broad Front).

Yet in the event, remarkably, despite the hype surrounding Lacalle Pou's campaign, and his <u>positive, inclusive message</u> (for him then, read Miliband and Labour: neither attacked the government in the way they might have done, both chose to focus on optimism and a 'better plan' instead), the FA actually increased their support on the previous election, held in 2009. Polling organisations were embarrassed: but later concluded they had failed to properly reach Uruguay's more distant, rural regions, a number of which lack regular internet access; some of which lack telephone lines. Even in Britain's fully developed society, were its internet pollsters failing to reach certain sections of older voters too?

There were, beyond that, a good number of more general reasons why Miliband was heading for defeat. Above all, strategy. Despite presiding over Labour's most progressive platform since 1992, he failed to appeal to enough young voters; or traditional Labour supporters heavily courted by UKIP; and especially those in Scotland. While Labour's message in England was often admirably positive and upbeat, in Scotland, it was the reverse: talking at, even condescending to its traditional vote; scaremongering about pensions and the SNP 'letting in the Tories' instead of offering positive reasons to vote Labour.

Much the same mistake was made during the Scottish referendum campaign: immediately following which, it was abundantly clear that UK Labour had no conception whatsoever of the seismic shift which had just occurred. At least three critical months were lost as Labour's leaders in London contemplated their navels, while the SNP made colossal political capital out of The Vow, and especially Cameron tying this to English Votes for English Laws the morning after the Union had been saved. The SNP mobilised furiously against the 'Red Tories'; Labour sat on their hands.

The remarkable failure to offer a referendum on EU membership also meant that those tempted by UKIP had no obvious reason to return to the fold. Given the colossal democratic deficit of the EU, its mounting unpopularity across much of the UK, and especially amongst the working classes in regions like the West and East Midlands, this was a huge blunder. The Tories wooed Kippers back into the fold by promising a referendum; Labour failed to counter this in any meaningful way.

Beyond this, given Labour's complete failure to challenge an absurd narrative regarding their 'responsibility' for a worldwide crash, the public, lied to every day by politicians and the press, continued to regard the Tories as far more economically competent. Cameron made particular hay of waving around Liam Byrne's note wherever he went. But Labour also had itself to blame for failing to properly articulate an altogether different reality. Regarding which, offering Ed Balls, who the public blamed for the crash almost as much as Gordon Brown, as prospective Chancellor, was tin eared beyond belief. Balls would lose his seat that fateful night of 7 May.

And then, of course, there was the SNP. At a loss on what to do regarding the extraordinary rise of Nicola Sturgeon's party in Scotland, Labour found itself squeezed, horribly, by English fears of a government 'being held to ransom' by those who want to break the UK up. Whatever Miliband did here, he could only lose. Joining Sturgeon in an anti-Tory alliance would've meant floods of English votes in those key marginals disappearing to either UKIP (a little) or the Tories (a lot); having nothing to do with it could only further alienate Scottish voters sick of being taken for granted for so long.

The SNP exploited the latter to such an extent that they left me, and more than a few others, suspecting that actually, their secret wish was for a Tory or Tory-led government: in which they could avoid any responsibility, and continue to build up support for independence ahead of a second referendum. There is no doubt that Sturgeon, Alex Salmond et al knew how their sabre-rattling played in English marginals: but then again, as a Scottish party increasingly winning the argument that as a political construct, the UK is bust, why should this have concerned them?

Miliband's 35% strategy was doomed the moment Labour campaigned alongside the Tories at the referendum. However difficult this was to avoid in a binary contest, far more thought should've been given to what this would look like; a far more distinctive approach, conducted as far away from Cameron as possible, was needed. It wasn't, and the tectonic plates shifted decisively and historically.

Finally, there was the leader himself. Other than the absolute fiasco over the 'Ed Stone', Miliband had a mostly good campaign: neutralising most of the media's attacks, rising to the occasion, even becoming one of politics' least likely sex symbols ever. But ever since his election as Labour leader, he had never convinced. An approach seen as too left-wing *and* too watered down meant he couldn't maximise either left or centre support; and he always lacked gravitas. Cameron possessed it: which was why Labour knew they were in danger the moment he became Tory leader. Miliband simply never did.

In this period of the last remaining calm before the post-2015 storm, style still mattered every bit as much as substance, if not more. Miliband was damned by what the electorate had come to expect in leaders such as Thatcher, Blair or Cameron, and unable to advance his rather different approach convincingly enough.

In the weeks leading up to the election, I spoke with close friends and family members who, were Miliband genuinely have been about to enter Downing Street, would almost certainly have all been voting Labour. But none of them were. My mother voted SDP during the 1980s; loathed what the coalition had done to the most vulnerable with all her soul… yet voted Lib Dem. A very close friend, disgusted by Blair's war in Iraq and Cameron's intervention in Libya, was very far removed from ever voting Tory… but told me he'd be going with either Green or Respect.

Another close friend, again all too conscious of this government's war on the poor, said she'd certainly be voting Labour if its leader's name had begun with 'David'… but as it didn't, was too alarmed by the prospect of Ed representing the UK internationally to do anything other than vote Conservative. My father is no right winger: but was horrified at the idea of Balls back in the Treasury, and unhesitatingly voted Tory to prevent this. And almost nobody amongst those I knew in Scotland - most of whom routinely voted Labour until 2010 - did anything other than throw their weight behind the SNP.

These were all mere anecdotes, but they spoke to a much wider story. Whether through English fears of runaway SNP influence, concerns over Miliband's lack of modern leadership skills, his failure to distance his party far enough from New Labour (whose reputation, thanks to both Iraq and the financial crash, was utterly toxic), or Scottish fury at the 'Red Tories', he simply hadn't done enough. Not to mention the broader, time honoured point that oppositions don't win elections, governments lose them; and in the absence of anything resembling a disaster under its watch, Cameron's government was still considered competent by enough of the electorate to be heading for a second term.

◆ ◆ ◆

And so it proved. Yet the result - this apparently cataclysmic shock - should have been foreseen easily, for the reasons I've explained above. In particular: the narrative on deficit reduction had been parroted so relentlessly by the increasingly hysterical Tory press, the BBC, and both the Tories and

Lib Dems, that when Miliband said perfectly reasonably that no, Labour had not over-spent before the crash, most viewers were horrified. How could they trust someone so irresponsible, he wasn't even prepared to apologise; and who'd been part of a government which, so everyone insisted, had 'run out of money'?

Never mind that no country in charge of its own money supply can ever run out of money (it simply prints more); never mind that Britain wasn't even remotely imperilled in the manner of southern European countries trapped in the eurozone and crucially, without control of their money supply or economic policy; never mind that the effect of coalition-imposed austerity was simply to remove huge amounts of liquidity from the system, grind the economy to a dead halt, and it only began to recover when those policies were significantly ameliorated; never mind that almost all macro-economists around the world (notably the Nobel Prize Winner, Paul Krugman; the Merton College, Oxford Professor, Simon Wren-Lewis; and even the International Monetary Fund (IMF) itself) had rejected austerity as a busted flush; never mind that not Labour, but the coalition, had doubled the national debt, and left it massively more exposed to an increasingly possible second crash; never mind that the economy had been growing rapidly when Gordon Brown was forced out of office; never mind that borrowing costs were historically low, with inflation then at zero; never mind that the welfare state itself had been built by the post-war Labour government at a time the country was technically bankrupt (so it simply borrowed instead, investing in infrastructure and setting a course for the Keynesian consensus); never mind that the now immortalised Byrne note was a playful aside to his successor in the manner of long established Treasury traditions; never mind that, mindbogglingly, the Tories were proposing a more extreme version of the very policy which had failed so completely in the first place... none of this mattered.

If a lie is repeated often enough, it becomes the truth. Thus both coalition partners asserted that Labour's much more balanced approach would 'pass our debts on to our children and grandchildren', even when Tory policy, by preventing growth or re-balancing, has done that very thing; both continued to espouse the risible nonsense that Britain's debt (which remember, they had doubled) was somehow comparable to a credit card debt, or that running a country is akin to running a household budget.

The press, run by barons who benefit enormously from the continuous upward funnelling of wealth to the super-rich, who would personally have been impacted by a mansion tax, the return of the 50p tax rate, and especially the removal of the absurd protection of non-doms, hammered the message home again and again: Labour would endanger everything. A shockingly economically illiterate public (so illiterate that, by this point, it was already all too obvious that this would pose an enormous threat to both public policy and certainly the UK's fiscal health) inevitably acquiesced: despite policies which do most of them ongoing financial and social harm.

And once the 'danger' posed by a party with the brass neck to have huge numbers of MPs democratically elected by Scottish voters was thrown into a wholly disingenuous, toxic mix, the die was cast: with public minds panicked into nonsensical comparisons with the 1970s, told that Nicola Sturgeon would 'drag' Miliband to the left... despite the SNP actually standing for slower, more drawn out austerity than Labour.

Yet having said all of that, when Miliband defended the Brown government's record during the televised debates, he needed to assert why it hadn't over-spent - but in keeping with serious communication issues which dogged him throughout his leadership, he couldn't. Instead, like a rabbit in the headlights, hoist by the petard of his own foolish commitment to austerity, he froze; and his failure to 'take responsibility' will undoubtedly have hung particularly heavy in undecided voters' hearts in the polling booths.

That the public continued to blame Labour for hardship caused by the coalition was a huge part of why Miliband's results at local, European and by-elections were so poor; and those results represented an enormous, critical warning: not only to Miliband, but the pollsters. Both ignored them; in the latter case, incomprehensibly so.

A week after the Scottish referendum, when most commentators were incomprehensibly expecting a Labour majority, and had not picked up on what was happening north of the border in any way, I stated that Labour would inevitably lose. When challenged, I even forecast the share of the vote: 37% or 38% for the Conservatives; 31% or 32% for Labour, and said:

I think we'll start the general election campaign, i.e. a month before polling day, with everyone anticipating a hung Parliament. We'll finish it, as a minimum, with the Tories as the largest party – and probably with a majority.

To me, this was the only logical outcome. As we moved towards the election, I treated any Tory lead as a sign of the inevitable; but was bewildered as Miliband appeared (according to the fatally flawed polls) to overtake Cameron during the campaign, then as things remained level pegging all the way to polling day. I grew more and more suspicious: what was wrong with the polls? Why were they all saying something which I could scarcely even conceive of being true?

The night before election day, as the nation slept before crunch time, and the likes of May 2015 asserted preposterous levels of hubris about the likely outcome, everything suddenly became clear. I had chanced upon the one and only forecasting hero of the campaign (in fact, one of very few in this entire decade): who had conducted comprehensive, demonstrably proven psephological research, and whose findings drove an absolute coach and horses through every single professional forecaster and polling organisation... as well as sending an unforgettably cold chill down my Labour-supporting spine. For the Conservatives, his work spelt Nirvana; for the opinion pollsters, it spelt Nemesis.

In an extraordinary tour de force, the best, most counter-intuitive piece of electoral research I believe has ever been conducted in the modern day (better even than Nate Silver's in 2008 and 2012), Matt Singh and the Number Cruncher Politics (NCP) website explained that, according to all possible indicators and variables, the polls were telling a wildly different story to that accepted by just about everyone.

As I did, NCP strongly suspected a repeat of 1992-style Shy Tory Syndrome; but unlike me, as the man behind it is possessed of the scientific expertise necessary to trawl through exhaustive amounts of data going back some 50 years and model it in various ways, he had the ability to conclusively prove it. By examining electoral data covering the previous 35 years, toplines from the last half century, and opinion polls from the 2010-15 Parliament, he identified a very clear statistical pattern, which repeated itself through three separate models. His main findings were as follows:

Opinion polls at British general elections are usually biased against the Tories and in favour of Labour. The exception, when both the Conservatives and Labour were a little understated in 2010, while the Lib Dems were wildly overstated, was easily explicable by the third party being squeezed under FPTP late on. The same demographic of voters who artificially inflated the Lib Dem position in 2010 had a similar effect on Labour in 2015.

The unusual fluidity of the electorate since 2010 (so many Lib Dem voters abandoning the party; Tory and Labour voters heading over to UKIP) had almost certainly undermined - perhaps even entirely negated - the adjustments made by pollsters after the debacle of 1992. Especially when it came to the usual method of reallocating 'don't knows': far fewer of these would vote for their traditional party, but amid a new, multi-party landscape, how could pollsters possibly determine who would, and who would not?

Every single one of 16 opinion polls ahead of an election over the preceding two years had fallen prey to a pro-Labour bias, at the same time as late swing to the Tories was occurring: unnoticed until the election itself. At the 2014 European elections, Labour's lead had been overstated by 3.3 points; while all by-elections since early 2014 had displayed a huge shy Tory factor, averaging 5.5 points.

Conflicting internal polling - which precipitated a dramatic change in strategy over the last week as a panicking Labour campaign desperately courted the notoriously unreliable young vote (again, the same voters who failed to turn out for the Lib Dems in 2010, despite so many of them having promised their support) - bore uncanny resemblances to 1992.

Since 1992, the overstatement of Labour and the Lib Dems had been almost uniform: ranging between 2.3 and 2.9 points.

Serious problems in weighting data from online panels; other problems in reallocating undecided voters in phone polls, and poor response rates to the latter.

Polling error averaging 5 points net over all general elections between 1983 and 2010.

Relative to the Tories, Labour's local election performances in non-general election years under Miliband had been the second worst by any opposition over the previous 35 years.

All three models - based on adjusted top-line numbers, polling internals and actual votes - were telling an astoundingly similar, unbelievably alarming story; and combined, when tested against the polls at every general election since 1983, outperformed them on all but one occasion (2010, when the difference was a mere 0.2 points).

What was that story? Namely, that the Tories were heading for a victory by between six and more likely around eight points, despite the opinion polls all suggesting things were dead level.

The sheer, overwhelming exhaustiveness of the research left no room for doubt. I was awestruck by what I had just read; and given my habitual sense that the polls were very, very wrong, knew it could only mean one thing. The Tories were heading either right to the cusp of an overall majority; or their first one since 1992.

Three final opinion polls were now due to be published before 7am. Inexplicably, none were; all appeared hours later instead, along with a fourth too. I tweeted the NCP research to May 2015, but got no response: instead, the New Statesman's forecast site happily updated the news that the final polls still suggested a tied race and Miliband premiership.

Section 66A of the Representation of the People Act, 1983 states the following:

(1) No person shall, in the case of an election to which this section applies, publish before the poll is closed—

(a) any statement relating to the way in which voters have voted at the election where that statement is (or might reasonably be taken to be) based on information given by voters after they have voted, or

(b) any forecast as to the result of the election which is (or might reasonably be taken to be) based on information so given.

Above, point 1(a) refers to exit polls: which of course, are never released until 10pm. But 1(b), while not explicitly doing so, appears at all elections in the past to have been taken to cover opinion polls released after voting has begun. This was the sixth general election I'd experienced; never before had opinion polls been published after 7am on polling day.

In fairness to the pollsters in question, the Act was hardly designed for an internet age dominated by social media and forecasting websites: all of which continued to apply the latest data despite point 1(b); while on Twitter and Facebook, various candidates re-tweeted endorsements from voters and voters declared who they had voted for. As The Telegraph noted, some form of mild campaigning still seemed to have been going on beyond that.

A mess, then; but there are two vastly more serious points here. First, for the duration of the campaign (and, for that matter, a good two years prior to that, according to NCP), all polling companies and forecasting sites had been publishing wildly, at times ludicrously inaccurate information which inevitably influenced the race, and the outcome. When parties are assumed to be tied, their strategy changes; media treatment of them substantially changes (never more so than in Labour's case in 2015); public responses change too. In the latter case, how many more voters are likely to vote a certain way out of fear that those they're opposed to are in touching distance of victory? And under FPTP, how many vote tactically who otherwise would not; and vice versa?

In practice, as the NCP model conclusively demonstrated, Labour were never ahead; and much as in 1992, were probably several points behind throughout the campaign. Yet that's not what the polling companies were saying. Should organisations with such disastrously flawed methodology and a consistent record of inaccuracy which, as NCP exposed, dates back to 1983, be allowed to dominate the agenda in such a way; and above all, have such heavy influence on debate and public discourse?

Remember: huge amounts of the Tory campaign were dedicated to frightening English voters into stopping a minority Labour government propped up by the SNP; but in practice, this was never the prospect it appeared, because Labour were doing much worse than was believed. Enormous amounts of discussion were put over not to policy, not to manifestos, but the electoral and parliamentary arithmetic; but this bore no resemblance to reality.

Is it any wonder the British public have such little understanding of macro-economics when whole election and referendum campaigns - leading to a decision hugely determining the futures of them, their families, their loved ones - are given over to constant reactions to never-ending opinion polls: even when these polls are completely wrong? Other countries (most notably, France) do not allow polling firms to play such a huge role during the final week of election campaigns; why on Earth does the UK?

Then there was the question of Ashcroft, whose data had indeed been awry. At The Telegraph, virtually ever since Miliband was elected Labour leader, Dan Hodges had consistently and brilliantly forecasted his demise. In February, he'd asked a question which the British polling world should already have been asking: 'What does Lord Ashcroft want?'

As Hodges set out, Ashcroft had morphed in public persona from hugely controversial non-dom to friend of the political process: opening up the business of polling to the public in a manner never seen before. But Ashcroft, contrary to what so many must assume, is not a pollster: he buys in polling from other companies, publishes the results, but won't reveal who these companies are. He's not a member of the British Polling Council either.

Not only that, but he's an extremely wealthy Tory peer, and former deputy chairman of the Party. During the campaign, he tweeted his admiration of Sturgeon: whose 'danger to England' just so happened, by purest coincidence, to constitute the central plank of the successful Conservative strategy. I have never known a Tory give such regular praise to a nationalist in the way Ashcroft did.

His final 'snapshot', released well after 7am on election day, had Conservative and Labour tied, and only added to the bigger picture that the two parties were deadlocked. But ask yourself, purely hypothetically: if you were a Tory who naturally desired your party to win, would you want the final poll to have them well ahead... or locked in a race too close to call, which would encourage maximum possible turnout? More to the point: purely hypothetically, if you were a Tory who wanted maximum possible negative exposure of Labour throughout an election campaign, scaring the public into voting against them, would you want them to be well behind... or seemingly on the verge of victory?

How far the obvious flaws in Ashcroft (sorry, I mean the companies which he buys his polling in from)'s data helped explain the almost identical flaws in every other firm's data, I couldn't possibly answer. But how had such an obviously self-interested individual become the most influential figure in opinion polling? Why were at least two very well-publicised forecasting sites so dependent on deeply flawed data? Why weren't more questions asked about his motivations?

One man who did ask such questions - many, many such questions - was the Labour peer, Lord Foulkes. He conducted an online pursuit of his Tory contemporary throughout the campaign: leading to frequently entertaining exchanges, but never leaving observers in much doubt over what he thought. Foulkes frequently hinted that the polls were wrong; and in February 2015, went a great deal further. Opinion polls, he fulminated, were increasingly:

Being manipulated at the behest of people with money, whether they be the media or individuals, as part of the political process... What is clear now is the media in particular, but others as well, are demanding instant polling, determining when it should be done and how it should be done. The academic rigour that ought to be carried out isn't being carried out.

Given what this chapter has set out, who could possibly argue true academic rigour had been carried out on a whole series of polls which weren't just a little wrong... but a lot wrong? Very wrong. Astonishingly wrong.

Similarly astonishing, when you stop and think about it for a moment, was how, after half a century's dominance of Scotland, the Labour Party found itself swept away just like that via a speeding yellow flash; meltdown triggered by The Vow and its ongoing fallout. But what's so often forgotten about the referendum campaign - the democratic event that changed Scotland forever - is that between August 2013 and polling day itself, just two opinion polls (and only one with a sample size of over 1000) put 'Yes' ahead. That latter poll, by YouGov and the Sunday Times, was publicised with unusual relish by Rupert Murdoch on Twitter, and sent shockwaves through the British establishment.

Its response to one solitary rogue poll? The Vow. As soon as it had been made, Labour were in no position to control what resulted; and when that involved Cameron cutting the rug away from Brown's feet on the steps of Downing Street, suddenly, a party which for so long had dominated Scottish politics was faced by an oncoming train it (because it was in government in neither England nor Scotland) could do nothing about: which flattened it completely, destroying its broader electoral hopes in the process.

Opinion polls, then, can be remarkable things with still more remarkable consequences. Especially when they're conducted for a newspaper de facto owned by someone with a surprisingly good relationship with the then First Minister of Scotland; even more when they help trigger the collapse of a party which had taken that someone on in a manner of, at the time, no other British political party in my lifetime. What did that someone's lead redtop do during the election campaign? Simultaneously support the SNP (against Labour) in Scotland; the Tories (against Labour, while banging home the message of dangerous, rebellious, left-wing Scots coming to rule over the English) in England.

Murdoch, of course, was humiliated by the Leveson inquiry into phone hacking; deemed 'not a fit person to exercise the stewardship of a major international company' by the British government, and has been investigated by both British and American authorities for bribery and corruption. This perhaps helps explain The Scottish Sun's enthusiastic support for the SNP; The Sun's vituperative opposition to Miliband, whose ideas threatened to end any remaining influence of Murdoch over the UK media, and its voicing of a narrative which would inexorably pull England and Scotland apart, threatening the imminent break-up of a 314-year-old Union.

Through his actions, Murdoch left no doubt regarding his open hostility to the UK and British establishment. Hell hath no fury like a global press baron scorned: as Cameron would himself discover the following year. At the same time as Murdoch fell from grace in Britain, Ashcroft's star rose dramatically.

The examples of both provide a heavy reminder of what can happen when vested interests collide with the democratic process.

As Foulkes noted, the ever more influential polling business is, incomprehensibly, entirely unregulated. In such a world, despite their consistent inaccuracy, all polls are effectively taken on trust: a remarkable state of affairs. Even more so given their colossal subsequent failings in 2016 and 2017.

To return, though, to polling day. Having read Singh's masterpiece and absorbed all that it meant, I was in the utterly bizarre position of, despite being thousands of miles away, knowing conclusively that the polls were hopelessly askew; while the dear old British public did not. Neither did the BBC presenters: who in tandem with the entire watching world (but not, at least, maybe two or three of us) greeted the exit poll with incredulity. The moment I saw that poll, I was entirely sure it was either (a) absolutely accurate; or (b) still underestimated the Tories' position. The latter was how it proved. I told my disbelieving friends that it was over. And indeed it was.

2015 was my first experience of appallingly inaccurate polls completely dominating the agenda, and palpably becoming corrupted by commercial and vested interests. Sadly, it would be far from the last.

4: COMETH THE HOUR: JEREMY CORBYN AND THE 2017 GENERAL ELECTION

'I would swim through vomit to vote against this Bill. And listening to some of the nauseating speeches tonight, I think we might have to' - John McDonnell

Shortly before 10pm on 7 May, 2015. Most within the Labour Party expected that next day, they'd be forming a minority government; Ed Miliband was even preparing a victory speech. Then one exit poll later, the party's collective chin hit the deck with a resounding crash. All sorts of certainties had vanished.

In the aftermath of its defeat, Labour behaved like a punch-drunk boxer: flailing around helplessly in all directions. Unable to find a coherent narrative under Miliband, most within the Parliamentary Party were still more unable to properly understand either why it lost, or what to do about it. Why? Under conventional circumstances, no clear path back to office existed: not given the ongoing decline of social democratic parties all over Europe; nor when we factor in Labour's long-term neglect of its core voters, grassroots members, activists and structures.

All sorts of narratives quickly emerged to explain the outcome: all of which had some merit, none of which painted the whole picture. None of them could; the answer was too complicated for anyone to perfectly encapsulate. Was Labour trusted on the economy? No, but that certainly didn't mean it should move rightwards. Did Labour shed support to the left? Yes, but FPTP would surely penalise it more than ever before if it did.

Labour's only successful living prime minister, Tony Blair, had no answers either. The electoral coalition he put together was only ever short-term; dependent entirely on him, a one-off political superstar, leading it; did a huge amount of long-term damage to the party; and enjoyed success amid economic conditions and social attitudes which no longer applied, and will probably never do so again.

That the party was so palpably bewildered and paralysed in the months after its defeat was entirely natural. Wherever it looked, whichever direction it might have sought to move towards, Labour was boxed in as never before. If it moved to the right and tried to become a more palatable version of the

Conservatives, not only would this have given up Scotland (without which, it could not win) as a lost cause, but it would have shed even more support to the now left-leaning Lib Dems, the Greens, the dispiritingly massed ranks of non-voters... and done itself lethal harm among its hollowed out grassroots. Upon whom any party depends to get its message out - but it must have a worthwhile, meaningful message with which to mobilise them in the first place.

If it moved to the left in a bid to recapture its core support and sound more authentic, it was still unlikely to make much headway in Scotland, where the rise of the SNP has been a fundamental, generational, maybe even irreversible shift, presaging independence in no more than the medium term; and it was *assumed* that this would achieve nothing whatsoever in Tory-dominated southern England: without which, it cannot win. Too right-wing for Scotland, too left-wing for England; or so it seemed, at least.

What changed this equation were the ever-worsening realities of austerity Britain. The country had become one of socialism for the rich and (portions of) the old; dog eat dog capitalism for the poor and young. A nation turned upside down, with young people overwhelmed with debt (which most will never pay off) even before entering an ever more insecure job market flooded with graduates, in which they've been formalised as second class citizens until age 25; expected to deal with skyrocketing rents; unable to ever hope of buying a home for love nor money; and if they come from an abusive home and have no support network, are quite likely to find themselves on the streets. Had Labour ignored all this, not only would it have lost the support of the young, but many would have been lost to politics and the democratic process altogether.

Even then, though, there remained the compelling question of what to do about the so-called 'grey vote'. Could it possibly afford to propose rent caps, a land value tax, any sort of pension reform, or remove any of the things which so many pensioners enjoyed through the coalition's 'triple lock' at the same time as hundreds of thousands in work found themselves plunged into poverty? To do so would have been electoral suicide. How had the Tories obtained the critical support of so many pensioners? Both through being much more trusted on the economy, and the outrageous pre-election bribe of allowing instant access for over-55s to their pension pots. A bribe supported and implemented by the Lib Dems: to their loss and their coalition partners' gain.

And then, there was UKIP. Amongst Labour's many election blunders in 2015, its implacable opposition to a referendum on the EU was maybe worst of all. This not only meant that it didn't trust the people and thought it knew better; it underscored its horrendous obliviousness to the effect of uncontrolled immigration from the EU into working class areas: *perceived* (and in politics, as in life, perception is nine-tenths of reality) by so many as pushing down wages and making work ever more insecure.

New Labour's whole attitude towards immigration - sneering at those who raised the issue as 'racist', and wholly impervious to its drawbacks - too often resembled that of cossetted, out of touch metropolitan liberals hectoring from an ivory tower. That it needed to develop a considerably more Eurosceptic stance, seeking real reform on freedom of movement, was greatly apparent.

Yet it also knew that if it did this, it would run the risk of losing the middle class, urban liberal support it had gained in London - its only election success story - and looking unprincipled: changing its position too much. Everywhere it looked, there was a huge problem; whatever votes it might have gained through any particular shift in policy, it would surely lose for the exact same reason.

Against such a backdrop, of course it was confused. Of course it looked a complete shambles. Any other party trapped in such a grim position would've done too. Yet it also made a series of decisions which, at the time, seemed like monumental blunders… but entirely by accident, ended up solving its great dilemma.

Decision/blunder/accidental success #1: with the final apparent misstep of his hapless leadership, Miliband stupidly stood down immediately instead of presiding over an orderly, Michael Howard to David Cameron 2005-style transition. This meant that, for the second Parliament in a row, Labour instantly ceded any control of the narrative to the Tories. Last time it had done that, a cacophony of gibberish about it having 'caused the crash' - the big lie which won Cameron the election - had been allowed to go entirely unchecked.

This time, the narrative shifted to social security (or as Cameron liked to pejoratively term it, 'welfare': Tory cynicism summed up in a single word), with Labour accused of being 'weak on welfare' if it did not support a whole series of horrific cuts which would plunge hundreds of thousands into poverty (including, staggeringly, many in work); socially cleanse the south of

England (given the Conservatives' planned boundary changes, a nakedly political move designed to drive any remaining non-Tory support out of more affluent constituencies altogether); remove £30 per week from the disabled and infirm; slash the already derisory amounts provided to asylum seekers and their children; remove access to housing benefit altogether for anyone under 21; and even require women who have a third child due to being raped to prove it.

During the 2010-15 Parliament, the coalition's narrative on the deficit was based, as we have seen, on the politics of bullshit. The narrative on social security was very similar. The housing benefit bill is what it is because of constant failure to do anything at all about exorbitant rents; and just as alarmingly few voters ever realised that George Osborne, not Labour, had doubled the national debt, so they were also unaware that by far the largest chunk of the 'welfare' bill went not on unemployment benefit, not on benefit fraud… but on pensions. The recipients of which, again for nakedly political reasons, the Tories protected and indulged.

Did Labour challenge this catastrophic narrative? Of course not. Instead, the left watched aghast as Harriet Harman, the disastrously incompetent acting leader, demanded the Parliamentary Labour Party (PLP) abstain on the Welfare Reform Bill on 20 July. Together, leadership contenders Andy Burnham and Yvette Cooper at least forced Harman to agree to a reasoned amendment; but whatever the whys and wherefores of parliamentary procedure, it was absolutely appalling politics. Those who accused Labour of being 'Red Tories' or 'Tory lite' were, quite rightly, greatly emboldened.

No such hesitation from Corbyn. Nor, for that matter, from John McDonnell either. This man, ludicrously demonised so often in recent years as some terrifying 'Stalinist', was one of very few grown-ups in the room that awful day. Like Corbyn and a handful of others, he had both a head and a heart. If you ever wanted to know exactly when Corbynism was born, why it rose as it then did, or why the Brexit vote went in such a way, this speech encapsulates the whole thing perfectly.

I would swim through vomit to vote against this Bill. And listening to some of the nauseating speeches tonight, I think we might have to. Poverty in my constituency is not a lifestyle choice. It's imposed upon people.

We hear lots about how high the welfare bill is. Let's understand why that's the case. The housing benefit bill is so high because for generations we've failed to build council houses. We've failed to control rents. We've done nothing about the 300,000 properties that stand empty in this country.

The reason tax credits are so high is because pay is so low. And the reason pay is so low is because employers have exploited workers, and we've removed trade union rights that would enable people to be protected at work. We now have less than a third of our workers covered by collective bargain agreements.

And the reason unemployment bills are so high is because we've failed to invest in our economy. We've allowed deindustrialisation of the north and Scotland and elsewhere. They're the reasons why the welfare bill is so high. And this Welfare Reform Bill, as all the other welfare reform bills in recent years have done, blames the poor for their own poverty and not the system.

On Friday, I brought together in my constituency in a poverty seminar, the welfare advice agencies, the local churches and religious groups, to talk about why there are poor people in my constituency. The reason they're poor is because rents are so high. People struggle to keep a roof over their heads. What this Bill will do on the cap is remove £63 a week from those families simply trying to keep a decent home over their children's heads.

The second reason... is low pay. They depend in my constituency on tax credits to live. Parents choosing whether they eat or the children eat that week. This will take £6 a week from every one of those families.

The other reason we've got poverty in my constituency is because people have disabilities. They struggle to work and can't do it. This will take £30 a week off people with disabilities who are desperately trying to work because they're in the work support group trying to get work.

That's the reasons for the poverty in my constituency. I find it appalling that we sit here in, to be frank, relative wealth ourselves, and we're willing to vote through increased poverty on the people back home in our home constituencies...

Some of the benefit cuts are going to be absolutely appalling. What is not in this Bill, but it's being sneaked through by the government, is the cut in support allowances for asylum seeker children. Cut by 30%. Some of the poorest children in our society we're about to ensure that we push into further poverty.

What we need now is an honest discussion about the reasons for that poverty, and how we can invest to ensure that we lift people out of poverty... and to come along and describe a derisory increase in the minimum wage as a 'living wage', when we know a living wage in this country is at least £10 an hour, I think is a disgrace.

Read that speech. Watch it too. Then tell me how McDonnell and Corbyn are the 'extremists', while all those Labour colleagues who abstained were the 'sensible' ones. What kind of country allows policies this grotesque to have happened on its watch? A country which needs both these men in government, desperately.

Decision/blunder/accidental success #2: on 18 May, thanks to Miliband having changed the rules around leadership elections, Harman threw the entire contest open to anyone prepared to pay just £3 for the privilege. The idea was clearly to elect a leader with national, not just party appeal; but it was initially ridiculed. Excoriated. Up popped The Telegraph to helpfully implore its readers to fork out three quid, vote for Jeremy Corbyn and 'destroy the Labour Party'.

Corbyn, though, was the beneficiary of another decision/blunder/accidental success, as well as the previous two. Never even wanting the leadership to begin with, he only agreed to stand because of the feeling that the left needed a representative; someone to put forward its ideas in the long contest ahead. McDonnell and Diane Abbott, both of whom had stood in the past, both ruled themselves out; yet Corbyn needed 35 MPs to nominate him, and at 11.15am on 15 June, 2015, 45 minutes before the deadline, he still required nine more.

Those nine individuals were Margaret Beckett, Jon Cruddas, Rushanara Ali, Sadiq Khan, Tulip Siddiq, Neil Coyle, Clive Efford, Gareth Thomas, Gordon Marsden, and Andrew Smith. Marsden nominated Corbyn at 11.58am, two minutes before the deadline; his was the decisive one, though amid the chaos and confusion, the Corbyn team had forgotten Efford's nomination, so Smith was initially declared the man who put Corbyn on the ballot.

Two minutes. In fact, according to McDonnell, ten seconds. Just imagine that; think of how different not just the Labour Party, but British politics itself would be, had those final few MPs not taken such a fateful decision. Which, I should add, was merely intended to broaden the debate; nobody thought Corbyn had an earthly of winning. Including even himself.

In the contest which followed, though, while his rivals, Andy Burnham, Yvette Cooper and Kendall, all competed to sound 'mainstream' and appeal to centrist or even centre-right swing voters, Corbyn, with nothing to lose, could simply be himself; and crucially, challenge the economic narrative around austerity and welfare cuts in a way none of the others were prepared to do. None of the positions he espoused were remotely 'extreme' even in centre-left terms; this contest suddenly had someone who looked like Labour and sounded like Labour. Whose rivals rapidly started to appear out of touch, disoriented and disconnected.

Instead of facing him down with conviction, authority, passion, vision, leadership, Corbyn's competitors were all cowed. Burnham embarrassed himself during the Welfare Bill fiasco and even gave way to Tory lies around Labour's spending in government; while Kendall, a tactic without a strategy, a Blairite who didn't seem to understand the first thing about Blairism, polarised the debate so much with a series of harshly expressed right-wing platforms that she unwittingly pushed many voters towards Corbyn. As for Cooper? She had nothing substantial to say about... anything really.

In part, this was because of AV. Last time round, this infernal, appalling system had delivered the wrong brother. This time, its emphasis on second preferences seemed to leave Burnham and Cooper frightened of even trying to articulate anything convincing; the latter's strategy of securing enough second choice votes to win failed completely. But in both her and Burnham's cases, their paralysis provided a reminder of just how many top-down machine politicians Labour had produced during the Blair/Brown era. When the going got tough, both went missing; Corbyn's authenticity was quite the compelling contrast.

Upon his crushing victory, in which he obtained 60% of the vote, and finished more than forty points clear of second-placed Burnham, Corbyn immediately found himself assailed by the British political commentariat. Most of whom had been miserably wrong about the general election months earlier; few of whom appeared to have reflected on this for a single moment. 'Labour have made a terrible mistake!', they cried in unison; but beyond the sheer chance of how Corbyn had got onto the ballot, much more powerful, centrifugal forces were now at work.

By this point - late summer 2015 - these had already been seen in action across Europe, notably in Greece, Spain and Scotland; and through both Bernie Sanders and, in a completely different way, Donald Trump, in the US. To merely look at the huge new intake of SNP MPs was to tell its own story: so many of them seemed like ordinary, authentic representatives of their people. Too many Labour MPs hadn't for far too long.

During the election campaign, squeezed by the vicissitudes of FPTP, Miliband found himself trapped into repeating a bunch of meaningless, vapid, insipid slogans. 'Working people'. 'A better plan for Britain'. Or as David Axelrod derisively put it, 'vote Labour and win a microwave'. 'Our politicians don't stand for anything anymore', despaired so many; and especially when it came to the left, they were right.

Compare and contrast Harman's inept handling of the Welfare Reform Bill - when Labour appeared to sell out as never before, and Corbyn effectively won the leadership just by knowing who the party was supposed to stand for - with the SNP. No such nonsense from them. They had long since understood the need to *be seen* as on the side of the most vulnerable. More to the point: what is politics *for* if not standing up for what you believe in and foursquare against those who threaten it?

Had Labour not so completely lost sight of itself, it is inconceivable that such an epic blunder could've occurred. The Tories weren't just mounting a huge attack on social security; they were even about to impoverish millions in work. Frank Field's brilliant analysis set it out in stark terms.

The only one who stood up for what they believed? Corbyn. For the first time since 1994, someone was not just standing up, but shouting traditional Labour values from the rooftops. Right when they most urgently needed to be expressed too.

I don't think it's much of a stretch to conclude that most of those pundits or politicians who, ever since 2015, have continually sneered at Corbyn's supporters and the man himself, haven't been affected by austerity. Do they know what it's like to be forced out of their home because of the bedroom tax? Do they know anyone sanctioned and left without any means of support for weeks, months or longer, because of either bureaucratic incompetence or (as many of us believe) deliberate cruelty? Can they imagine what it's like to have to choose between heating their home and feeding their children? Are they aware of the horrific impact of cuts on social care up and down the land? At any point, have they bothered to research the shocking numbers of deaths within weeks of those found 'fit for work' by the DWP?

Austerity isn't some medicine to be swallowed with a few mild side-effects. Austerity *kills*. Specifically: it kills the poorest. Those least able to protect themselves. If the Labour Party isn't there to help, support and protect them, what is it there for? So at length, it made its choice. At last, it rediscovered its soul; and stuck two fingers up at Britain's mad voting system: in which affluent, suburban homeowners had long been far more electorally significant than single mothers from broken homes; the mentally ill, losing their benefits in their hundreds of thousands every year; or the disabled.

FPTP, surely, was what led to Miliband's otherwise incomprehensible acceptance of the urgent need for deficit reduction. During the leadership contest, Burnham stated that Labour had 'spent too much' while in office; but it had not. The public being so flat out wrong about something so important is no reason to accept the falsehood. Yet all Burnham, Cooper and Kendall had offered was mostly more of the same to those already horrendously affected.

After the general election, John Curtice, doyen of British psephologists, highlighted that not only would Scotland be a hopeless cause for Labour if it did not move leftwards; but intriguingly, a clear public desire for a compelling alternative economic narrative. While Kendall took this to mean 'we must reassure the public over our economic competence', Corbyn, quite rightly, was emboldened. At a time of 40% cuts to Whitehall budgets; 'welfare' being deliberately turned into a dirty word, with vulnerable recipients scared off even trying to claim it; and the worst, slowest recovery in 300 years (the third worst in 650 years, topped only by the South Sea Bubble and the Black Death), if this didn't call for a distinctive alternative, what on Earth would?

Something else was now playing its part too, though. Namely, to increasing numbers (especially amongst the poor and squeezed middle), the failure of neoliberalism itself. Until 2008, there was always a sense that democracy and capitalism went hand in hand in delivering, if not a land of milk and honey, at least progress: each generation doing that bit better than the last.

Not anymore. Now, for the first time since the war, twenty- and thirty-somethings would do _worse than their parents_; and the prognosis for those younger is even worse than that. If someone is born into property wealth in the UK, they'll probably do fine. If they're not, they probably won't. Social mobility has been static for decades; very soon, it will go into reverse.

The only individual who put forward a real plan to deal with all this? Corbyn. He tapped into huge amounts of support from young people who simply hadn't counted enough under FPTP for successive governments of both hues to have cared about; he inspired them. Purely by telling a story they could relate to.

More broadly, the sense that, since 2008, Western capitalism had mutated into a rich-get-richer-sod-everyone-else scam was wreaking havoc upon social democratic parties across Europe. Most of which were in power at the time of the crash; many of which had embraced free market economics and moved away from their core support in the decade or so beforehand; none of which had come up with any serious response since. In the absence of any viable alternative to capitalism, the best they could do was say 'the system's terrible. Vote for us, and... er... we'll make it slightly less terrible', but that's no platform at all. So radical, populist parties of the left had begun to emerge instead.

More than that: as Creasy continually reiterated during her strong but unsuccessful Deputy Leadership campaign, Labour 'had to become a movement again'... but a grassroots movement cannot exist if it stands for nothing worth standing for. Especially given Cameron was threatening to take an electric chainsaw to Labour's critical trade union funding. For it to survive, let alone prosper, Labour needed the hundreds of thousands of new members delivered by Corbyn; and to keep them, a return to the top-down triangulation of the past just wasn't an option. Its task now was to build towards the long term and a genuinely new, bottom-up politics of the left instead.

I voted for Corbyn in 2015. As far as I was concerned, only he had even a ghost of a chance of somehow bringing disaffected working class voters back from the SNP and UKIP; reaching out to those who'd viewed Miliband as 'Tory lite', so had gone Green or Plaid Cymru; while holding together Labour's young, liberal, multi-ethnic support across the cities. Yet I still had the gravest of doubts about him. I was extremely sceptical that he could lead effectively; and knew that the PLP, so few among whom had even wanted him in the contest at all, would never stand him.

So it was that, instead of launching a whole new Labour Party to the public, poor Corbyn found himself spending much of the next 20 months dealing with impossible colleagues. In retrospect, this period - the PLP doing its utmost to bring their leader down, and only amplifying the message of an implacably hostile media - probably cost Labour a majority at the 2017 general election. Called by May in an attempt to destroy both it, and any remaining opposition to hard Brexit.

Yet in fairness, many of those MPs who went on to oppose him, call for his resignation and agree a motion of no confidence didn't do so because they are all enemies of what progressives everywhere want. They did so because on all available evidence, to go to the left meant certain disaster. No left-wing platform had won a majority since 1974, nor a convincing majority since 1966; and since Blair's departure, as Labour had inched leftwards, its position had grown substantially worse.

These MPs, like almost all political data analysts, could only go on what they knew; or rather, what they *thought* they knew. And what they thought they knew was as follows:

Young people and traditional non-voters wouldn't vote.
Corbyn would lead the Labour Party to oblivion.
Corbyn's team were a bunch of fanatics with no idea what they were doing.
Brexit was a sign of socially conservative attitudes and identity politics sweeping the West.
UKIP voters would desert to the Conservatives in their droves.

Theresa May's 'strength and stability' was exactly the leadership the country wanted.

The electorate thought Labour had caused the financial crash.

The electorate blamed Labour for uncontrollable immigration.

The electorate thought Labour meant benefits for the workshy.

The electorate would never trust Labour again with the levers of the economy.

The extent to which many so commentators in the liberal media are themselves, for want of a better term, Blairite, may be a matter of correlation; but in the gargantuan failure of all polling companies except YouGov and Survation to predict what happened on 8 June 2017, it's tempting to attribute causation too. As Nate Silver noted in a much misunderstood piece, conventional wisdom is invariably wrong because it's guided by confirmation bias. Not by what we know; but what we *think* we know. And this bias - however unconscious, subtle, or well-intentioned - affects all analysis.

But in any democracy anywhere, voters cannot be pigeonholed. The point of leadership isn't to cravenly accept public opinion, but to change it, and transform millions of lives in consequence. So if Corbyn's platform at last offered working class voters and young people real hope and dignity, highlighted the clear alternative to austerity which has always existed, was massively more in tune with an electorate split 52-48 on Brexit, and the man himself responded to vicious personal attacks which demean British politics by always being positive, always reaching out, why wouldn't he have been successful?

In the analysts, commentators and insurgent MPs' defence, though, they weren't only guided by opinion polls which had Labour 20 points or more behind. They were also informed by real results at by-election and local level: which in May, had left the main opposition party on a miserable 27%. Never in history had such a party increased its share of the vote at a general election held the following month; to have done so by fully half was unthinkable. But again: what we think is not what we know. History is just that; the future can always confound.

Why did it do so? To be sure, it had little to do with the efforts of far too much of the mainstream media. In only the second week of the campaign, Loughborough University found that, weighted by circulation, Labour's net balance of positive to negative articles in the written press was over 100 times worse than the Conservatives'.

The European Broadcasting Union, moreover, has a net trust index, which surveys public attitudes to the written press across the whole of Europe. In 2016, the UK finished bottom by fully 14 percentage points: a figure which should shame the whole industry.

Yet it's not only The Sun, The Express or The Daily Mail - parasites, not patriots, as Aaron Bastani[4] of Novara Media memorably referred to them - who are culpable here. The BBC, funded by the public on pain of imprisonment, is too; alarmingly so.

While May's speech responding to the London Bridge terror attacks was front and centre of the BBC website's coverage, Corbyn's could barely be found anywhere. One of the most widely read articles of the whole campaign was a Laura Kuenssberg piece on Corbyn's attitude to shoot-to-kill which the BBC Trust itself had ruled was misleading, yet the corporation refused to take down.

When its flagship show, The Daily Politics, ran an opening feature on the two leaders' approaches to terrorism and security, images of May featured the captions that 'the police budget (had been) protected since 2015', and that 'counter-terrorism funding (was) increasing'; while images of Corbyn stated that he 'faces questions about associations with terrorist groups', and shamelessly juxtaposed him alongside Osama bin Laden.

When discussing the future of the NHS - the number one issue at the election for many voters - incomprehensibly, the BBC featured a former Tory councillor and private consultant as an 'ordinary voter'. When Amber Rudd, the Home Secretary and lead Tory spokesperson throughout the campaign, had one of her hustings opponents *censored* for the crime of asking awkward questions, other websites covered this; the BBC, naturally, did not.

And on election night itself, as a parade of the same old tired figures trotted out for every such night for decades on end droned on endlessly, what was so remarkable was how few Corbyn supporters - how few people who *actually understood what was going on* - were interviewed.

For the most part, this is not an issue which other broadcasters tend to have. Channel 4 News' coverage was informative and hugely analytical. ITV's combination of Osborne and Ed Balls worked extremely well. Even Sky's coverage was modern, topical and thought-provoking. Auntie, by comparison, was astonishingly biased.

Shortly into its election night show, Emily Thornberry was interviewed by

David Dimbleby. Once more, the Tories' 'coalition of chaos' line was trotted out, despite the BBC's own exit poll showing it would be May's party which would have to form one. When Thornberry asked why the BBC hadn't questioned the Tories about this, Dimbleby's response was horribly instructive. 'Well no, they all say they're going to have a majority'.

Guided by polls. Guided by confirmation bias, which played a huge part in those polls. Guided by conventional wisdom; not leaving that wisdom to the electorate. Think of it: at no point during the campaign, despite her only holding a wafer-thin majority to begin with, did a single journalist anywhere ask May, 'if there's a hung Parliament, who will you talk to?' Just as during the EU referendum, at no point were Northern Irish politics mentioned at all, despite the colossal implications of a Leave vote for the UK-Irish border. How does any of this inform the public on decisions of such profound consequence?

Given all this, it should scarcely be a surprise that from the very start of his leadership, Corbyn's team saw little point in working with much of the mass media. Electoral rules at least demanded some semblance of balance in the broadcasters' coverage, and voters suddenly discovered that Corbyn wasn't the dangerous ogre he'd been made out to be at all. But just as, if not more important, was how brilliantly Labour utilised social media: through platforms such as Novara and Facebook. In the final week of the campaign, one in four of all UK Facebook users saw a video by Momentum, another frequently misunderstood, derided movement; yet which helped deliver millions of voters to Labour.

Sure enough, some commentators still couldn't grasp what had happened even in the aftermath. A few moaned that 'Labour still lost'; others espoused the absurd proposition that under any other leader, Labour would have won. This was both lunatic, and a sign of just how hermetically sealed the bubble which some pundits reside in had truly become; because only Corbyn could've expanded the membership so much. Only Corbyn could've attracted such huge crowds the length and breadth of the country at rallies which, again, the BBC did not cover.

Only Corbyn, by offering something truly different through old-style, straight-talking, honest campaigning, could've enthused young people in such a way; and only Corbyn could've somehow put together a voting coalition incorporating Greens and Kippers, working classes and metropolitan liberals, whites and BAMEs: which meant that places as different as Kensington, Liverpool and Kensington, London (average house price: £1.4m) were now both red; and that Corbyn delivered the biggest increase in Labour's share of the vote since 1945.

All this was achieved despite a pessimistic, overly defensive Labour HQ, itself suffering from chronic confirmation bias, under-funding marginals. Despite a Parliamentary Party which had wanted Corbyn to be removed ever since he became leader; spent most of the campaign expecting to be wiped out, plainly canvassed the wrong people (!), and missed the surge of new voters entirely. Despite an electoral map which had suggested that votes would pointlessly pile up in core areas, while marginals would fall by the bucketload. Despite a media which had barely taken Corbyn seriously at any point, and never given him a remotely fair crack. Despite a prime minister who called the election in a seemingly invincible position, with everything in her favour.

As for the Tories? Even at this point, before Brexit would drag the country into near total disrepair, their problem was and remains simple. They're toxic. Toxic to millions of voters who've watched their living standards fall and wages plummet during the so-called 'economic recovery'.

Toxic to working class communities destroyed by decades of 'There Is No Alternative' neo-liberalism. Toxic to aspirational working and middle classes in a country with the lowest social mobility and one of the highest levels of inequality in the developed world. Toxic to the unemployed and disabled; scapegoated, scorned and punished with often lethal cuts.

Toxic, perhaps above all, to Britain's young. Its future. On election night, Justine Greening, the Education Secretary for heaven's sake, patronised the 'idealism' of young voters: only further confirming that her party had irretrievably lost the plot. It's not idealistic, Justine, to believe that better things are possible than being swamped with unsustainable levels of student debt, most of which won't even be fully paid off (a looming time bomb every bit as dangerous to the public finances as the property bubble or credit card debt).

Nor is it idealistic to believe that when a whole generation benefits from free healthcare, free university education, cheap housing and generous pension schemes, pulling up the drawbridge and expecting their children and grandchildren - grappling with insecure employment, pathetic wages, out-of-control rental prices and a housing market which resembles a Ponzi scheme - to pay for their pensions, healthcare, winter fuel allowances and free TV licences is somehow reasonable. It's not. 'Free stuff', Daniel Hannan? In Britain, that's long been the preserve of the wealthy and (some of) the old, not the poor and young.

To be fair, as he's a far better man than I'll ever be, Corbyn didn't go remotely as far as I just have; which really ought to tell us something. In any society with horrendous, inexcusable levels of inter-generational injustice, attacking those who've benefited from it is no answer at all. What is? The plain and simple redistribution of wealth which all governments have shied away from since 1979.

Almost 13 million people voted Labour because they know that the current system does not work. They know it's been rigged against them. This awareness was what, above all, drove Brexit: not hatred of the EU, but of the same old miserable status quo propagated by machine politicians who'd systematically abandoned the working class and had no idea about the lives of most people. And hallelujah, along came someone offering a real alternative at last.

So terrified were the Tories of being rumbled, they made zero effort - none at all - to encourage anyone to register to vote: and may even have used dark advertising designed to actively suppress it. They'd already made every effort to gerrymander constituencies and de-fund opposition parties. Having brought in individual registration as a deliberate attempt to make it harder for students and those living in shared households to vote, they want to introduce ID cards for future elections. The pattern is clear. This is not a party which cares about anyone but a privileged few, or even democracy itself.

Desperate to avoid echo chambers, I have plenty of Tories on my Twitter feed. Throughout the 2017 campaign, there was scarcely a single re-tweeted message which had anything positive to say at all about the party they supported. Instead, just about everything focused relentlessly on Corbyn, the IRA, or Abbott; it was personal and hysterical in tone; and featured never-ending, instantly demonstrable lies. This party does not understand the people it purports to govern.

For Labour, by contrast, the future was suddenly brighter than at any point since the Iraq war. It now had strongholds all over the country; a burgeoning membership and hugely innovative activist base, both online and on the ground; an electoral map which favoured it; and the government it opposed was mired in absolute, ongoing turmoil, from which it had no escape.

No, Labour didn't win the election. But it won something which, in the long run, should prove far more significant. It won back hope; it won back the prospect of real, radical, transformational change; and above all, it changed the contours of the debate completely. Now the impossible wasn't just possible. All of a sudden, it beckoned.

5: APOCALYPSE NOW? THE EU REFERENDUM

'Britain faces a simple and inescapable <u>choice</u> - stability and strong Government with me, or chaos with Ed Miliband' - David Cameron

'Absolutely <u>nobody</u> is talking about threatening our place in the single market' - Daniel Hannan

Getting on towards 25 years ago now, in Politics A-Level class at school, I remember arguing passionately that a referendum on Britain's membership of the European Union (EU) must be held. Only a referendum, I reasoned, would educate the public on the costs and benefits of being part of the EU; and only a referendum would finally give the electorate a voice on the rapidly changing nature of the Union, denied them for so long.

In the two decades which followed, those in favour of British membership had opportunity after opportunity to explain what the advantages were. They failed: mirroring the high-handed, craven attitudes of technocratic elites in Brussels in so doing. The constant refusal to allow the people to decide enabled the whole question of the EU to fester at the heart of political discourse, playing into the hands of its many opponents.

Yet this - and my hopelessly idealistic viewpoint expressed while still a teenager - is to reason without the extraordinarily pernicious influence of the British press. For which, fake news about the EU was a staple for decades before the referendum plunged the UK into a state of purgatory; from which it has yet to re-emerge.

So this chapter has several aims. First, it looks at the very real, reasonable arguments employed by good faith, principled Leavers. Then it examines what actually happened; how the referendum campaign was taken over by interminable nonsense from both sides, especially Leave; and dark money, which the UK media has been extraordinarily reluctant to expose. It concludes with a reminder of the underlying causes of Brexit which had nothing to do with corrupt donors, foreign interference or lies; causes which, needless to add, are very much still with us today.

It's easy to forget now; but until the mid-1980s or so, much of the British left favoured withdrawal from the then European Economic Community

(EEC), while the Conservative Party was split. So much so that pro-European Tory MPs and ministers, infuriated by Margaret Thatcher's mounting antipathy towards the European project, brought the Iron Lady down in 1990, for reasons which seem remarkable now. After her fall, the whole issue of Europe would poison the party, root to tip; while the highly Europhile New Labour grasped the political nettle. Even entry into the euro seemed likely at one point.

Yet the British left's quarter-century-long enthusiastic support for all things Europe wasn't only at odds with UK public opinion; but in many ways, the facts on the ground. The euro experiment became a political, economic and social disaster: impoverishing huge swathes of southern Europe, tying it to a currency with no escape, and even robbing member states of anything resembling democracy or control of their own destinies. Freedom of movement, the dream of so many pro-Europeans, has substantially imploded in tandem with the Schengen agreement.

EU political institutions not only profoundly lack democratic legitimacy, but proved themselves inert, all but helpless, in the face of the greatest refugee crisis since 1945. National governments can hardly agree on what day of the week it is, let alone how to respond holistically; anti-immigration sentiment has risen across much of the continent. By the middle of the decade, the question was being posed: was the very thing which was designed to bring help bring peace and stability to a region so often ravaged by war now unwittingly provoking not unity, but mounting anger and division?

The forerunner to the Common Market, the European Coal and Steel Community (ECSC), was the brainchild of extraordinarily enlightened French and West German ministers. Twice in the preceding 36 years, their countries had done each other untold levels of human suffering; and Europe's longer history had involved constant cycles of violence and misery. The peace we all take for granted now was a dream to statesmen such as Robert Schuman of France and Konrad Adenauer of West Germany: both of whom displayed immense courage and remarkably far-sighted vision. Countries which trade with one another do not fight each other. The European project, based on supranationalism and interdependence, was born.

Yet given how recently the two countries had been at war, and the natural mistrust of both their peoples, what would have happened had the ECSC, founded in Paris in 1951 (where Belgium, Italy, Luxembourg and the Netherlands joined France and West Germany as co-signatories), been put to a democratic vote? And where Europe was concerned, lack of demonstrable popular consent would prove a constant and ever-mounting problem.

Jean Monnet, founding father of the ECSC, has often wrongly had the following apocryphal words attributed to him:

> Europe's nations should be guided towards the super-state without their people understanding what is happening. This can be accomplished by successive steps each disguised as having an economic purpose, but which will eventually and irreversibly lead to federation.

In fact, these weren't Monnet's words at all - but those of the Conservative politician and author, Adrian Hilton, in _The Principality and Power of Europe_, published in 1997. Yet this is almost by the by. That so many have ascribed them to Monnet is because so many have been so shocked at what the European project has since become.

The ECSC morphed first into the Common Market, then the EEC. Britain joined in 1973, and its public approved membership by two to one in the 1975 referendum: where recently elected Tory leader, Mrs Thatcher, campaigned passionately for a 'Yes' vote. But what the electorate was sold then - a mutually beneficial club based on free trade and nothing more - was not remotely what would transpire; and gradually, the penny began to drop.

Contrary to her reputation of fire and brimstone (and especially, the myths she indulged following her downfall), Thatcher went on to sign the Single European Act: the first substantive revision of the Treaty of Rome since 1957, which codified not just economic, but political co-operation between member states. With the sole exception of the Lisbon Treaty, no single piece of legislation did more to accelerate the EEC's transformation from free trade zone to political behemoth.

Under pressure from various key Cabinet ministers - Nigel Lawson, Sir Geoffrey Howe, Douglas Hurd and John Major - and greatly against her better judgement, Thatcher even acceded to Britain's membership of the Exchange Rate Mechanism (ERM): where sterling would shadow the deutschmark, but as events would prove, at entirely the wrong rate. When when it came to proposals for a single currency, however, the prime minister balked.

In the House of Commons, Thatcher focused on the obvious threat which a common currency would pose to national, economic and parliamentary sovereignty. Her autobiography, paraphrased by The Telegraph in 2010, set out her broader fears with stunning levels of prophecy:

> (Thatcher) warned John Major, her euro-friendly chancellor of the exchequer, that the single

currency could not accommodate both industrial powerhouses such as Germany and smaller countries such as Greece. Germany, forecast Thatcher, would be phobic about inflation, while the euro would prove fatal to the poorer countries because it would 'devastate their inefficient economies'.

To watch the famous 'No! No! No!' debate in the Commons in October 1990 is to observe two things. First, a prime minister in absolute command of the issues: who foresaw with impeccable prescience that no country which loses control of its money supply can retain control over financial policy, parliamentary sovereignty, or even its democracy itself. And second: support which came more across the floor from figures such as Tony Benn or David Owen than her own party; especially, her own Cabinet.

Thatcher's increasingly autocratic style - going over the head of Sir Geoffrey, her deputy, and ignoring collective Cabinet government in the process - would bring her down within weeks. Yet her words have echoed down the years since. The Iron Lady got all manner of things wrong during her final years in office and divided the country horrendously throughout her premiership; but on Europe, she foresaw with perfect clarity exactly what was coming.

The President of the Commission, Mr. Delors, said at a press conference the other day that he wanted the European Parliament to be the democratic body of the Community, he wanted the Commission to be the Executive and he wanted the Council of Ministers to be the Senate. No. No. No.

History carries many strange, bitter ironies. Precisely because Thatcher had become so enormously unpopular by the end of her time, and thanks to the fratricidal nature of her removal, instead of these words being heeded, two things began to happen. Under her successor, Major, the Conservative Party, unable to forgive itself for what it had done, descended into poison and acrimony: with the amiable prime minister undermined at every turn by Eurosceptic backbenchers, egged on by an embittered ex-premier. The suddenly renascent Labour Party, meanwhile, defined itself against the hopelessly split Tories: the more the latter obsessed with Europe, the more Tony Blair guided his unified troops towards embracing Britain's destiny at the heart of the European project.

Yet however unelectable the Tories undoubtedly were, or obsessed with Europe they had plainly become, the detail of matters of profound importance - economic, political, social, and above all, democratic - was never properly discussed. The left simply embraced Europe as a fundamentally good thing; it never really stopped to ask itself why.

To be sure, what had now become the EU appeared to offer the kind of social protections which Thatcher had sought to remove; certainly, a spirit of open-minded, outward-looking internationalism chimed in perfectly with the broad church which New Labour had become. Yet even as it basked in public approbation, Blair's government never sought to explain the benefits of the EU to the British people, nor allow them any say (for example, on the proposed EU Constitution) via a referendum. There was simply no serious attempt by Europhiles to set out the merits of their position.

During this time, like so many of my friends and contemporaries, I was an EU enthusiast myself. Beyond some warm, fuzzy sense of peace on Earth and goodwill to all men - an aspiration of what Europe could be, not what it actually was - and blinkered antipathy to anything the Tories stood for, I never really thought about it in much depth. The Maastricht Treaty was so dense, so impenetrable, so voluminous, it seemed better suited as an offensive weapon than a vitally important document. Goodness knows, I had little or no knowledge of the intricacies of the European Council, European Commission, or European Parliament. Which of these bodies had what powers, I couldn't have begun to articulate; nor could anyone else I knew either.

Mind you, there was one detail I'd repeat to anyone who challenged me about my Europhilia. Freedom of movement. The idea that, should I so choose, I could up, leave, live and work in any other member state was marvellous as far as I was concerned: but in implementing this, the EU had begun to sow the seeds of its own downfall. In the UK, at least.

For there's a flipside to freedom of movement. Not merely mass immigration but uncontrollable immigration; nations which lose control of their own borders. And in a globalised world, that inevitably means those from poorer member states migrating to wealthier ones. Migration on such a scale - the largest wave of inward migration ever to hit the British Isles - is perceived (mostly wrongly, but try telling that to those who feel they are victims of it) to push wages down and local people, especially those living in poorer areas, out of jobs: generating anger, resentment, alienation, atomisation. The political and media narrative in Britain began to change. In line, it should be noted, with much of northern Europe.

Yet as public frustration grew, still the British people were denied any say on anything to do with the EU. And even in places where referenda were held - in France, the Netherlands, or (twice) in Ireland - rejections of the Nice Treaty, EU Constitution, or Lisbon Treaty were met with studied indifference on the part of EU leaders. The Constitution was turned into the Lisbon Treaty, and when the Irish people - the only national electorate anywhere in the EU to be allowed a vote on the most far-reaching, seismic piece of legislation in its history - vetoed this, after a few amendments, they were asked to vote again.

Why was Lisbon so important? In amending and consolidating the Treaties of Rome and Maastricht, it:

Moved the Council of Ministers from requiring unanimous agreement to qualified majority voting in at least 45 areas of policy

Brought in a 'double majority' system: which necessitates the support of at least 55% of European Council members, who must also represent at least 65% of EU citizens, in almost all areas of policy

Established a more powerful European Parliament, which would now form part of a bicameral legislature along with the Council of Ministers

Granted a legal personality to the EU, enabling it to agree treaties in its own name

Created a new long-term President of the European Council and a High Representative for Foreign and Security Policy

And made the Charter of Fundamental Rights, the EU's bill of rights, legally binding.

Whether you agree with these changes or not is beside the point. The point is: the peoples of Europe were never given a vote on it. Instead, all this was just pushed through over the European public's collective head. In the twenty-first century, how can such profound constitutional changes, which impact on all Europeans whether they recognise it or not, be allowed without democratic consent?

In any polity, if leaders or legislators do not accede to their position through the ballot box, this lack of accountability breeds out of touch, unanswerable governance about which the public can do nothing. Yet in many ways, that is the reality of the EU. The President of the Commission is approved by the Parliament; but this happens unopposed. All Commissioners - who together, comprise the executive of the EU - are nominated by member states.

The President of the European Council - the de facto *President of Europe*, the EU's principal representative on the global stage - is chosen by the heads of government of the member states. And even the European Parliament, whose members are all directly elected by the public, (1) Oversaw constant falling turnout between 1979 and 2014, with even this year's best figures since 1994 still barely scraping through 50%; (2) Cannot formally initiate legislation; (3) Does not contain a formal opposition.

In terms of genuine democracy, most of the above is unrecognisable. If more and more people believe that powers are shifting away from their hands and national legislatures towards a group of illegitimate, unelected bureaucrats and apparatchiks, it might well be because they're right.

One such apparatchik was Herman Van Rompuy, the European Council's first full-time President. An individual less cut out for the position of global ambassador for Europe, it's impossible to conceive of; and following his appointment, one man wasn't about to allow him to forget it.

As the EU's institutions have steadily fallen into disrepair, and publics across Europe grown more and more infuriated at the acquiescence of their national assemblies and established parties, populists have increasingly flourished. Ugly, lowest common denominator populists, in many cases; but when it comes to Europe, that doesn't mean they don't sometimes have a point. So it was that as the sheepish Van Rompuy, who probably isn't even a household name in his own household, presented himself to the Parliament, UKIP leader Nigel Farage gave it to him with both barrels:

> Who are you? I'd never heard of you. Nobody in Europe had ever heard of you. I would like to ask you, President! Who voted for you? And what mechanism do the peoples of Europe have to remove you?

In Farage's case, that old line about broken clocks being right twice a day springs to mind here. Few people in British politics have ever been as cynical and nakedly self-serving as him. But by and large, he's only gained a position of such influence because of the enormous disconnect between Eurocrats and European voters. Which in 2008/9, was highlighted in no uncertain terms by Václav Klaus, then President of the Czech Republic.

In December 2008, Klaus met with the leaders of various European parliamentary groups at Hradcany Castle, overlooking Prague. His country had yet to sign the Lisbon Treaty. You might imagine this would have been a convivial meeting, with full respect shown towards a democratically elected head of state. Quite the reverse.

Daniel Cohn-Bendit, leader of the European Greens, complained bitterly that the EU flag was not in evidence above the castle, and plonked his own flag down on the table. He then informed the Czech President: 'I don't care about your opinions on the Lisbon Treaty'.

After the appalling Hans-Gert Pöttering, President of the EU Parliament, weighed in on Cohn-Bendit's behalf, it was the turn of the Irish MEP, Brian Crowley: who fulminated against Klaus' apparent support of the successful 'No' campaign in the recent referendum. When Klaus replied: 'The biggest insult to the Irish people is not to accept the result', Crowley bawled: 'You will not tell me what the Irish think. As an Irishman, I know it best'.

If this was bad, it would get worse. Far worse. Two months later, Klaus was invited to speak to the European Parliament as head of a member state. Europe's MEPs - supposed servants of the people - were clearly very unused to being told anything other than how wonderful and important they all were. Instead of engaging in the standard empty platitudes, Klaus took the opportunity to deliver one of the most important, far-reaching speeches ever made in the continental legislature:

> Are you really convinced that every time you vote, you are deciding something that must be decided here in this hall and not closer to the citizens, i.e. in the individual European states? ... In a normal parliamentary system, a faction of MPs supports the government and a faction supports the opposition. In the European Parliament, this arrangement is missing. Here, only one single alternative is being promoted and those who dare think differently are labelled as enemies of European integration.

As if to prove Klaus right, jeers and whistles now began to ring out around the chamber. Undeterred, the President continued, reminding his audience of his country's tragic recent history under Communist rule: 'A political system that permitted no alternatives and therefore also no parliamentary opposition... where there is no opposition, there is no freedom. That is why political alternatives must exist'.

At length, Klaus delivered the *coup de grâce*. In a few softly spoken paragraphs, he not only punctured the pomposity of the delegates as no-one ever had before; he also set out exactly what was wrong with the EU, and why this fundamental problem could not be resolved:

> The relationship between a citizen of a member state and a representative of the Union is not a standard relationship between a voter and a politician, representing him or her. There is also a great distance (not only in a geographical sense) between citizen and Union representatives, which is much greater than it is inside the member countries.
>
> This distance is often described as the democratic deficit; the loss of democratic accountability, the decision-making of the unelected - but selected - ones, the bureaucratisation of decision-making. The proposals... included in the rejected European Constitution or in the not much different Lisbon Treaty would make this defect even worse.
>
> Since there is no European demos - and no European nation - this defect cannot be solved by strengthening the role of the European Parliament either. This would, on the contrary, make the problem worse and lead to an even greater alienation between the citizens of the European countries

and Union institutions.

There followed a quite extraordinary spectacle. Unable to bear the laser guided truth missiles raining down on them from the lectern, 200 MEPs rose to their feet and walked out. In a dispiriting sign of just how impervious the British left had become on the whole question of the EU, many of those doing so were Labour MEPs. As demonstrations of the farce European 'democracy' so often is, it will never be bettered.

In his speech, Klaus had set out just how counter-productive the European project had become. Something designed to bring Europe closer together was, in fact, threatening to drive its peoples apart. Without democratic consent, and in the absence of a European nation, how had the public agreed to what was being implemented over their heads, in their name?

It was also increasingly clear that Europe could only be a super-state, or a collection of sovereign states. It could not be both, operating under the same institutional umbrella. The former required Europe-wide consent which had never been asked for, let alone provided; the latter would only lead to paralysis, with the various members unable to agree on common policy and pursuing often wildly diverging national interests.

The democratic deficit referred to in such devastating terms by Klaus has been spoken about with deepening alarm for 25 years and more. Not only has nothing been done to change this, but the Union's institutions have accrued considerably more unaccountable (in many respects, illegitimate) powers over that time. Uncontrolled immigration has helped facilitate the rise of right-wing populism across huge swathes of Europe, both East and West.

And then, of course, there's the euro. Nowhere has the intransigent, indifferent, fanatical nature of much of the Union been displayed more openly than over the economic catastrophe it has overseen. As Thatcher noted in her autobiography, tying so many hugely different economies together under one monetary unit was bound to lead to disaster. Yet this was compounded by (1) No public mandate for this in any of those countries; (2) Eurozone states, in theory if, unhappily, not in practice, keeping control of their budgets and tax affairs; (3) German monetary discipline in the face of appalling repercussions elsewhere; (4) Despite all being part of one currency, member states remaining responsible for the debts they accrue.

The latter point has meant that far and away the euro's strongest member, Germany, has had its cake and eaten it: flooding the market with cheap exports, while deliberately holding wages down at home, and building up the largest trade surplus anywhere in the world. That surplus automatically grows simply thanks to prices being artificially low in Germany, artificially high elsewhere. Its own domestic and political priorities have trumped those of many other euro members.

When others get into difficulty, they don't have the option of devaluing and recovering. Instead, all they can do is put taxes up again and again (destroying their competitiveness in the process) and cut, cut, cut: with profound social consequences. The result was youth unemployment across southern Europe of eye-watering levels: a whole generation written off just to preserve a currency which nobody with an ounce of economic literacy believes can work.

Meanwhile, member states trapped inside the euro's economic prison have found themselves unable (or rather, not permitted) to change course, even if they wanted to. Ireland was told it would have to have its budget approved by the EU and International Monetary Fund (IMF) before it could hold elections. In Italy, euro architect, Mario Monti, appointed as a lifetime senator just three days earlier, was parachuted in to lead an entire government of wholly unelected technocrats in implementing harsh austerity reforms, regardless of the public's wishes. And in Greece, the cradle of democracy, events had to be seen to be believed.

Greece, of course, is the ultimate example of an economy which should never have been part of the euro to begin with; whose then leaders conspired with Goldman Sachs in cooking the books to gain admission. The moment it was accepted into, in William Hague's famous words, a 'burning building with no exits', its fate was sealed.

A great deal of nonsense has been spoken about Greece somehow being responsible for the unmitigated economic catastrophe in which it finds itself: how, in the parlance so beloved of austerians, it 'maxed out the credit card, then expected others to pay the bill'. In practice, Greece has been the world's most enduring victim of the 2008 global crash. This was caused by the toxic sub-prime mortgage bubble bursting; in consequence of which, the private exposure of the banks was piled onto the public across the developed world.

For Greece, already a weak service economy hugely dependent on tourism, the downgrading of national bonds via the corporate sector and credit rating agencies was especially crippling: piling up interest payments to the point where they became a noose around the country's neck. Greek government 10-year bond yields, generally sailing along at around 5% until

2010, soared to an unthinkable 48.6% by March 2012.

This meant that of the so-called European Central Bank (ECB)/IMF 'bailout' loans which Greece received, fully three-quarters went towards debt and interest repayments, paying back the IMF, and recapitalising the banks. Just 11% was used for government cash needs. The loans barely went towards stabilising the Greek economy at all; and were accompanied by austerity packages so lunatic, they should have come with a public health warning.

When George Papandreou, the Greek prime minister, announced the government's desire to hold a referendum on the 2011 'bailout', he was forced out, and replaced, as in Italy, by a technocratic, puppet administration. There was no election; and Lucas Papademos, the new premier, was a former ECB vice-president. The Greek people had been warned.

Entirely predictably, given skyrocketing repayments and strangulating austerity, the package failed; in the meantime, Papademos intensified the mass sell-off of public assets. Pushed almost beyond breaking point, the public had had enough: voting in a government led by radical leftists, Syriza, in 2015; then rejecting another draconian bail-out via referendum on 5 July of that year.

The new government had frantically sought a sensible accommodation with the group of euro finance ministers. Any such agreement would self-evidently feature an enormous write-off of debt. But as the maverick Yanis Varoufakis, not so much Don Quixote as Don Quick Quote, rapidly discovered, the Eurogroup wasn't interested in helping a stricken member along the path to sustainability and any kind of viable future. Instead, for nakedly political reasons, it wanted its pound of flesh. Papandreou had been punished for insurrection; so too must the new prime minister, Alexis Tsipras.

The aim, plainly, was to bring Tsipras' anti-austerity administration down as quickly as possible. The outbreak of democracy in Greece was a threat to be treated with contempt. Varoufakis found himself confronted by the ultimate blockhead: Wolfgang Schäuble, the ultra-conservative German finance minister.

The other side insisted on a 'comprehensive agreement', which meant they wanted to talk about everything. My interpretation is that when you want to talk about everything, you don't want to talk about anything… There were absolutely no (new) positions put forward on anything by them.

(Schäuble was) consistent throughout… His view was, 'I'm not discussing the programme – this was accepted by the previous (Greek) government and we can't possibly allow an election to change anything'.

So at that point, I said: 'Well perhaps we should simply not hold elections anymore for indebted countries', and there was no answer.

65 years previously, the ECSC had been born amid a spirit of solidarity: nations putting aside their differences and working together for the common good. Through no fault of its own (other than having signed up to the euro, that is), Varoufakis' country was trapped in the worst depression seen anywhere in the developed world since the 1930s; but the EU was now a purely political project, driven by self-interested nation states. Those governments which had accepted austerity packages - in Portugal, Spain, Ireland or Italy - were horrified at the idea of Greece winning substantial concessions, because it 'would obliterate them politically: they would have to answer to their own people why they didn't negotiate like we were doing'. Greece was cornered from almost all sides.

What happened when Varoufakis tried to discuss economics in the Eurogroup?

There was point blank refusal to engage in economic arguments. Point blank. You put forward an argument that you've really worked on, to make sure it's logically coherent, and you're just faced with blank stares. It is as if you haven't spoken. What you say is independent of what they say. You might as well have sung the Swedish national anthem - you'd have got the same reply.

The day after the referendum, Varoufakis resigned, and rode off into the sunset. In his absence, the following weekend, the whole world witnessed just what a grotesque spectacle the EU had become. Far from seeking to accommodate Tsipras, Eurozone leaders and finance ministers simply piled on more and more pressure; and were armed with the ECB's threat of unlawfully cutting off liquidity to Greek banks. Even the central bank was now a political tool to be used by politicians as they saw fit. The Eurogroup - which please note, isn't even a legal entity - didn't want a workable solution for Greece. It wanted dominion.

The subsequent 'agreement' was even harsher than that rejected at the plebiscite: Varoufakis described it as a 'new Versailles Treaty'. The Greek left now began to split; but Tsipras had been shown where the true power lay in Europe and had no way out. On 22 July 2015, he won a parliamentary vote clearing the way for Greece to agree talks with its creditors on the horrendous new package; but this was no victory. To this thunderstruck observer, for all the world, it was like watching a national Parliament vote itself out of existence.

Earlier this year, Tsipras and Syriza were voted out of office. The euro duly claimed its latest victim; but the people of Greece will continue to pay an intolerable price.

How does the euro ever recover? Ever become genuinely sustainable? The only way I can envisage is if a super-state is formally agreed and approved of at the ballot box by its members; and in the manner of the federal US, it then takes on responsibility for all economic and taxation policy, as well as all debts accrued. The chances of this? Zero. The Eurozone publics and almost all its governments would never stand for it.

The great mistake of the EU's architects was to assume that, in a world of ever-closer interdependence, nation states could gradually be swept away in the name of a greater cause. In fact, as this important article explains, Europe's elites knew that disaster was inevitable even before the euro was launched:

> Specific crises of national sovereignty were needed, i.e., socially perceived problems that could not be solved within the national framework. The occurrence of such crises was a window of opportunity for the progress of the unification process and determined its direction: an economic crisis would favour developments towards economic integration… Crises were opportunities for the development of a federalist 'initiative'.

'An economic crisis would favour developments towards economic integration'. In other words, the woes which would befall the euro's southern states would, or so the Eurocrats believed, inevitably force those states into a federal super-state, whether the people liked it or not.

Yet both nationalism and especially its benign cousin, patriotism, will always be innate and powerful forces; people will always need a place called home. And when those people have the right to formulate their own policies and forge their own national destinies at the ballot box removed from them, they react. It's inevitable. 'Europe's nations should be guided towards the super-state without their people understanding what is happening'… but more and more people do understand what is happening, and they don't like it one bit.

Thus, in the face of the worst humanitarian crisis since the Second World War, the response of a good number of Eastern European states - notably Hungary, Slovakia and the Czech Republic - was one of fear. It's true that leaders such as the appalling Viktor Orbán, Hungarian prime minister, have irresponsibly whipped this fear up; but it's also the case that peoples across Europe simply did not vote for migration of whatever nature on this enormous scale.

Meanwhile, what can other governments do but respond to these fears? The Danish government took to placing advertisements in the Lebanese press warning refugees of the hurdles they would face should they come to Denmark. The French government had to keep often alarming levels of support for Marine Le Pen's National Front in check. The British authorities unconscionably deport 18-year-old Afghan refugees taken in as children back to their country of origin - an approach which is not only disgracefully inhumane, but as with its treatment of non-EU graduates, constitutes economic self-harm - and did not fully clarify whether the same might apply to the shamefully low numbers of Syrian children granted asylum.

Goodness knows what Monnet, Schuman or Adenauer would have made of Europe's shambolic response (or rather, non-response) to this crisis; but a great deal of it is predicated on the forces which the European project has unwittingly unleashed.

◆ ◆ ◆

I write all the above despite not having voted Leave. I did flirt with it for a good six to nine months or so until early 2016 - but became a born again Remainer when I realised just how false a prospectus Leave were offering. Yet what I've set out in this chapter illustrates just how complex the arguments around the EU were and still are. That's a large part of why, when Leave voters are denounced as 'thick' or 'racist', it's so unreasonable; it so completely misses the point. There's a huge number of things horribly wrong with the EU as presently constituted.

But the key point is this. Very little of the above applied to Britain. Thank heavens, it never joined the euro; nor is it part of the Schengen agreement. Even on freedom of movement, at any point, it could've introduced ID cards and done what many EU members do: namely, to make it essentially impossible for anyone without work who stays for more than 90 days to assimilate into the tax, social security, healthcare and employment system. I bet you didn't know that. I didn't either until only a couple of years ago. It wasn't mentioned in the referendum campaign at all.

Britain, in fact, really did have 'the best of both worlds'. While the core of the EU accelerated towards ever closer integration, the UK - along with a few other states in the north and east - stood to one side: with both the single market and enlargement enabling it to advocate, often very successfully, for a more flexible economic approach. And as it retained full economic sovereignty at all times (as the UK government's own Brexit White Paper actually admitted), it was free to make its own political decisions.

Ask yourself. If Brussels really does dictate everything, why are there proper building regulations in Germany, which therefore hasn't had its own Grenfell disaster? Why are railways still nationalised in many EU countries? Why do so many EU members have completely different income and corporate tax rates? Austerity was forced upon southern Europe by the EU; but in the UK, it was forced upon the public by the Tories.

Not only that, but the reason the EU currently behaves in such a right-wing, neoliberal way is that most of its member states' governments are right-wing and neoliberal. If their makeup changes, so inevitably must the EU itself. Especially in the cases of those member states which remain outside the euro, but even some which don't, the real power resides with them. It always has.

When it came to the referendum campaign though, instead of a mature, grown-up discussion about a decision of the most compelling, far-reaching nature, in which the various nuances were acknowledged, all we got was noise. Lies. Narnia on stilts. And in Remain's case, the most pathetic, miserable, inept campaign I've ever seen.

I could see the Leave vote coming a mile off. For the second consecutive year, I thought the polls were completely wrong; again, because the story they were telling just didn't make sense to me. There were a variety of reasons for that.

The 2015 election had been a battle between Cameron - scarcely a beloved figure, but generally considered a competent one - and Miliband: who the public just did not view as competent. All Cameron had to do was be better than his opponent. But this time? With such a small Commons majority and given his announcement that he'd be standing down before the next election, Cameron's authority was fast ebbing away: not merely over his party, but the electorate too. As prime ministers go, he was already a lame duck.

Who was most people's idea of his likely successor? Boris Johnson: at the time, the most popular politician in the UK. The moment that Johnson announced for Leave, this spelt disaster for Cameron and Remain: who could suddenly no longer count on bringing undecideds and Tory moderates with them. Worse: Johnson and Michael Gove would ensure that the Leave campaign was not hijacked by the electorally toxic Farage. The latter nonetheless made a series of spectacularly stupid comments; but the presence of the sober Gove and popular Johnson meant that little or no damage was done.

Thus Vote Leave were able to combine a patriotic message appealing to voters' hearts with one focused on their heads too. Nobody did so more effectively than Daniel Hannan: whose optimistic, even idealistic view of Britain's future chimed in with a world in which voters were thirsting for real change.

Remain, on the other hand? Negative. Scaremongering. Appealing to voters' fears, not their hopes. In tone, Remain sounded exactly like all those Brussels bureaucrats towards whom voters across Europe, never mind the UK, feel such disdain.

Why were Remain so negative? Very simply, they found themselves up against the exact same barrier which stopped so many British governments (notably Blair's) from calling a referendum in the first place. It's perfectly possible to make a series of dry, technocratic arguments explaining why EU membership is a good thing; but it's close to (though not entirely, as this wonderful video proves) impossible to do so via the kind of simple, emotive language required in contemporary election campaigns. Especially in binary referenda.

Even Remain had to acknowledge how many problems the EU clearly has: Cameron did so again here, for example. But this simply muddied the waters: 'If the EU has so many issues', voters were bound to ask, 'which have only grown throughout our membership, why should we stay?'

Compounding this was the charade around Cameron's 'renegotiation', which scarcely a soul could have taken seriously: most of the 'concessions' he achieved were already in place beforehand. How could he have stood before the British people, as he did at the general election, and insist he'd recommend a 'Leave' vote if serious concessions were not forthcoming; achieve next to none of these, then invoke the shadows of doom in the event of a Leave vote? The prime minister was hoist by his own petard.

Labour, meanwhile, was completely at war with itself. It shrunk before our eyes: practically to vanishing point. The entire campaign instead became a battle between the two wings of the Tory Party; rather than the desperately needed positive one explaining how the EU could be reformed for everyone's benefit. This was a generational opportunity for the British left to come together, stand up for workers' rights and against deregulation, and exploit how unpopular Tory ideas are among so many. It didn't so much fail as barely even try. Lamentable. A genuine tragedy.

In 2015, a hugely controversial move to individual voter registration removed almost 800,000 from the electoral roll. Most of these voters were young: much more likely to support Remain. Some would not have been reached by the Remain campaign's efforts to publicise the need to register; others would have been completely unaware of their removal from the roll.

This was always especially likely among what we might term the 'soft progressive' vote: whose poor levels of turnout meant that Labour did far worse in 2015, and the Liberal Democrats far worse in 2010, than the polls had suggested. To an extent, the problem even ate into the 'Yes' vote at the Scottish referendum: where the ultimate ten-point margin was beyond that predicted by any poll just before referendum day, and where turnout in strongly 'Yes' areas like Dundee or Glasgow was well below that in 'No' areas.

At the EU referendum, as in Scotland in 2014 and on 7 May 2015, which group of voters were always most likely to turn out? The old. Which group were always least likely to do so? The young.

More than that: the sheer lily-livered weakness of Remain's argument meant that psychologically, those who wanted change were that much more likely to make their electoral voices heard: which is why UKIP performed so much better at the European elections in 2014 than the general election a year later.

Remain's case was nothing like clear or passionate enough to engage those whose support it desperately needed. The opposite applied with Leave. The results were inevitable.

On top of this, Cameron's government voted down a measure to allow the vote to 16 and 17-year-olds; while expatriates (most of whom, comfortably well off, predominantly older, were likely to support Leave) were granted the franchise and EU citizens living in the UK were denied it. Both this and the electoral registration changes would only have made sense had Cameron led the Leave campaign; but that he allowed it to happen despite placing his entire political legacy on a Remain vote was extraordinary: evidence of an unfathomable level of carelessness, even devil-may-care insouciance.

Then, there was the power of media magnates too. So much of the anti-EU debate of the last 25 years has been led by the right-wing press: which has never displayed such disdain for facts and objective argument as it does now. The mounting corporatism of the media is the reason for that: but regardless, this was the opportunity which right-wing oligarchs had been waiting for.

On which basis, it should scarcely be a surprise that so much of the debate turned towards immigration, Leave's ultimate vote winner. As it never spelt out what I have above - that ID cards can fix the problems around freedom of movement - Remain was always on the defensive. And thus, it was doomed.

There was a further problem for Remain too: a critical one. Led by many of those who'd run Labour and the Lib Dems' disastrous campaigns in 2015, Remain failed even to properly challenge the dozens of different versions of Brexit which Leave could happily offer. Thus, it promised that the UK could be like Norway, or Switzerland: we could have our cake and eat it. Or it promised that we could control immigration while being Norway or Switzerland (without ID cards, an impossibility). And almost nobody suggested we'd be leaving the single market, let alone the customs union. Did the majority of the UK electorate even know what the latter was?

The public, indeed, had been fed all sorts of never-ending lies about the EU for decades. It was the failure of so many governments, including Blair's, to counter these lies which laid much of the groundwork for Brexit. How had they become so powerful? Here's how. Six days before the EU referendum, Martin Fletcher, former Brussels correspondent for The Times, wrote the following:

For 25 years our press has fed the British public a diet of distorted, mendacious and relentlessly hostile stories about the EU - and the journalist who set the tone was Boris Johnson...

... Johnson, sacked by The Times in 1988 for fabricating a quote, made his mark in Brussels not through fair and balanced reporting, but through extreme euro-scepticism. He seized every chance to mock or denigrate the EU, filing stories that were undoubtedly colourful but also grotesquely exaggerated or completely untrue.

The Telegraph loved it. So did the Tory Right. Johnson later confessed: 'Everything I wrote from Brussels, I found was sort of chucking these rocks over the garden wall and I listened to this amazing crash from the greenhouse next door over in England as everything I wrote from Brussels was having this amazing, explosive effect on the Tory party, and it really gave me this I suppose rather weird sense of power'.

Johnson's reports also had an amazing, explosive effect on the rest of Fleet Street. They were much more fun than the usual dry and rather complex Brussels fare. News editors on other papers, particularly but not exclusively the tabloids, started pressing their own correspondents to match them. By the time I arrived in Brussels editors only wanted stories about faceless Brussels eurocrats imposing absurd rules on Britain, or scheming Europeans ganging up on us, or British prime ministers fighting plucky rearguard actions against a hostile continent. Much of Fleet Street seemed unable to view the EU through any other prism. It was the only narrative it was interested in.

Stories that did not bash Brussels, stories that acknowledged the EU's many achievements, stories that recognised that Britain had many natural allies in Europe and often won important arguments, almost invariably ended up on the spike.

That the man behind all this is now prime minister should alarm the hell out of you. Never trust a single thing Johnson ever says. He's only out for one thing: himself. What the media did throughout this time, though, was like a test run for what it would do on all sorts of issues during this decade; including the very thing we'll come to in the next chapter.

◆ ◆ ◆

No review of the referendum would be complete without exploring the truly dark side of the campaign: encompassing dark money, corruption, foreign interference, and rather frightening use of data. To say nothing of Farage's despicably racist banner, unveiled on the very morning that Jo Cox would meet a tragic end at the hands of a far-right lunatic; this utterly shameless Vote Leave video about the NHS: so full of lies, it should've been illegal in any grown-up country; disgustingly racist misinformation here or here; or the notorious £350m for the NHS on the back of a bus: a promise made by those who actually want to privatise and sell it off to US pharmaceutical giants.

And that's just scratching the surface. Vote Leave broke electoral law; Leave.EU was funded by the darkest of dark money, with suspicions pointing towards Vladimir Putin's Russia. The role of Cambridge Analytica, meanwhile, which harvested data from Facebook on an epic scale - data used to target millions of voters across the country - was like something out of *1984*.

Yet the BBC and much of the written press has barely reported on it at all. Imagine the US media burying Watergate to protect Richard Nixon, and you get somewhere close to the extraordinary chicanery that's gone on here. In Uruguay, I'm an English teacher; and in July, an intermediate level student of mine, only a teenager, mentioned a Netflix documentary he'd just seen on the role of both Cambridge Analytica and Facebook in both Brexit and Donald Trump's victory later in 2016.

He was shocked. Appalled. He wondered if he should delete his Facebook account. Then he became a lot more shocked when I said, 'the thing is, the vast majority of the British public doesn't even know about this'. How can a teenager in Uruguay now know more about the criminal corruption of the referendum than most British people? How has it not been front and centre of the UK media for the last three-and-a-half years?

International newspapers, who actually care about such things as reporting the truth, unearthing corruption and holding the rich and powerful to account, have discussed Cambridge Analytica very often. They even know things about Farage which the British people don't. Two-and-a-half years ago, *Die Zeit* asked him a <u>series of questions</u> the nature of which no UK outlet ever has.

Interviewer: Who financed your Leave campaign?

Farage: Who financed the whole Remain campaign for over 50 years? The government.

Interviewer: You didn't answer the question.

Farage: Individuals. Individuals from the UK.

Interviewer: And with money from Russia?

Farage: No Russian money at all. That's ridiculous. What you are talking about is conspiracy. I never received a penny from Russia. I wouldn't have taken it, even if it had been offered. This campaign wasn't about money. It was about messages, good clear messages.

Interviewer: Have you ever received external money for your political work?

Farage: No, of course not.

Interviewer: You never received any money for your appearances on Russia Today?

Farage: Which I do twice a year. Or three times last year. I am doing global media. I am talking to you as well.

Interviewer: Why did you meet with Julian Assange in the Ecuadorian Embassy in London?

Farage stops for a moment to think. Following his visit to the Ecuadorian Embassy not long ago, he told reporters directly after his meeting with Assange that he could no longer remember what he had done in the embassy.

Farage: Oh, for journalistic reasons.

Interviewer: What? Because you want to write a story about the Wikileaks founder?

Farage: For journalistic reasons. I will not say anything more about that. But I did it for journalistic reasons, not for political reasons.

Interviewer: What do you mean when you say, 'journalistic reasons?'

Farage: I will not say anything more about that. If you look at what I do today, I used to do politics 100 hours a week. But now I do politics for 40 hours a week, so I have got a lot of time to do other things…

…

Interviewer: So you were sent by someone to speak to Julian Assange? What did you talk about?

Farage: It has nothing to do with you. It was a private meeting.

Interviewer: You just said it was a journalistic meeting, for the public.

Farage: Of course.

Interviewer: Are you going to publish an article soon about your connections to Wikileaks and your meeting with Assange?

Farage: You will have to wait and see. I meet lots of people all over the world. I always help them.

Interviewer: You once said you admire Russian President Vladimir Putin.

Farage: In 2013, as a political operator, he was the best in the world. Yes, this is what I said. But I wouldn't like to live in his country. I didn't like a lot of things he did. But as a political operator, he is to be admired.

Interviewer: One of Russia's foreign policy goals is dividing and weakening the EU. Could it be that in the case of Brexit, you were directly or indirectly used for this Russian goal?

Farage: It is obvious that the EU wants to expand to the east and threatens Russia. That's completely mad.

Interviewer: What you say isn't true. It wasn't the EU that triggered the revolution in Ukraine, but the Ukrainians who wanted better relations with the EU.

Farage: I want the EU to be destroyed and it doesn't matter if God or the Dalai Lama wants it as well. The EU is an anti-democratic, failing structure. You know, you are the first person who has asked me if Russia supported me. Maybe you have a special German mindset. No other journalist in the world has asked these questions.

Interviewer: I just want to understand your role.

Farage: We have no links to Russia.

Interviewer: You didn't meet with the Russian Embassy's deputy chief-of-mission in London?

Farage: Nope.

Interviewer: Not in 2013, before the Brexit campaign was conceived?

Farage: Ah, hang on. He came to the EP office. Or I met with him in London. So what?

Interviewer: Why did you meet with him?

Farage: I think you are a nutcase! You are really a nutcase! Brexit is the best thing to happen: for Russia, for America, for Germany and for democracy. And that's the key point…

…

Interviewer: … What is your role?

Farage: Changing public opinion. That's what I have been doing for 20 years. Using television, media. Shifting public opinion. That's what I am good at.

Interviewer: And that's why you had to meet with Julian Assange?

Farage looks to his press spokesman and pauses again.

Farage: That, that is a different angle in this.

Interviewer: It's an angle that I want to understand.

Farage: Well, you will not get it. I went to meet him very briefly. We talked about a lot of things.

Interviewer: But you didn't want to be seen going into or out of the embassy? Your visit was only publicised because somebody took a picture of you.

Shortly afterwards, the interview was cut short. Exit Farage, pursued by awkward questions. Which include:

Why are you a person of interest to the FBI?

Why are you so close to Donald Trump, who publicly praised Assange and Wikileaks, and openly encouraged it to leak anything which might embarrass Hillary Clinton?

Why were you so quick to announce Leave's supposed defeat on referendum night? Was it so you could short the financial markets because you already knew Leave had won?

Why did you and other UKIP MEPs only start filling out EU transparency reports, including for the reimbursement of office expenditure, in 2009, despite your already having been an MEP for a decade by then?

Hilariously, Farage presents himself to the public as a regular man of the people: John Bull himself. In practice, not only is he extremely wealthy, funded to the tune of £450,000 by Arron Banks (yet contrary to its rules, this was not declared on the European Parliament's register of interests); but the very day after the referendum, he appears to have applied for a German passport. Asked about whether he now holds one, he has consistently refused to deny it.

No problem for him, then, if the No Deal Brexit he advocates goes ahead: which it will if the Conservatives win this election. Unlike his fellow Brexiteer, Lord Lawson (no relation, thank goodness): whose application for French residency, rather delightfully, fell at the first hurdle. Meanwhile, the city firm co-founded by Jacob Rees Mogg has set up not one, but two investment vehicles in Dublin, after it warned of the dangers of Brexit; John Redwood, who passionately advocated for Brexit for decades prior to the referendum, has advised investors to take their money out of Britain; and Sir James Dyson, champion businessman of Brexit, has relocated to Singapore.

However much Remain completely botched its campaign, however many real issues there are with the EU, and however real the structural causes of the Brexit vote (decades of betrayal and neglect by both major parties, plus both neoliberalism and especially austerity) were and still are, that is the reality of the lie these people sold the public. A lie which brought British politics and discourse into disrepute as never before, whose social and economic repercussions continue unabated even now; and if the Tories win, these will get worse. Far worse.

And then, there's Isabel Oakeshott. Maybe best known for co-authoring a scurrilous biography of David Cameron with Lord Ashcroft, she appears very regularly on BBC *Question Time*. Quite what qualifies her as an expert commentator, I've never understood: for this is someone who sold out her source, Vicky Pryce, to the police, which led to Pryce being jailed; and has never provided any verification for her most salacious story about Cameron. A story which got the whole country talking (and oinking) for weeks afterwards.

Much more serious, though, is what she did to Carole Cadwalladr, one of Britain's few genuine investigative journalists, whose work on the (very) dark side of Brexit has been magnificent and heroic. On the BBC sofa, Oakeshott publicly ridiculed Cadwalladr for 'chasing unicorns', *when at the very same time*, she was in possession of a whole trove of emails confirming Banks' regular contact with Russian officials between 2015 and 2017.

Instead of taking these emails, which show that along with his Leave.EU colleague, Andy Wigmore, Banks had multiple meetings with high-ranking Russian officials; that Banks visited Moscow in February 2016, and was introduced to a Russian businessman by the Russian ambassador who allegedly offered him a multibillion dollar investment opportunity in Russian goldmines, to the Electoral Commission - or better still, to the police - Oakeshott sat on them purely to benefit her own book, *White Flag?* An attitude which mysteriously changed when informed that The Observer had obtained the emails.

Hilariously - part of me almost admires this - this born hustler (or should that be, grifter?) then somehow convinced The Observer to hold the story for its sister paper, The Guardian, on the Monday; while The Sunday Times went to work and splashed with it. Rather less hilariously, Oakeshott appeared on Question Time that very Thursday, and absolutely nothing was mentioned about any of this. The BBC clearly didn't want the public to know.

You may also recall the story which broke some months back, and cost Sir Kim Darroch, the UK Ambassador to the US, his job. It came from Oakeshott: a Leave.EU member and like Ashcroft, her sponsor (in effect, she's his public spokesperson), a strident supporter of the hardest form of Brexit possible. I don't think it's grasping at straws to speculate that she, personally, has plenty to gain from No Deal coming about.

Yet despite everything I've written here, we still shouldn't forget the very real structural causes of Brexit. Those causes, in fact, are a theme of this book: for without austerity destroying millions of lives, there's simply no way Brexit would've been supported in enough numbers. Just as it wouldn't have been backed had governments of all hues not turned their backs on working class people for decades. Ultimately, the Brexit vote falls on them. As does a quite colossal cultural divide between urban and rural Britain; social liberals and social conservatives.

I attempted to explain that divide, which mirrors that in the US, here. But it only underscores how incredibly foolish ultra-Remainers are to assume everyone thinks like them; half the country feels rather differently about all this. And moreover, that if Labour had a 100% pro-Remain leader, not only would it have no chance of reaching out to Leave voters, but it'd only be compounding the divide even further. If Britain is ever to heal from all this, both Leavers and Remainers must be listened to and their concerns heeded. And only Labour are doing that.

Beyond that: the many problems with the EU which I've set out in this chapter mean, very obviously, that such a narrow Leave vote should've resulted in the UK leaving the political institutions... but staying in the single market and customs union. This was a no-brainer. It remains so even now. It would avoid both economic harm and the intractable reality of the Irish border: which shamefully, was barely even mentioned at all.

But after the result was announced and Cameron resigned, two things rapidly became clear. (1) Staggeringly, there was no plan from either the government or the Leave campaign about what to do in the event of a Leave victory; (2) The Tories would do their utmost to take full advantage, twist the vote into something it never was, and brook no compromise with anyone. Their needs, not the country's, came first.

Faisal Islam's memorable revelation that there was no plan was the exact moment British politics fell into the abyss. It has never climbed back out since. Since that point, and exactly contrary to what Cameron had famously boasted on the eve of election night, all has been chaos. Tory chaos.

Any serious government remotely interested in the common good would immediately have sought cross-party negotiations and, for that matter, a cross-party team to lead them in Brussels. But then, had we been a country which hadn't already lost the plot, the referendum would never have been conducted in such a laughable, disgraceful way to begin with. The tenor could not have been more unserious... on both sides, Leave in particular.

Chapter 7 takes up from where we leave off here. The next chapter, however, is about how the power of the media - so complicit in Brexit, as we have seen - to lie, lie and lie some more has corroded public discourse and turned the most sensitive issue imaginable into a political football. With all sorts of horrendous consequences.

6: THE POLITICAL WEAPONISATION OF ANTISEMITISM

'The charges of anti-Semitism against Corbyn are <u>without merit</u>, an underhanded contribution to the disgraceful efforts to fend off the threat that a political party might emerge that is led by an admirable and decent human being' - Noam Chomsky

I'm Jewish. I'm the grandson of a Holocaust survivor. My grandmother, who died in 2017, was the one true hero of my life. Brought up in the village of Papa, Hungary, she, along with her parents and two sisters, was deported to Auschwitz in mid-1944. Her father - my great-grandfather, Geza, who she idolised - did not survive. Somehow, my grandmother, her mother and sisters <u>all did</u>: on a journey which took them to Frankfurt-am-Main, Zillertal, Ravensbruck, and Mauthausen, encompassing unimaginable horror.

She was experimented on with malaria, the symptoms of which persisted until 1982, by Mengele himself. She watched an SS officer tear a new-born baby from its mother's arms and smash its head against a wall. On arrival at Ravensbruck, she saw a woman so desperate, so desolate, she'd been reduced to eating human excrement. She wept in despair as a group of small boys, no more than 10 years old, were all told they would be gassed next day... and responded by praying that they'd soon be reunited with their already fallen mothers and fathers. She was taken on death marches barefoot in freezing cold; when if anyone stopped to catch their breath, they were immediately shot.

Had it not been for the filthy mood of a drunk Mengele, who stood at the front of the Auschwitz lines and pointed some to the left, others to the right, but after slapping my great-grandmother and insulting her, bizarrely gestured rightwards in sheer anger, I would not be sat here typing this now. Nor would I be had the officer who, two days before she was liberated, pointed a revolver at my grandmother and told her to come with him - only for her to respond, with typical heroism: 'I am going nowhere. You will pay for your crimes' - killed her as he had killed her best friend at Mauthausen only days earlier: trampling her to death in front of my gran.

In the years before they were deported, the family had taken in small children, sent by relatives in Slovakia. The relatives hoped the children would be safe. One day, the family received a knock on the door. The children were taken away, never to be seen again; and outside, scores of people cheered and *celebrated*. Later, the local general wanted to speak to my great-grandfather, who invited him in for tea. The general told him his girlfriend had been Jewish. Geza felt momentary relief; perhaps his family would be alright?

The general continued: 'So she had the honour of being shot by me'. Geza went up to the bathroom. He was muttering and chuntering away to himself. My grandmother told me this was the only time in her life when she ever saw her father scared.

On the train to Auschwitz, various things happened. When someone tried to escape through an impossible tiny metal grille, they were discovered. And instantly shot. Also on the train, in impossibly airless conditions which reeked of faeces and urine, was a sex worker who'd been discovered hiding Jews in her home. Suddenly she fell down in front of my grandmother. A bullet had somehow penetrated the grille. From that day forward, my grandmother would never hear a bad word said about sex workers.

After the four women had stuck together and somehow survived Auschwitz, their journey took them to Frankfurt: where they were charged with helping construct a runway. They stood in freezing conditions and next to no clothing, being beaten by Nazis just for the hell of it. Yet their next stop proved critical, for reasons which will likely astonish you.

At Zillertal, Austria, there was a camp; but the local factory owner had done some sort of deal with the local Nazis. As a result, the workers had clean running water and real food. Over Christmas, the family were therefore able to rebuild their reserves of strength. A picture of Zillertal hung in my grandmother's corridor. She would point to it and say, 'that place saved my life'. That picture is one of my most cherished possessions.

Things, though, got far worse from here: encompassing death marches; Ravensbruck, a camp overwhelmed with lice and disease; and Mauthausen: where Jews were thrown down the 'Stairs of Death' by laughing Nazis, and everyone around the area could see it. That is why, when locals later claimed they had known nothing of what had been going on, they were lying.

At one point, my grandmother was herself in a line headed for the gas chambers. Whereupon an old woman, in terribly poorly condition, *swapped* with her. 'You are young; you have your whole life ahead of you'. Imagine the guilt my gran carried with her for the rest of her life because of that extraordinary sacrifice.

How did my grandmother, great-grandmother and two great-aunts survive all this? They stuck together and lived on their wits. My gran spoke fluent German: which meant she could eavesdrop on Nazi officers' plans. As a result, she had an uncanny instinct for knowing who'd be targeted next; and in the hours beforehand, would carefully usher herself and her family away.

Yet she always did her very best for everyone in the camps. She stopped someone trying to escape through barbed wire to their inevitable death; mercifully, the Nazis did not discover this. And when someone in the family discovered a piece of bread, she demanded everyone take it in turns just licking it. Trying to make it last as long as possible.

Upon liberation, many survivors immediately perished; they were given too much food, and their stomachs exploded. Yet the Americans didn't have enough clothes for the survivors. Instead, she and her family *had to wear SS uniforms* on the train back to Hungary. Upon arrival, they found their home had been ransacked and taken over by a Russian general: who offered them just one room in their own house.

It is a measure of how much my grandmother's self-esteem had been destroyed that she always spoke of this man with reverence; with gratitude. But she was able to access the cellar… where a true miracle occurred. She leant against a panel in the wall - and suddenly, all this jewellery fell out! Somebody - maybe her father, maybe a maid, maybe someone else - had hidden it there. It had escaped the clutches of all those who'd turned the whole house over; and she was able to pawn it and use the money to emigrate to England. But not before, very shortly after her return from the camps, a neighbour remarked on her unimaginably emaciated condition, 'I see you finally learned to work, then'.

It took until 1990 for my grandmother - who upon her liberation, weighed just 20kg - to even begin speaking about her experiences. Until then, if anyone so much as mentioned the word 'Germany' or a German company like Bosch, Audi or Volkswagen in conversation, she would shut down and not say another word. And back then, there was no counselling; no understanding of what trauma did to people.

Trauma which she, like the rest of her family (only one of whom, my great-aunt, still survives now) would carry with them for the rest of their lives. She only bathed, never showered; cut her own hair; made her own clothes; repaired her shoes constantly; only ever had one light on; always shopped at 99p stores despite becoming independently wealthy; and her kitchen had enough food to last at least two years, enough drink for at least five years.

There was no point telling her this was unnecessary. It had happened to her. She'd experienced it. So why couldn't it happen again? It was the greatest privilege of my life to know her as well as I did; but however much she rebuilt her life through the most astounding courage and strength - which included helping smuggle her mother and sisters over the Hungarian-Austrian border in 1956, from where they travelled to safety and work in the UK - and even included working until she was 90, she lived in perpetual fear of it happening again.

At the very core of our being, I think all Jews live with that fear. I'd describe it as a constant anxiety nagging away at me; it's like being born with uncommonly sharpened antennae, alerting us to any possible danger. Just to give one example: sadly, my great-aunt has dementia. When she travelled with us to my grandmother's funeral, she looked at me and plaintively asked, 'which organisation are you from?' For a brief moment, I could picture what it had been like for her; the impossible levels of trauma she'd experienced, the panic she'd known ever since, the fear of strangers coming to take her away all over again. It had been a struggle to convince her to come with us, for precisely that reason.

The bottom line is this. It's no good telling Jews that something cannot happen when we all know that it has, many times over; when our family histories are dominated not just by the Holocaust, but an endless history of pogroms and persecution, hatred and horror. The number one cause of that history? Our lack of a homeland. This enabled scores of tyrants, charlatans and opportunists to keep the Jews out of mainstream society, then turn on us whenever anything went wrong, accusing us of 'polluting' the national bloodstream. And it also meant that as the situation across Europe deteriorated dramatically during the 1930s, there was next to no help from its governments; growing hostility from its peoples; and for so many, nowhere to turn.

That was the backdrop behind Israel coming into being. As my grandmother often said to me: 'Shaun, we Jews had always been weak. The lesson of the Holocaust was we had to be strong'. Europe had completely betrayed the Jewish people: to the extent that by as late as 1952, there were still over 250,000 Jews living in refugee camps. Only one place offered salvation.

◆ ◆ ◆

It's surely because of Britain's historic role in that - through both the Balfour Declaration, and partition agreed by the United Nations of British-mandated Palestine - that Britons of both left and right have remained so impassioned and opinionated about the subsequent tragic conflict. The Holocaust is part of my and millions of other families' history; Israel-Palestine has its genesis, in many ways, in British history. And of course, the UK has a large, thriving Jewish community.

On which basis, when one of Britain's two major political parties stands accused of institutionalised antisemitism, it is inevitably a huge story. Labour MPs throw their hands up in disgust; newspaper editorials condemn the leadership of Jeremy Corbyn; Jewish leaders do likewise. 'What has happened to Labour?', they cry. And is, as Margaret Hodge apparently claimed in July 2018, Corbyn a 'fucking anti-Semite and a racist'?

Well no. He's not. Few figures in British public life have dedicated their whole careers to fighting against all forms of racism in the way Corbyn has. To the best of my knowledge, no other party has set up a full, comprehensive investigation into possible antisemitism within its ranks in the way Labour has either. Yet when Baroness Warsi states that Islamophobia is 'very widespread' within the Conservative Party, and the Muslim Council of Britain calls for an inquiry, the response of both the government and almost all the media is nothing. Narratives, apparently, are much more important than facts.

In that sense, a rather brilliant trap has been laid for the Labour Party. The media smears Corbyn and his supporters as 'anti-Semites'. It doesn't matter if it doesn't provide proper evidence; only the smear counts. Because it means that if anyone challenges it - if anyone calls out the idea of 'endemic antisemitism on the left' as the offensive nonsense, disproved by research, it undoubtedly is - they will be denounced as either enabling antisemitism or an anti-Semite themselves. This is the catch-22 which Labour has been caught in for at least the last 16 months; and is why it's not challenged the allegations in the way I'm about to.

Before I go any further, let me make something abundantly clear. Of course antisemitism exists on the left. The reason is because it exists *everywhere*. It is a horrific cancer which the Jewish people have been fighting for over 2000 years. Jewish people like my late grandmother and her whole family. Jewish people like myself too.

What I expect anyone fighting against it to do is call it out wherever they see it, with zero tolerance. But in Britain in 2019, that is not what is happening. Instead, not only is antisemitism on the right, considerably more prevalent than on the left, disgracefully ignored; but thousands of good, decent, anti-racist Corbyn and Labour supporters have been smeared, bullied, attacked in positively McCarthyite fashion: simply for being Corbyn and Labour supporters.

The reason for this? It's political. In a country with a racist prime minister, a racist government, a governing party which ignores all calls for an inquiry into institutionalised Islamophobia, whose belatedly added guidelines on antisemitism don't even apply to its members - only its representatives - and with many on the right (including Leave.EU) routinely repeating a hideous, vile trope against George Soros while much of the media barely says a word, this is the only possible explanation.

Nigel Farage has even publicly blamed Jewish conspiracies! Has he been banished from public life? Don't be silly. He's not on the left, so of course not. Why would the media even care given that the Soros trope has been spread by, amongst others, The Sun and even The Telegraph?

As if to confirm just how much British political life now resembles an entirely alternative universe, even the Jewish Chronicle (JC) has been in on the act. Imagine an article about Jews which repeats not one, but two antisemitic tropes. First, that the Jewish community's main priority is wealth and hording it away; and second, which even refers to the Rothschilds. Any denunciation of this? Of course not; it didn't come from someone on the left. Just the obviously unimportant City Editor of the Daily Mail.

This whole discussion is polluted with so much hypocrisy, so much cynical politicking and self-seeking, so many stones being thrown from the glassiest of houses, we shall all be subject to a great clattering from the sky at any moment. And as I'll set out later, this wasn't the first such example from the JC either. Far from it.

◆ ◆ ◆

At this point, I'm going to do something which apparently, almost every journalist in the UK is clinically incapable of. I'm going to look at actual, real data: from the Campaign Against Antisemitism (CAA)'s Antisemitism

Barometer, published in April 2018; and a comprehensive report by the Institute for Jewish Policy Research (JPR), 'Antisemitism in Contemporary Great Britain', published in 2017. The CAA found the following (click on the links to view the graphs):

The number of people across society endorsing antisemitic statements is falling.

Antisemitism is considerably more prevalent among Conservative voters than Labour voters.

This roughly confirmed both the JPR and The Economist's recently reported findings too.

Yet despite this, the British Jewish community believes that antisemitism is infinitely more common on the left (in the graph here, 1 = low levels of antisemitism among the party's members and elected representatives; 5 = high levels of antisemitism among the party's members and elected representatives).

How do we explain this extraordinary gap? Lamentably, research has already found the British public to be quite astonishingly wrong about very many different issues. It's unutterably wrong about the figures concerning benefit fraud, illegal immigration, ethnic minorities, crime (including violent crime), teenage pregnancy, foreign aid, JobSeekers' Allowance, and pensions.

It's just as wrong on matters relating to the EU too. Embarrassingly wrong about the number of EU citizens living in Britain, the amount of money the UK sends the EU each year, and the amount of benefits paid to EU migrants. Almost a quarter of Britons even believe that ever-pervasive myth that 'bendy bananas' are banned.

This level of ignorance is so profound, it's an ever-growing national security threat: as we've seen given the public's disastrous acceptance of austerity; and equally disastrous belief, prior to the referendum, that the UK would be better off out of the EU. The consequences are all too evident in our paralysed Parliament and political process: as Britain endures its gravest national crisis since May 1940, and perhaps its greatest constitutional one since 1689.

Who is responsible? The answer is the UK's appalling political class and media: frequently joined at the hip in the never-ending nonsense they spout. Remember what Martin Fletcher said about how all journalistic discourse around the EU had come to be <u>wilfully distorted</u> for decades? Something awfully similar seems to have happened around antisemitism in Britain. The narrative - that there's a huge problem on the left, and only an apologist or anti-Semite themselves would deny it - is all that counts, despite what the data and evidence consistently say. And there is, I'm afraid, comprehensive proof, which you can see in the graphs <u>here</u>, <u>here</u>, <u>here</u>, <u>here</u> and <u>here</u>.

Meanwhile, anti-Muslim hate crime is at its <u>highest</u> level since records began. In London, it <u>increased</u> by 40% in a single year; in Nottingham, three out of every five Muslims have been <u>victims</u> of hate crime. The UK government's own statistics reveal that 52% of all hate crimes recorded by the police in England and Wales occur against Muslims; 12% against Jews (see Table B1 <u>in this</u> Excel file). Given this, you might imagine there'd be at least four times more coverage of Islamophobia than antisemitism in the UK press. But <u>not a bit</u> of it. This <u>graph</u> tells its own story.

That is the kind of media coverage which Jeremy Corbyn, Labour and British Muslims are faced with. Which has been consistently <u>biased</u> to a quite mindboggling <u>extent</u>. Of course, that there were 672 hate crimes recorded against Jews in England and Wales in 2017-18 is shocking and appalling. It's a reminder of the challenge we all face in combating this evil cancer. But when public figures make <u>preposterous</u> comparisons between antisemitism on the left and Germany in 1936 or 1938, it should be an instant red flag to any media outlet remotely interested in the truth.

There will, naturally, be those who highlight that the JPR and CAA surveys paid no account to Labour members. But even there, there have been a few hundred cases among a membership of around 550,000: less than 0.1%. Comparing this to Nazi Germany is grotesquely offensive and quite laughable; but not to the UK media, whose narrative is the only thing that matters.

I must emphasise here that in no way whatever am I seeking to downplay the lived experiences of British Jews. Anyone who has suffered any form of antisemitism has my full support, sympathy and solidarity. But given all we already know about how wrong the British public has consistently been about everything else, it'd be quite miraculous if the Jewish community were somehow uniquely immune from that. Which is precisely why when the editor of the JC is an avowed <u>opponent</u> of the left, and has been for well over a decade, very loud questions should be asked.

Most of the UK media is right-wing and corporate owned. Oligarchs do not buy newspapers for the fun of it. They do so to influence and drive opinion; protect and expand their interests. Rupert Murdoch bought The Times and Sunday Times in 1981. Since then, he has never - not even once - been on the losing side of any general election or referendum: 12 in total. If that doesn't give the British public serious pause, I have no idea what would.

Here, moreover, is some more data: about Islamophobia in the Conservative Party. In June of this year, a poll of Tory members for the anti-racist campaign group, Hope Not Hate, found the following:

40% wanted limits on the numbers of Muslims allowed to enter the UK
43% 'would prefer to not have the country led by a Muslim'
45% believe 'there are areas in Britain in which non-Muslims are unable to enter'
67% believe 'there are areas in Britain that operate under Sharia law'
39% believe that 'Islamist terrorists reflect a widespread hostility to Britain amongst the Muslim community'
And to cap it off, despite all the above, 79% do not believe there is a problem with Islamophobia in the Conservative Party.

A follow-up released two weeks later confirmed that:

54% of Tory members believe that Islam is 'generally a threat to the British way of life'
60% think that Islam is 'generally a threat to Western civilisation'.

These are absolutely shocking findings. When two-thirds of Tory members hold disgustingly racist, Islamophobic beyond belief attitudes, you'd think the media would be all over it... wouldn't you? But in Britain in 2019, the truth is: Muslims don't count. They're irrelevant. Like the poor, the sick, the disabled, the unemployed and, as we shall see, Jews who support Corbyn and Labour, they're treated as non-people. We've all effectively been disappeared.

It's precisely because his members are so grotesquely racist that Boris Johnson has offered them periodic dog-whistles. As well as likening Muslim women who wear the burqa to 'letterboxes' and 'bank-robbers', he has also written:

To any non-Muslim reader of the Koran, Islamophobia - fear of Islam - seems a natural reaction, and, indeed, exactly what that text is intended to provoke... The problem is Islam. Islam is the problem.

To be sure, Johnson certainly knows what plays well with his base. And this racist, who leads an institutionally, endemically racist party, is now prime minister... while the country obsesses about a lifelong anti-racist instead. The world turned upside down.

The Tories have a (very) long list of party members and elected representatives who've been guilty not only of Islamophobia, but all manner of horrendous, unspeakable things. Dominic Peacock, a councillor for East Riding, was suspended for saying 'I've just donated the steam off my piss' to Jo Cox' memorial fund, just days after her murder. Tom Davey, of Barnet Council, wrote on Facebook of 'benefit claiming scum', stated that his job-hunting might be easier if he were a 'black female wheelchair bound amputee who is sexually attracted to other women', described himself as 'more excited than Harold Shipman in a nursing home', 'smacking his bitch up... that'll teach her for ironing loudly while the football is on!', and was even caught advocating social cleansing.

Enfield councillor, Chris Jonannides, was expelled for comparing Muslim women and children to bin bags; Erdington councillor, Gareth Compton, was arrested for saying that Yasmin Alibai-Brown, a Muslim journalist, should be 'stoned to death'; James Heappey, then MP for Wells, told a schoolgirl she should 'fuck off back to Scotland'; Solihull councillor, Ken Hawkins, was suspended for suggesting that Grenfell activists and campaigners demanding justice should be hung; various individuals have dressed up as Nazis and/or performed Nazi salutes; and no less than three MPs have all used the phrase, 'n***** in the woodpile'. The most recent of these, Anne Marie Morris, was quite unconscionably allowed to return to the Parliamentary Party. That is what the Conservatives think of racism within their ranks.

All this is a tiny snapshot; the tip of an enormous iceberg. There's been much, much worse - the most grievous stuff imaginable - and you can read all about it here. Warning: it may take you some considerable time to get through it all.

Just as it will if you explore the very many cases of antisemitism in the Conservative Party. Which include Boris Johnson, our prime minister, publishing a racist article by Taki Theodoracopulos when editor of The Spectator. Theodoracopulos wrote about the 'Jewish world conspiracy' and declared himself a 'soi-disant anti-Semite'. Johnson did not fire him; Theodoracopulos was free to continue his vile racism.

In October 2014, Andrew Bridgen, MP for North West Leicestershire, said 'the political system of the world's superpower and our great ally, the United States, is very susceptible to well-funded, powerful lobbying groups and the power of the Jewish lobby in America'. In May of that year, Patrick Mercer, formerly MP for Newark, referred off-camera to an Israeli soldier as a 'bloody Jew'.

In 2004, an unnamed Tory MP told the late Simon Hoggart of The Guardian that 'the trouble is that the party is being run by Michael Howard, Maurice Saatchi and Oliver Letwin - and none of them really knows what it is to be English'. All three individuals are Jewish; this was the hideous 'dual loyalty' trope being played in disgusting fashion. And in 2015, a Conservative local council candidate said she could never support *'Al Yahud'* Ed Miliband. *'Al Yahud'* is Arabic for 'the Jew'.

As with Tory Islamophobia, there's plenty more: which you can read about here. And regarding our beloved PM: as well as having spread Islamophobia and enabled antisemitism, he has described African people as 'piccaninnies with watermelon smiles'; gay men as 'tank-topped bumboys', and many, many more. Only days ago, he attended Theresa May's unveiling of a statue of Lady Astor: the woman who speculated that Hitler could be a 'solution' to the 'world problem of Jews'. Did you hear much from the media about that?

Meanwhile, Dominic Cummings, his special adviser, wrote a deranged blog which included the following:

> **They've literally written into their manifesto that they will cheat the second referendum -** apart from giving millions of foreign citizens the vote, they will rig the question so the "choice" is effectively "Remain or Remain", they will cheat the rules, they will do anything, supported by *the likes of Goldman Sachs* (my italics) writing the cheques like they did in 2016, to ensure Remain win.

'The likes of Goldman Sachs'. That's an antisemitic dog whistle *par excellence*, coming from a man whose Vote Leave campaign is being investigated by the police; and who behaves like this to MPs when they receive death threats.

Yet what does the media do in the face of all this? It treats anything to do with Johnson as a laugh; even continually referencing him by his first name, as though he's some cheeky chappie who's everyone's mate. Which perfectly explains how he's risen all the way to Downing Street despite a record of racism, lies, sexism, misogyny and narcissism which shames not only him, but the country he now leads.

That country's press isn't remotely interested in detail, nuance or complexity of any kind. Only slogans and soundbites, preferably of five words or less, which it doesn't challenge or question; it simply repeats them again and again and again. Until what's false is treated as true; what's wrong is treated as right.

◆ ◆ ◆

What was it, though, that truly thrust the issue of antisemitism on the left into the heart of British political discourse? The answer is David Collier's apparent expose of Corbyn as either an anti-Semite himself, or someone who consorted with many anti-Semites. Collier compiled a two-part report on the Facebook group, Palestine Live. Corbyn was likely added to this group without his consent, as frequently happens with Facebook groups; but did make a few posts, including 'a suggestion on the vote on recognising Palestine, which I supported, and inviting a doctor to speak at an event'.

An alarming number of posts in that group were disgustingly, revoltingly antisemitic. Labour promptly suspended any members involved. My own view is that Corbyn, however busy his then backbench life undoubtedly was, plainly should have performed comprehensive due diligence before writing anything. But that is naivete; it is not a crime. Not many Facebook users scroll through a group's entire content before posting something perfectly innocently.

Collier's thesis effectively judged Corbyn as guilty by association. That has been the consistent theme of the whole argument. He met with Hamas members in Parliament; at a debate, he once referred to them and Hezbollah members as 'friends' (something he regrets); depending on what or who you believe, he held and/or laid a wreath at a monument commemorating Palestinians murdered by the Israeli government in 1985, and/or near the graves of several Munich terrorists; he failed to notice anti-Semitism in a mural he commented on. Regarding which, he should certainly have done better; but all he was guilty of was treating the mural (and the artist behind it) in good faith. As crimes go, it's hardly earth-shattering.

This is someone who has spent almost his entire parliamentary career as a backbench MP. As recently as during the 2015 general election campaign, had anyone suggested he would become the next Labour leader, they'd have been strongly advised to spend a considerable period of time in a padded room. And as someone on the backbenches, he naturally had other interests: in his case, Israel/Palestine.

Anyone in politics who cares about this ever-protracted conflict and wants to help resolve it is bound to meet some deeply odious individuals, with whom they entirely disagree. Do we think, for example, that Theresa May agrees with Saudi head-choppers? Obviously not, yet that didn't stop her. Business is business, you see: what's contributing significantly to the worst humanitarian catastrophe on planet Earth when set against billions of pounds for British arms manufacturers?

If the British media could be bothered to do its job and cover the hideous realities in Yemen - in the manner of, say, Michael Buerk's celebrated report on the Ethiopian famine in 1984 - the Tories' position would probably evaporate overnight. Ethiopia was almost entirely a natural disaster. Yemen is man-made: with Britain profiting from the wanton slaughter of its people.

Here, meanwhile, are two cases of British prime ministers meeting terrorists. For which they were not excoriated... but praised. Both were examples of the appalling reality of politics and international relations. Every British leader there's ever been has done business with some of the most grotesque individuals imaginable. Margaret Thatcher didn't just oppose sanctions against South Africa (while Corbyn was arrested for protesting about it) or support the mass-murdering fascist Augusto Pinochet (while Corbyn campaigned to bring him to justice). She even - get this - helped Pol Pot.

There is, however, one thing I think Corbyn should be castigated for. His appearances on Press TV, an Iranian propaganda channel, whose view of the UK is as follows; in particular, an appalling comment he made about 'suspecting the hand of Israel' behind a 2012 terrorist attack in Egypt.

In my judgement, this is the one and only time he's ever said anything which could reasonably be deemed antisemitic. It was an incredibly crass, offensive thing to say. But when compared to Thatcher's support for Pol Pot - every bit as evil an individual as Hitler - Pinochet, or Saddam Hussein; Tony Blair's disastrous bombing of Iraq (regarding which, Corbyn was once more on the right side of history); Churchill's gassing of the Kurds; or the current UK government's despicable backing of Saudi Arabia, it's quite literally nothing. Further: if someone utters an antisemitic comment once in their lives, it categorically does not make them an anti-Semite.

The International Holocaust Remembrance Alliance (IHRA) have a working definition of antisemitism, which we'll come to in a moment. At this point, purely because this is how I think it's understood by the vast majority of the public, I'll add my own.

Antisemitism is hatred and/or persecution of, discrimination and/or prejudice of any kind towards Jews *because* they are Jewish.

The idea that any of this applies to Corbyn in any way, shape or form is risible nonsense. In fact, all the evidence suggests this prolific signatory of early day parliamentary motions - regularly condemning any form of antisemitism, praising the heroism of Jews during the Holocaust and expressing dismay at the poverty encountered by many in London - has been a continual friend to the Jewish community.

Let's take just one example. On 22 February 2010, a pathetic 31 MPs signed Diane Abbott's motion calling for Yemeni Jews to be afforded refugee status in the UK. Corbyn and John McDonnell were among them. Riddle me this. What kind of country - what kind of Parliament - keeps bombing and killing them for profit, opposes their rescue altogether, while denouncing someone desperately trying to save the lives of Jews as an 'anti-Semite'?

What kind of country, indeed, allows Tony Blair's government to portray Howard as 'Fagin', thinks nothing of Blair's subsequent all too cosy (and enormously profitable) relationship with the grotesquely antisemitic House of Saud, ridicules a Jewish Labour leader for how he eats a bacon sandwich, and even attacks his father for 'hating Britain'? The whiff of antisemitism - the Mail's obvious, slanderous insinuations over divided loyalties - during that disgusting saga was all too pungent. Strange how nobody was prepared to say so when someone on the left was under attack, isn't it? Nobody, that is, except - how awkward - Corbyn himself.

You may recall the furore surrounding both Corbyn's co-hosting of a meeting in Parliament on Holocaust Memorial Day 2010, entitled 'Never Again - For Anyone'; and his referral to certain Zionists as 'not understand[ing] English irony'. There is a direct link between the two. At the former, the late Holocaust survivor, Hajo Meyer, appeared to liken the Israeli government's treatment of the Palestinians to the Nazis' treatment of the Jews. Not, please note, in the death camps - which would be absurd and horrendously offensive - but during the 1930s.

Controversial, certainly; hurtful to many, I've no doubt. But while it's not something I agree with, it's also not an analogy entirely without merit, given the open air prison camp, some of the worst conditions on the planet, in which the Palestinian people are held stateless, helpless, voiceless; killed, maimed, tortured and brutalised, while the rest of the world does nothing.

At this event, a tiny group of ultra-Zionist hecklers turned it into a fiasco. Whenever any other genocide victim tried to speak of their experiences, they bellowed 'Boring!' One heckler made a Nazi salute and shouted the German phrase meaning 'All Hail!' at Meyer, a Holocaust survivor. Jonathan Hoffman - who on a separate note, was convicted earlier this year of disorderly behaviour likely to cause harassment, alarm and distress, before denouncing the Crown Prosecution Service and police for doing their jobs - even continued to disparage Meyer as 'the amazing dancing bear' until his death in 2014. He's a truly delightful fellow.

Predictably enough, none of this background was mentioned when the media went to town on Corbyn. Yet it is precisely these thugs to whom Corbyn was referring in his 'English irony' comment. He's a long-suffering veteran of how they behave. 'Zionists' meant only these few individuals.

So when the media went ballistic and demanded answers from the Labour leader, they took the side, unwittingly or otherwise, of fascists and hooligans against a deceased Holocaust survivor. That is how far through the looking glass we now are; and all those who did so, including a vast array of journalists who think of themselves as voices of reason, should be ashamed. Sadly, even Jonathan Freedland of The Guardian was still ignoring this rather uncomfortable truth when repeating this smear against Corbyn in a recent piece.

Then let's look further afield. It might sound absurd to ask; but is Benjamin Netanyahu an anti-Semite? Not only did he invite the abhorrent neo-Nazi, Viktor Orban, the man far and away most responsible for the antisemitic abuse which Soros receives every day, for a friendly chinwag in Jerusalem; not only does he do geopolitical deals with Saudi Arabia, where government officials and religious leaders actively promote the idea that the Jews are trying to take over the world, and even cite the Protocols of the Elders of Zion as a factual text.

Not only was he beside himself with joy as the US relocated its embassy to Jerusalem, the opening prayer being led by Robert Jeffress, a pastor who once declared that Jewish people were 'going to hell', with the closing benediction delivered by John C. Hagee, a televangelist who'd claimed that Hitler was 'part of God's plan to return Jews to Israel'. An unusual twist on evangelical Christians' standard claim that the Jewish people will all be destroyed by their longed-for rapture: the very thing which makes their support for Israel so total. They're a bunch of disgusting anti-Semites.

No: there's even more than that. In 2015, the Israeli prime minister doubled down on an outrageous claim that the Holocaust was all the fault not of Hitler, but the Palestinian grand mufti of Jerusalem. Perverting the truth about the Holocaust is a form of Holocaust denial. Be in no doubt: Netanyahu did this for shameful political expediency.

Taken together, Netanyahu's comments and behaviour are about a thousand times worse than anything Corbyn has said or done. And that's even before we remind ourselves of the ongoing injustice of the Palestinian people at the hands of the Israeli Defence Force.

Come to think of it, are May and Johnson anti-Semites too? They're both huge fans of doing deals with Saudi Arabia, one of the most Jew-hating countries on the planet. Moreover: apparently not satisfied with David Cameron having already relocated Conservative MEPs into the European Conservatives and Reformists (ECR), a political grouping containing fascists and homophobes, May did nothing to stop them voting *against* a rule of law procedure censuring the Hungarian government under Article 7 of the Lisbon Treaty. Even most of the yet further right European People's Party (EPP) bloc voted for it. British Tories stood in shameful isolation.

That is how unhinged the narrative has become. While the Tories, the far right and even the leader of the world's only Jewish state commit antisemitic behaviour or are apologists for it, it's Labour and the left who are under permanent attack: from the media and its own MPs, in particular.

◆ ◆ ◆

We'll look at each of these: beginning with a ludicrous furore in July 2018, when a drama was turned, quite deliberately, into a full-blown crisis. This was when Labour opted to put together its own code of conduct on antisemitism. 'How dare Labour think it knows better than Britain's Jews?', was the general accusation. 'How dare it think it knows better than the IHRA?'

But the reason for that was simple. Several examples below the IHRA working definition of antisemitism (which in and of itself, Labour fully endorsed) can and do have the effect of minimising, even suppressing, legitimate criticism of Israel. How do we know that? Because of what the author of that very working definition (adapted by the IHRA from the European Monitoring Centre on Racism and Xenophobia (EUMC)) himself set out to Congress in November 2017.

Kenneth S. Stern is Executive Director of the Justus & Karin Rosenberg Foundation, and has spent his whole career combating hatred and antisemitism. Few people anywhere are better qualified to comment on this whole issue than he is. Yet to his dismay, as he explained to the House of Representatives, the definition has been abused on various US university campuses to 'restrict academic freedom and punish political speech', and had the effect of 'chilling pro-Palestinian speech'.

Stern also paid particular heed to alarming developments in Britain.

(The) 'working definition' was recently adopted in the United Kingdom and applied to campus. An 'Israel Apartheid Week' event was cancelled as violating the definition. A Holocaust survivor was required to change the title of a campus talk, and the university mandated it be recorded, after an Israeli diplomat complained that the title violated the definition. Perhaps most egregious, an off-campus group citing the definition called on a university to conduct an inquiry of a professor (who received her PhD from Columbia) for antisemitism, based on an article she had written years before. The university then conducted the inquiry. And while it ultimately found no basis to discipline the professor, the exercise itself was chilling and McCarthy-like.

This has already been the impact of the definition: which in practice, has proven less legal than political. The examples are still being misused too: although in this case, Paul Jonson was at least reinstated by Dudley Council after a campaign to clear his name. So let's examine the four examples which Labour either slightly altered, or left out of their code of conduct.

Denying the Jewish people their right to self-determination, e.g., by claiming that the existence of a State of Israel is a racist endeavor.

Also in July 2018, Israel passed the highly controversial 'nation-state law': which states that Jews have a unique right to self-determination in Israel, and relegated the status of Arabic. Through law, Israel is now actively denying the right to self-determination of both Israeli Arabs and Palestinians. It is impossible to see how such a law is not, by its very nature, both racist and ethnonationalist.

There is, indeed, an ever-growing contradiction at the heart of Israel. It always insists it is a democracy; but the need for it to remain a specifically Jewish state is abundantly borne out by the history I set out above. The mounting problem is it cannot be both. It turns away Syrian refugees despite being the nearest safe country of refuge. It illegally uproots Palestinians from their homes, resettled in by Jews. It keeps almost 2m Palestinians in an open-air prison camp: denying them nationhood, escape, or the remotest semblance of dignity. Appallingly frequently, it kills hideous numbers of often complete innocents too.

More than that: if you read this, by the brilliant Rula Jebreal, it is impossible to conclude that Israel affords its own Arab citizens the same equal rights as it does its Jewish citizens. Jebreal, like so many of her fellow Palestinians, finds herself subject to all manner of indignities just when travelling back to her home in Israel; and as she'd surely admit herself, she's one of the lucky ones.

The Labour Party has long supported both Israel's right to exist and the Palestinians' cause. But when Israel, in effect, denies the latter their right to self-determination, how can any Labour government hold its Israeli counterpart to account if it accepts the full implication of this IHRA example? It cannot. Not only that; but this example means that if any Palestinian who has lost their home or loved ones to Israeli expansion describes this as 'racist', they are apparently being 'antisemitic'. What disgraceful, offensive, dehumanising nonsense.

And while 'Zionism' as originally understood simply meant support for a Jewish homeland (which is precisely why I'm a Zionist myself), in recent decades, to many entirely non-racist people, it has come to mean something else. As Israel has continued to build illegal settlements and carry out ethnic cleansing in defiance of international law, not to mention blockade Gaza for what is now 12 years, to many, 'Zionism' has come to mean 'racist expansion'. That is not a position I personally agree with; but I do understand it.

The IHRA example appears to delegitimise it; and worse, conflate anti-Zionism with antisemitism. That is utterly nonsensical. There is precisely zero that is antisemitic about opposing racist laws, racist policies, or the continued contravention of international norms. In any case, Labour's code of conduct highlights that the term 'Zionist' should only ever be used 'advisedly, carefully, and never euphemistically or as part of personal abuse'.

Applying double standards by requiring of it a behavior not expected or demanded of any other democratic nation.

This example is, to say the least, extremely strange. When some focus their ire on the behaviour of the Trump administration, it is not because they are anti-American. When others focus on the Brexit shambles, it is not because they are anti-British. And when still others grieve over so many lost

Palestinian lives and seek to hold the Israeli government to account, it is not because they are antisemitic. It's because they are human: with empathy and compassion for those continuing to endure profound injustice.

When Israel is condemned for gross disproportionality in its military campaigns in the Gaza strip, these are not 'double standards'. It is expected to comply with the norms of democratic states: minimising civilian casualties as far as is humanly possible. Instead, it behaves *ab*normally. Through its ally on the UN Security Council, the US, it attempted to block an independent, transparent investigation into what happened in Gaza on 14 May 2018. Why would any country do that if it had nothing to hide?

It considers a law which would ban the photographing or filming of IDF soldiers. It bans left-wing groups which criticise the army from schools. It passes the racist nation-state law mentioned above. And when a soldier is captured on video killing a wounded Palestinian, he is released... after just nine months in jail. Palestinian children who throw stones, by contrast, face a mandatory minimum of four years' imprisonment; while the 16-year-old girl who slapped two Israeli soldiers was given just one month less than the soldier: who was convicted of the manslaughter of one of her compatriots.

These are the real double standards: how Israel treats its Arab citizens and especially, the Palestinians; in comparison to its Jews. The example has the effect of quieting criticism of its conduct; in other words, of Israel not being held to the standards of other democracies at all. And it carries the potential for those who do hold it to those standards to be called 'antisemitic' for rightly calling out its government and military.

Drawing comparisons of contemporary Israeli policy to that of the Nazis.

Note here the specific language. Not 'suggesting equivalence between contemporary Israeli policy and that of the Nazis'; nor 'suggesting that contemporary Israeli policy is identical to that of the Nazis'. Either formulation would be profoundly offensive and indeed, extremely antisemitic.

Instead, the wording simply speaks of 'drawing comparisons'. This is bizarre. When someone suggests, with innocence and dismay, that 'the abused have become the abusers', that is not antisemitic. It is reality. That there are the most profound psychological reasons for Israel's political and military conduct - embedded in the collective trauma and fears of its people -

is not even a controversial statement. As it is for an individual or a family who have endured unimaginable trauma, so it can also be for a nation: above all, one founded against a backdrop of the murder of six million people for no other reason than that they were Jewish; especially when, ever since its inception, it has been surrounded by enemies bent on its destruction.

In fact, in 2000, the celebrated BBC documentary, *Five Steps to Tyranny*, made precisely such a juxtaposition. Commenting on the ongoing Israeli-Palestinian tragedy, Louise Christian, the acclaimed human rights lawyer, noted (at 46:34 in the <u>video here</u>):

> It's one of the great ironies... in Israel, that the Israelis were people who originally came together out of a sense of common, shared nationhood and identity, because of the Holocaust they'd been subjected to, not just in Nazi Germany but in Europe generally... and that they should have come together, but have done so at the expense, as it's perceived, of another people. And I think that illustrates the way in which human rights abuses may perpetuate themselves, and one abuse may create another abuse.

In my own case, the trauma of my grandmother and her family was passed down to her children, and on to my siblings and myself. My father grew up all too aware that something was horrendously wrong amid a home environment of absolute emotional emptiness; but my grandmother, whose emotions had been literally crushed out of her by the Nazis, but was desperate to protect her children, said nothing. Something very similar occurred throughout my and my siblings' childhoods too. This is how trauma works its way <u>down the generations</u>; what the Nazis did to my ancestors still has a profound impact on me and my loved ones even now. Much the same has undoubtedly been true of so many similar families and communities in Israel itself: for entirely understandable, human reasons.

Labour's <u>code of conduct</u> referenced the <u>Chakrabarti Report</u>, which 'warned of the need for all members to resist Hitler, Nazi and Holocaust metaphors, distortions and comparisons'. Certainly, such comparisons do nothing to advance serious, mature discussion of the enormously complex Israeli-Palestinian conflict, and only cause further anger and division; but in my experience, they're most often expressed by people who are simply bewildered that the Palestinians are suffering such a plight at the hands of people whose families suffered so much themselves. They're expressed, in other words, however ill-advisedly at times, mostly by human beings who care.

Accusing Jewish citizens of being more loyal to Israel, or to the alleged

priorities of Jews worldwide, than to the interests of their own nations.

Of all the examples underneath the IHRA working definition, this was the only one whose theoretical omission by Labour gave me huge room for pause. On the face of it, it's a classic racist dog whistle: employed for centuries against the Jewish people, who found themselves systematically isolated, stigmatised and ostracised as an 'other'. In many ways, it's precisely this which led to the Holocaust itself.

Yet in point 14, the <u>code of conduct</u> expressly states: 'It is also wrong to accuse Jewish citizens of being more loyal to Israel, or to the alleged priorities of Jews worldwide, than to the interests of their own nations'. In other words, the code covers this in almost the exact same way as the IHRA example does. There was never any case to answer here.

Labour's full code of conduct on antisemitism can be <u>viewed here</u>. Read it, and ask yourself: 'Is there anything in this which justifies the absurd lengths so many have gone to attack it?' Brian Klug, senior research fellow at St Benet's Hall, Oxford, correctly <u>described it</u> as a 'constructive initiative'; but already appreciated the mountainous task which evidence-based views like his <u>would face</u> amid such a ludicrously disingenuous climate. 'A part of me feels the hopelessness of appealing to reason, a sense of swimming against a mighty and unmindful current of opinion'.

Klug very much recognised which way the wind was blowing. For throughout the long, fractious political summer of 2018 (and ever since too), almost nobody in the mainstream media was prepared to report remotely accurately on the issue. Instead, for the crime of carrying out an inquiry, publishing a report, then doing far more in its proposed code of conduct than anything any British political party had ever done before, Labour was denounced as 'institutionally antisemitic'. The JC, Jewish News and Jewish Telegraph went even further: describing a lifelong campaigner against all forms of racism, who tends to his allotment and makes his own jam during his spare time, as an <u>'existential threat to Jewish life'</u>. This was madness parading as reason.

Chief among those excoriating Corbyn, of course, was Hodge. Rather than examine whether there's any substance in her depiction of the Labour leader, predictably, many of her 'moderate' colleagues instantly rallied behind her;

while journalists condemned the leadership for underlining her. Yet of course it did: because calling Corbyn a racist or an anti-Semite is to spread a disgraceful, libellous trope with no basis in fact at all. Which to his eternal shame, Sajid Javid was only too quick to pick up on.

Hodge is one of all too many so-called 'moderate' Labour MPs whose motives in all this appear deeply dubious. Her record is not one which any Labour MP should be proud of; quite the opposite. In 2016, she was quoted as saying this about Corbyn, who she has known and worked with for over 40 years:

> I was fighting the BNP between 2006 and 2010. Jeremy must have come down two or three times, brought a car full of people from Islington to help me. And that's Jeremy - I think he appeared more often than any London MP. I was fighting fascism and that would be completely up his street... He's always, always courteous. I've never seen him lose his temper.

How in the world did, according to Hodge, this 'courteous man' for whom fighting fascism was 'completely up his street' morph into a 'fucking racist and anti-Semite' only two years later? Indeed, also in 2016, the Home Affairs Select Committee also noted serious issues with some of the IHRA examples, so proposed two clarifications. Hodge had no objections at all.

Hodge, incidentally, only succeeded in beating back the BNP in Barking by, much to its delight, copying its racist policies. A quite remarkable number of Corbyn's opponents in the Parliamentary Labour Party have similarly appalling pasts of being apologists for racism. In Hodge's case, though, it gets worse, far worse.

In May of this year, Geoffrey Alderman, Professor of Politics at the University of Buckingham, wrote a piece for The Spectator. In it, he revealed the following:

> In 1987 the West London Synagogue approached Islington Council with a startling proposal: to sell its original cemetery to property developers, destroying the gravestones and digging-up and reburying the bodies lying under them. This cemetery (dating from 1840) was not merely of great historic and architectural interest - in the view of orthodox Jews, the deliberate destruction of a cemetery is sacrilegious. So when Islington Council granted the planning application, a Jewish-led and ultimately successful campaign was launched to have the decision reversed. I was part of that campaign. So was Jeremy Corbyn. Meanwhile, the then-leader of Islington Council (1982-92), whose decision to permit the destruction of the cemetery was eventually overturned, was none other than Margaret Hodge.

Those reading the above might like to ask themselves: what kind of campaigner for Jewish people would allow such a thing under their watch? And what kind of 'anti-Semite' would step in to help stop it?

There's more still. While leader of Islington Council, Hodge failed to take reports of child abuse seriously. Potentially, thousands of people were abused physically and sexually by paedophiles in Islington Council-run care homes between the 1970s and 1990s. Hodge was confronted about this <u>by survivors</u> only last month. Yet as Matthew Norman <u>explained</u> in The Independent:

> She was guilty of rather more than a casual failure of oversight. She dismissed the detailed, accurate reporting of the London Evening Standard - whose editor, Stewart Steven, battled with typical ferocity to hold her to account - as 'a sensationalist piece of gutter journalism'. Not content with shutting her eyes to his front pages, our latter-day champion of the whistle-blower closed her ears to the courageous whistle blowing of a social worker, Liz Davies. In an open letter to the BBC after it investigated a range of monstrous abuse (child prostitution, torture, alleged murders), Hodge libelled one of its victims as 'seriously disturbed'.

And just to cap it all off: in 2012, while she was chair of the Public Accounts Committee, The Telegraph <u>reported</u> that Stemcor, the steel company founded by Hodge's father, run by her brother and in which she owned shares, had paid just 0.01% tax on its UK-based revenue. Also in 2011, she was among the beneficiaries of the winding-up of a foundation based in Liechtenstein, a tax haven, which held shares in Stemcor.

How, you may ask, had Stemcor become so successful (boasting a turnover of £1bn by 2000; and ranking as the third-largest private company in the entire UK a decade later)? The answer, at least in part, lies in doing brisk business in <u>apartheid South Africa</u> during the very period when the anti-apartheid movement rightly called for extensive economic sanctions and disinvestment.

In 1973, Coutinho, Caro & Co (CCC), as Stemcor was then known, formed a joint venture in South Africa with the multi-sector conglomerate, Protea Holdings. The joint venture was called Protea International: which was split 50-50 between CCC and Protea Holdings. Initially, Protea International worked primarily as an importer, bringing steel into the South African market. But from 1976, this was reversed, and it became a net exporter of South African steel.

Like both CCC and later, Stemcor, Protea International produced none of its own steel. Instead, it acted as an intermediary for existing producers: including the state-owned giant, Iscor. By 1980, it was selling 100 million rand's worth of South African steel and other products: including in Argentina and Brazil, then both under murderous fascist dictatorships; and even in Augusto Pinochet's Chile.

During the 1970s, Protea Holdings was linked to a series of gross human rights violations. In 1971, the South African Institute of Race Relations found it was paying poverty wages to its black staff. But there was something altogether worse too; something completely horrifying. In 1963, the South African government had allowed private companies to set up psychiatric facilities on its behalf. The website, the Daily Maverick, takes up the story:

> By 1975, 11,000 mentally ill patients were housed in these private camps, of which 9,000 were black. Public leaks, parliamentary questions in the UK and a detailed investigation in the UK's *Observer*, revealed the horror of the prevailing conditions. Black patients were made to sleep 30 to a room on flimsy mats. They were treated by part-time physicians with ghoulish attitudes to African psychiatry. The death rates were terrifying: in 1973 at one facility called Randwest, 207 of the 3,200 black inmates died.
>
> The source of the influx of black patients was equally disturbing. By and large the populations of the camps were made up of the detritus of apartheid's devastation, 'those who are found wandering, drunk, or collapsed in the streets'. A brief review by a white psychiatrist and a rubber stamp from a magistrate was all that was required to declare the thousands of black Africans insane, rather than simply indigent. After being admitted, they were put to work, making leg irons and coat-hangers, or sent out as a private labouring army.
>
> Contemporaneous investigators dug deep to find the primary corporate power behind the camps - a company called Intrinsic Investments, of which [Richard] Lurie was a director. According to an investigation in the US, led by the Congressional Black Caucus, Intrinsic 'was linked to Protea Holdings, specialising in chemicals, drugs, hospitals and medical supplies'.

When the American Psychiatric Association conducted a series of site visits, its findings 'substantiate[d] allegations of social and political abuse of psychiatry in South Africa. Its President, Alan Stone, who headed the visits, said 'the most shocking finding of our investigation was the high number of needless deaths among black patients. There was evidence of patients being allowed to die who had treatable illnesses'. That is what CCC and Protea Holdings' partner, Intrinsic Investments, was doing during that time; and Hodge went on to profit from it.

Taken together, this is an absolutely monstrous record. I have no idea what such an individual is even doing in the Labour Party. It's precisely this record which recently saw her threatened with deselection: because much of her local party association has had enough. Naturally so. Yet to our execrable media, she's become a latter-day heroine and champion of anti-racism. Utterly absurd, gratuitously so... but the perfect embodiment of how Britain has lost the plot.

As an absolute bare minimum, it is rather unfortunate that almost all those Labour MPs who attacked Corbyn during the IHRA saga had essentially been against him right from the very outset of his leadership. Labour's dramatic recovery at the 2017 election owed considerably to Corbyn's personal popularity and appeal; its most progressive manifesto in at least 25 years, arguably longer; and the brilliant grassroots work of Momentum, whose utilisation of social media made an enormous difference.

But these same Labour 'moderates' wanted Corbyn out at various points during his leadership; wrongly believed he would take the party to electoral collapse; and regularly attacked Momentum. Too many of them remain spectacularly oblivious to just how much of an irrelevance Labour had become before Corbyn became leader. It was viewed as standing for nothing, believing in nothing; and at least some of its MPs had become horribly distant automatons, held in increasing contempt by their constituents. So much so that after the 2015 general election, Labour were effectively bankrupt. Only Corbyn could've re-energised the whole party in such a way, massively expanded its membership, and brought in desperately needed funds.

Some of these MPs want to have their cake and eat it. To benefit from Momentum's remarkable work (without which, many would no longer hold their seats), but not be subject to the democratic principles which govern it. The media has spoken in dark terms of 'Stalinist purges' about constituency associations democratically choosing their candidate! The message seems to be that activists should be seen, but not heard; pay up, and shut up.

Hodge, at least, was not among the Labour MPs who, in April 2018, disgracefully spent a week on a 'fact finding mission' in Saudi Arabia: which commits war crimes in Yemen on a daily basis, does indefensible arms deals with the UK, and whose role in Islamist terrorism was buried by the British government. Among the MPs on that trip was John Woodcock, who resigned from the Labour Party three months later. Comically, this resulted in him being hailed as a man of principle: a word which has been entirely redefined by the British media. To it, 'principle' apparently now means avoiding a sexual harassment investigation, attacking individuals on Twitter several hours after an innocent misunderstanding had been resolved, so prompting a pile-on on someone with mental health issues; and supporting Saudi war criminals.

What sort of 'moderate' wrongly accuses Jeremy Corbyn of antisemitism, only to themselves kowtow to one of the worst, most notoriously Jew-hating regimes on the planet? A 'moderate' which the Labour Party is much better off without. And if you wanted to know how other 'moderates' have behaved, this tweet, from Ian McKenzie, is the perfect example. 'The anti-Semitism stuff is cutting through... we've a real chance of winning NEC seats back'. The sheer, unadulterated cynicism takes the breath away.

In Britain in 2019, the truth is this. The more outrageously someone behaves, the better. The more lies they tell, the better. The more they seek their own advancement, not that of the country or its people, the better. This is a country which has produced not one, but two compulsively lying, malevolent Tory buffoons, who large sections of the population actually *admire* for their buffoonery. This is a country which voted itself poorer on a pack of lies, is still mired in austerity based on a pack of lies, after having gone to war in Iraq on a pack of lies.

This is a country where, when he's not being called everything from a traitor to a spy to an anti-Semite to Lucifer himself, the Leader of the Opposition is routinely derided as 'weak': despite having miraculously forced a hung Parliament - the very thing which has prevented a hard Brexit - from a 20-point starting handicap; and inflicting more defeats on the government than the opposition to Cameron, Gordon Brown, Blair and John Major combined. This is a country whose Parliament which, charged with preventing the worst national catastrophe since Norway 1940, spent an entire session before Christmas 2018 conducting a witch hunt based on a lip-reading exercise. This is a country where reality has ceased to matter altogether.

Throughout all this, centrist commentators - who decry Corbyn as 'unelectable' and yearn for some impossible return to Blairism - simply haven't had the first clue. It is they who stood back and cheered as New Labour abandoned the working class. It is they who disgracefully considered Cameron and George Osborne's devastation of the welfare state and the supply side of the economy as 'centrist' and 'moderate'. It is they who obsessed with nonsense like Miliband looking awkward while eating a bacon sandwich. It is they who swallowed economically illiterate poppycock like 'running a country is like running a household budget' and 'we have to live within our means', with all the catastrophic consequences that has led to.

It was their complacency, their arrogance, which helped Remain lose the EU referendum via the worst political campaign ever seen (with one exception). It is they who've constantly written off Corbyn and dismissed over half a million members and 13 million voters as a 'cult'. It is they who are so clueless, so hermetically sealed, that they think Labour should replace Corbyn with a chief architect of the Work Capability Assessment, who also brought in Atos.

At some point, you'd think they might ask themselves: 'How exactly did we get here?' But as the answer would involve looking in a mirror, there's no chance of that. Britain has, in my honest opinion, the worst, most pathetic, most oblivious, most out of touch, most conceited, most pleased with itself media and political class anywhere in the democratic world. And very possibly, the most corrupt one too.

We live in a political age in which not only have facts ceased to matter, but narratives based almost entirely on myths and lies have gained such sway that they have decided important elections, and taken whole countries down entirely different, increasingly dark routes. 'Labour overspent and caused the crash'. 'Welfare is a lifestyle choice'. 'Let's take back control and give £350m to the NHS'. 'Turkey is about to join the EU'. 'We've had enough of experts'. 'Hillary Clinton's email server is a national security threat'. 'Lock her up'. 'No deal is better than a bad deal'. 'Stop talking the country down'. 'Enemies of the people'. 'Corbyn and Labour are riddled with antisemitism'.

On and on it has gone. For many years now, the vast majority of the media has utterly failed to do its job of holding truth to power. Instead, it's enabled the powerful - and the destruction of so many people's lives - by spreading their lies. Any media which is not holding the exact same microscope to Islamophobia in the Conservative Party (in fact, given the extent of its prevalence, a much more magnified one) as it has with antisemitism in the Labour Party is simply not doing its job.

Speaking of the former, here's another snapshot. From a Facebook group called 'Conservatives Against the EU'. Click on these links at your own risk… but if you do, ask yourself: how come this wasn't reported in the media? And how come May wasn't hauled over the coals for it?

Yet when someone comes along who might challenge a quiescent, pliant, failed beyond imagination status quo, look what he gets. Smears, slander and never-ending disinformation from those who insist they are so appalled by fake news; smears and slander of his supporters too. Many of whom are poor, vulnerable, unwell, disabled, homeless: battling through lives unthinkable to those who sneer at them from their bubble. Many of whom have friends and family whose lives have been destroyed (often, literally) by wanton Tory cruelty. To paraphrase the great Ian Martin: wake the hell up, centrist bobbleheads, and stand with those with nothing. They're the ones who need power, not you.

◆ ◆ ◆

There remains, though, the more general issue. In April 2018, Luciana Berger, then MP for Liverpool Wavertree, gave a powerful, moving speech on the horrific antisemitic abuse she has been subjected to throughout her life. Quite rightly, she highlighted the online environment: a 'cesspit', as another MP referred to it during her speech.

Yet listening to her speech begged the question: just how much abuse which she and her colleagues have received has come from Labour members? Many Twitter accounts are not under someone's actual name. The online world was all but taken over by Russian bots ahead of the 2016 US presidential election, the EU referendum... perhaps even the Scottish referendum in 2014.

In no way whatever is this to downplay the horrendous abuse which Berger and many of her Labour colleagues have experienced. As she herself said, one antisemitic Labour member is one too many. But if the vast majority of abuse has come from outside the Labour membership, then beyond commissioning a comprehensive investigation (which he did) and a new code of conduct (as the NEC did), and removing any members found guilty of antisemitism (which they have been, albeit the process still needs improvement), what on Earth is Corbyn supposed to do?

As his leadership prospects dramatically grew during the 2015 Labour election, extraordinary numbers of vile antisemitic tweets seemed to emerge more or less out of nowhere. Were these genuine Corbyn supporters? Or bots and operatives (including paid Tory ones), seeking to wreak havoc? As long as there are bad people on the internet anywhere in the world - bad people who can be made to *look* like Corbyn supporters (not at all difficult, as both the US and Britain's experiences in 2016 bear testament to: chaos agents ruling the roost) - it won't stop. That's the whole point; the whole cynical, nefarious, despicable exercise. Played out in a country which has entirely lost all sense of what it's supposed to stand for.

Take a trip to any of the Daily Mail, Daily Express, The Spectator, or Guido Fawkes' websites' comments sections; or simply glance at the Twitter pages of those on the right or far right. All are packed with never-ending Islamophobic and, regularly, antisemitic abuse. Perhaps some of these commentators might be Russian operatives too; but many others will be Tory voters. Strangely, no demands have been made of May or Johnson to somehow magic away all the horrible people on the internet. So why has precisely this been demanded of Corbyn?

Celebrities have been in on the act too. 'Jeremy Corbyn has made me a Tory', wails Maureen Lipman... before, in a quite remarkable interview, first condemning him for meeting with 'the wrong people' (in other words, 'the wrong Jews') at a Seder night; then, with stunning Islamophobia, exclaiming that 'we have not committed thousands of appalling crimes... we're not bombing or beheading'. Who are, Maureen? Muslims?

Not only that, but Lipman mysteriously failed to mention that, along with 86% of the British Jewish community (it's not Corbyn who lost the support of British Jews. It was Ed Miliband), she in fact abandoned Labour four years ago. And why? In her case at least, because of its support for a Palestinian state. Think about that for a moment: she denounced the Labour Party for its backing of Palestinian self-determination. Would she prefer the Palestinians to rot forever instead?

'The Chuka Harman Burnham Hunt Balls brigade? I can't, in all seriousness, go into a booth and put my mark on any one of them'. Fair enough, Maureen, neither could most of the country... but that's precisely why Labour had to move leftwards afterwards. Yet you condemn that too.

On Twitter, others declare with pure self-righteousness that they 'won't throw British Jews under the bus'. In practice, oh yes they will. Because there's plenty of poor Jews in the UK; and plenty of other Jews who've suffered just as much under this atrocious excuse for a government as anyone else. Why do so many care so little about them? Why are so many happy for their suffering to continue, or get even worse? To these people, I can only ask the following.

Do you seriously care more about the omission of a few problematic examples under the IHRA definition (which its own author has strongly critiqued), which has been fully endorsed in any case, than you do about the poor? The infirm? The disabled? The unemployed? Doctors? Nurses? Teachers? The NHS? The fire service? Police? Immigrants and refugees? Grenfell? Windrush? EU citizens at the mercy of a no-deal Brexit? Those forced onto zero hours contracts? Those who can never hope to buy a home, and who pay disgusting rent charges amid often squalid conditions with no protection at all? Those who have been led down the garden path by the most incompetent, corrupt government in living memory? Do you care about any of *them*?

But on the subject of suffering: if, in the event of a Labour government, we'll finally have a prime minister prepared to call out the Israeli government on its treatment of the Palestinians, that is very much a good thing. Over the last 20 years, their situation has grown profoundly worse; and the international community has, by and large, remained silent. Quiet, sweet nothings about supporting a two-state solution (which Israel has itself abandoned, and never been truly serious about since the collapse of the Oslo Peace Process) have achieved zero; while the language around the conflict has continued to change in favour of Israel, in spite of the ever more bleak reality.

Let's return to that BBC documentary I mentioned earlier. With no bias, nothing other than a desire to calmly report the truth, its narrator, Sheena McDonald, set out the realities facing the Palestinian people (at 43:50 here):

In Israel, the Palestinians often live in appalling conditions, not far from impressive housing developments built by Jewish settlers. As the gulf between the two groups widens, with restricted human rights for Palestinians, there's ongoing violence. The Palestinians throw stones and sometimes open fire. The Israelis retaliate with live rounds and rockets, and the force of law.

Until September 1999, Israel effectively legalised torture, under the term 'moderate physical pressure'. This enabled the secret police, the Shin-Bet, to brutalise suspected Palestinian terrorists, using shackling, shaking, and isolation. A liberal, middle class nation stood by and tolerated this behaviour, for years…

… The Israeli Army's use of 'moderate physical pressure' has led to the jailing and torture of some 10,000 Palestinians over the last decade. They have their day in court, but only with the veneer of a fair trial.

That documentary was broadcast 19 years ago. Try imagining the BBC ever broadcasting something similar now. The political climate is such that the producer might, ludicrously, find themselves accused of 'antisemitism': purely for focusing on the Palestinians' horrendous plight.

In July of this year, Auntie took it to a whole new level. Its edition of *Panorama*, which purported to be an expose by John Ware, was nothing more than a hatchet job. An appalling one. As I wrote on Twitter at the time, any serious investigative programme would've done the following:

It would've noted the huge amount of research which shows how small a problem antisemitism on the left actually is.

It would've noted that antisemitism in Labour has *fallen* since Corbyn became leader.

It would've asked surely the most important question of all: why is there such an enormous chasm between what the data says about antisemitism on the left and in Labour… and what the British community perceive? Perceptions which cannot and must not be ignored.

As well as those it interviewed, it would've sought out accounts from British Jews who support Corbyn and Labour. There's plenty of us. The media just likes to pretend otherwise.

It would've taken a thoughtful, serious approach to understanding the difference between antisemitism and anti-Zionism. Which I'll attempt to do later in this chapter.

There was precisely zero attempt to explore or analyse any of this. What the programme did instead was provide a series of anecdotal accounts set to mood-influencing music; accounts which often featured extraordinarily little specific detail.

Other, that is, than from Ben Westerman: a Labour Party investigations officer from 2016 to 2017, who was dispatched to the Liverpool Riverside Constituency Labour Party (CLP) to probe allegations of antisemitism and bullying. On the programme, Westerman stated the following:

And we finished the interview. The person got up to leave the room, and then turned back to me and said, 'where are you from?' And I said, 'what do you mean, where am I from?' And she said, 'I asked you, where are you from?' And I said, 'I'm not prepared to discuss this'. And they said, 'are you from Israel?'

What can you say to that? You are assumed to be in cahoots with the Israeli government. It's this obsession with the fact that just spills over all the time into antisemitism.

In fact, a full recording of what *appears* to be the interview in question features merely the following exchange:

Witness: I'm just curious, because I haven't been in the Labour Party very long, and I've certainly never been to anything like this informal interview before… so I'm just curious about… what branch are you in?

Westerman: I don't think that's relevant… I hope that's ok… I just don't think where I'm from is at all relevant to the investigation… you're more than welcome to ask questions, but I reserve the right to not answer them and I feel that's a question about my personal situation which I don't think is relevant to the situation.

Witness: No, it might not be. Just, but it might be interesting.

Westerman: I'm not prepared to discuss my address, basically.

At no point in this exchange was Westerman asked if he was from Israel, nor for his address. Yet despite its public service remit requiring balance, nobody from Liverpool Riverside was asked for their side of the story ahead of Panorama's airing. They were all just airbrushed out instead.

Worse: an email by Seumas Milne, Labour's Director of Strategy and Communications, was deliberately edited to make it look as though he had said something he had not (Milne's email concerned Jewish members accused of antisemitism: including one with a Holocaust-surviving parent); a lie about Jackie Walker, which the BBC had admitted was inaccurate only week earlier, was quite unbelievably repeated; and Jennie Formby, Labour's general secretary, who has done a vast amount to speed up and sort out disgracefully inept complaints procedures she inherited from Iain McNicol, was repeatedly demonised; while the latter, whose gross incompetence should've been highlighted by the programme, was instead indulged like an expert witness. Astonishing.

Two of those interviewed by *Panorama* had also featured in Al-Jazeera's *The Lobby*: a behind-the-scenes series which exposed an Israeli diplomat seeking to 'take down' a UK government minister and Labour MPs. Shai Masot was promptly recalled by an embarrassed Jerusalem. It was, to say the least, rather curious to see Ella Rose, who'd been filmed threatening Walker with violence by al-Jazeera, now weeping in front of the BBC cameras and again, treated as a scrupulously objective witness.

I don't know what they teach at journalism school nowadays, but a beginner's guide to critical thinking is as follows:

1. Who is telling me this?
2. Why are they telling me this?
3. In whose interests are they telling me this?

These three basic rules are seemingly well beyond the grasp of all but a handful of journalists in the UK; as, indeed, is the basic GCSE History requirement of contextualising sources and looking behind them. With regard to which, it should come as no surprise for you to learn that Ware, who produced and presented the programme, has a whole history of both Islamophobia and describing Jews who oppose Zionism - a perfectly legitimate, respectable position, albeit one I don't share - as 'marooned on Judaism's furthest fringe'.

When the BBC employs such an individual for a documentary on such a serious, sensitive topic, it knows full well what it's doing. It's seeking to fan the flames, sensationalise, and scrape the bottom of the barrel... all while single mothers go to prison for not paying the licence fee.

◆ ◆ ◆

And then, there's the Jewish Chronicle. The paper of record for British Jews. The one publication which, you might imagine, would surely be beyond reproach when it comes to reporting antisemitism and seeking to protect Jews everywhere. Think again.

The JC's editor is Stephen Pollard. He gets rather angry if anyone suggests he is a racist. Well Stephen, in that case, I'd like you to explain the following. In April 2006, when Blair's premiership still had more than a year to run, Pollard declared that 'the Left, in any recognisable form, is now the enemy'. In 2009, reviewing Bruce Bawer's *Surrender: Appeasing Islam, Sacrificing Freedom*, he opened with the hyperbolic drivel that 'there is no more important issue facing the West than Islamism, Islamofascism or - to use yet another label - radical Islam'.

Climate change threatening all humanity? Nuclear war? The 2008 financial crash, the consequences of which are still with us over a decade later? But do go on. Bawer's book featured the following excerpt:

> The pernicious doctrine of multiculturalism, which teaches free people to belittle their own liberties while bending their knees to tyrants, and which, as we shall see, has proven to be so useful to the new brand of cultural jihadists that it might have been invented by Osama bin Laden himself.

Channelling his inner Enoch Powell, Pollard concluded: 'Bawer is unquestionably correct, and that fact is quite simply terrifying'.

In 2015, when Farage disgracefully accused British Muslims of having 'split loyalties' - the very same trope which rightly incenses British Jews if it's ever levelled at us - how did Pollard respond? With this. This was barely a year after Pollard had acknowledged that Farage had allied with extremists and anti-Semites. But when the right is guilty of vile antisemitism, Pollard seems only too quick to forgive and forget.

And in 2011, we had the worst case of all. Remember that shameless front page which the JC and its sister papers ran in July 2018? Following the London riots, a British Jew, along with his family, faced a very real existential threat: from neo-Nazis. This is his story.

> Back in 2011 the Jewish Chronicle ran a piece on me, which also included mention of my parents and their politics, and my childhood and education, none of which had any bearing whatsoever on the story. One of the consequences of them running this piece is that my parents and I were profiled by far right racists and fascists. Some fascists got hold of my parents' address, and some details about all of us were shared on extreme far right forums like Stormfront. I received death threats, while my parents had to find ways to secure their home. In all cases these threats were explicitly linked to us being identified as Jewish, by far-right anti-Semites.
>
> At the time my parents and I wrote to the editor, Stephen Pollard, and requested, given these grave antisemitic threats, that the article be removed from the Jewish Chronicle website (it had already gone out in a print edition). He refused and the article remained online.
>
> So excuse me when I can't quite believe my ears, when you protest there is an 'existential threat' to Jews. The one time in my life I was profiled and violently threatened by known anti-Semites because I

was Jewish, you refused to help. It turns out safety should only be guaranteed to the 'right' sort of Jews, and only when it serves your political agenda.

The individual's father adds this detailed, disturbing commentary:

It was the Jewish Chronicle's editorial decision to report this case in such a way that it gratuitously provided details of other family members and their left-wing political views. It was the decision of the editor, Stephen Pollard to leave the report online, after it became apparent that neo-Nazis were using it to make threats and incite acts of violence against us.

In an email dated 14th August 2011 we wrote to Stephen Pollard, copied to two members of the Board of the Jewish Chronicle (Richard Burton and Jennifer Lipman), which said **'under the circumstances we would request that you urgently remove the article from your website'**. On neo-Nazi websites they had published photos of our son with the crosshairs of a target superimposed on his face.

We had also pointed out factual inaccuracies in the Chronicle's report. Pollard fixed these and wrote an email back to us on 15th August saying: 'You do not point to any other inaccuracies in our piece **and I see no reason to remove it'**. Neither of the Board members copied in responded to us.

Just a few weeks before this incident, a Norwegian neo-Nazi, Anders Breivik had massacred 77 people, mostly children at a socialist summer camp, having been inspired by online hate material. Pollard's argument for keeping the material there was that it was factually accurate. And yet by doing so once he was aware of the threats, he was increasing the danger to us...

... We were and still are very shocked that the editor of the leading community newspaper could have behaved like this in response to a clear case of a murderous antisemitic threat against a member of the Jewish community.

That is what Pollard thinks of his fellow Jews if they face real danger. Antisemitism only matters to him if it's from the left; and for over a decade, the only thing that's mattered to him is stopping a Labour government, at any cost. Anything from him on the patently antisemitic coverage of Ed Miliband and his father? No. Or from his newspaper when, in September, Jacob Rees-Mogg employed one of the world's oldest, most vile antisemitic tropes, when describing Sir Oliver Letwin and John Bercow as 'illuminati'? Astoundingly, also no.

Quite what this avowed opponent of multiculturalism and, when it suits him, effective enabler of neo-Nazis is doing editing a newspaper as hitherto august as the JC, I have absolutely no idea. And on a similar note: quite what journalists at that publication are doing supporting members of Farage's Brexit Party and even employing the Soros trope *against* the Jewish poet and author, Michael Rosen, I couldn't tell you either. This is Alice in Wonderland stuff at times. I've been on the receiving end too, albeit in a milder way: have a look at the images highlighted here by Jack Mendel of the Jewish News, and see if you can spot any 'personal abuse'. (Helpful hint: there isn't any).

Incidentally, have you ever wondered where the Soros trope originates from? Astonishingly, it was concocted by George Birnbaum and Arthur

Finkelstein, two brilliant but almost nihilistically cynical political operatives. To my shock and real pain, both also happen to be Jewish. In Birnbaum's case, his grandfather was shot by the Nazis in front of his son, Birnbaum's father, and later survived Auschwitz. The Jewish school Birnbaum attended was often defaced with antisemitic slurs.

Yet in 2008, Birnbaum and Finkelstein worked together to elect Orban. They did this by constructing an all-pervasive external Jewish enemy. Extraordinary. Just as extraordinary was that Finkelstein truly broke through into worldwide prominence by devising a hideously negative campaign which enabled Netanyahu to achieve a shock, wafer-thin victory against Shimon Peres in 1996: the true modern-day political turning point in Israel. Peres had pledged to uphold the legacy of his great friend, Yitzhak Rabin, the heroic man of peace. Netanyahu immediately took Israel off on a rejectionist path, from which it's never truly recovered.

This article lays bare the full detail of what Finkelstein and Birnbaum did to Soros, their fellow Jew. It's a deeply disturbing, chilling read. And it provides an awful reminder that, just as with any other people, some Jews do turn on their fellow Jews; even, in a few cases, they seek to destroy them.

Harpin, too, also seeks to destroy others. A journalist so completely without scruples, he was arrested and had his computer confiscated during the phone hacking investigation, one of his recent targets has been Audrey White, the very woman who paved the way for legislation against sexual harassment, and was portrayed by Glenda Jackson in the award-winning *Business as Usual*.

In the JC, Harpin alleged that White had been 'expelled' from the Labour Party during the 1980s; and had 'lied' about her date of birth upon applying to rejoin the party in 2015, 'on the day Jeremy Corbyn became leader'. Harpin further alleged that White 'had been amongst a group of militants who repeatedly interrupted' their MP during a speech; 'had received a number of formal warnings from the party over allegations of bullying against party members'; and had 'falsely claimed that a Labour councillor was under investigation by the police for having cruelly taunted a disabled pensioner suffering from cancer'.

Disgracefully, the JC had taken no steps to verify any of this. It has provided no evidence whatever - with a recording of the CLP meeting in question confirming that the crowd had not been 'rowdy' at all.

White complained to the Independent Press Standards Organisation

(IPSO), which ruled entirely in her favour. It also found that a councillor had indeed been under police investigation for abusive behaviour towards a disabled pensioner; and most tellingly of all, found the JC extremely uncooperative throughout its investigation. The paper repeatedly failed to respond to questions put to it; with its conduct so 'unacceptable', it's been referred to IPSO's standards department.

You can read the full ruling here (and may also care to note that White happens to be a member of the same Liverpool Riverside CLP reported on by Panorama). This is what both Pollard and Harpin think of basic journalistic standards, of facts, or of not smearing a pensioner: with all sorts of horrendous consequences for her reputation based on a pack of lies. What IPSO should be doing is investigating the JC from top to bottom. It is yet another example of our wretched, disgraceful, still unregulated press.

But then, in a country where The Spectator publishes racism every week from Theodoracopulos or Rod Liddle; The Sun allowed Katie Hopkins to describe immigrants as 'cockroaches'; or even James O'Brien, so quick to denounce the fake news and racist dog-whistles surrounding the EU referendum, shares a studio with Farage and, to his eternal shame, described Labour as the 'party of Holocaust denial', there's surely no room for surprise any longer. The British media doesn't hold truth to power. It protects power at all costs and does its dirty work for it: pumping out never-ending lies and hateful, destructive smears.

Regarding the Jewish community, this involves a loud, daily drumbeat of 'Labour is antisemitic! Corbyn is antisemitic!' So of course British Jews are scared. Of course their perceptions of antisemitism on the left are extraordinarily out of kilter with reality. Their only crime in all this is to trust the media. But what is abhorrent - what is absolutely disgusting - is for that media to play on that inner fear which deep down, all Jews (certainly including myself) have. 'What if? What if it happened again?' Exploiting the horrendous suffering of my people's tragic history, for nakedly political reasons.

Sam Kriss has described this as 'The war against the Jews'... and he's absolutely correct. It's a war which even involves rabbis telling their congregation that they must vote for whichever party can stop Labour: which presumably includes the racist Conservative Party and even more racist Brexit Party. It fell to Rabbi Howard Cooper to provide urgent perspective and draw exactly the correct conclusion.

This situation requires a calm thoughtfulness rather than an emotive, fear-fuelled enactment which merely mirrors the hostility that some Jews feel themselves subjected to.

Jews are understandably upset, angered and fearful when they hear about, or witness, antisemitic remarks or actions. But thoughtful rabbinic leadership at this moment in our history should be helping people manage their anxieties about these trends - which are part of larger, disturbing trends in the society around us: all that toxic swirl of aggression, anger, hatred and victimisation that courses through public discourse and on social media.

A rabbi's job, I believe, is to help the Jewish community contain its worries and its emotional distress, not by telling people how to cast their vote (as if they didn't have a mind of their own) but by strengthening their psychological and spiritual wellbeing.

Rabbi Romain's intemperate action can only stoke Jewish fears, increase people's anxieties, collude with our historically deep-seated impulses towards paranoid thinking.

And the message it may send to non-Jews? I fear that it colludes with a fantasy that Jews are a homogenous group who are only concerned about themselves rather than the larger shared issues of the society we all live in. And for some it may fan the flames of a belief in Jewish conspiratorial networks that seek to undermine the country's wellbeing.

Jews are not threatened with organised violence in this country. If it comes, as it might, it will come from the populist right - who have no internal countervailing voices, as the left do. We will then realise that we had our eyes on the wrong ball all along.

One hopes that Ephraim Mirvis, the Chief Rabbi, read Rabbi Cooper's comments. If so, they fell on deaf ears. On 26 November, he made an unprecedented intervention, denouncing Corbyn as 'unfit for high office', inquiring about the 'moral compass' of a country which elected such a man, and stating that 'the very soul of our nation is at stake'. To which I can only say: at least he got the last bit right.

This is someone who welcomed Boris Johnson's accession to the premiership; that is to say, he welcomed the election of a racist to Downing Street. Throughout his time as Chief Rabbi, there hasn't been a peep from him on Islamophobia in the Tory Party; or any of the unspeakable things being done to the poor, the disabled, the defenceless, the voiceless, which this book has set out. I have no idea where his 'moral compass' is... but quite where in the Torah it says that abandoning the sick, the vulnerable, the needy because of a pack of lies is the correct form of behaviour, I'm none too clear. Perhaps he could enlighten us.

To be frank: this hasn't even been a campaign against antisemitism. It's been a campaign of unimaginably bad faith against the left, period. When even the Liberal Democrats see fit to play the pettiest of politics with disgraceful Twitter videos, that is the only conclusion which can be drawn. And one of very many reasons why all the evidence is pointing in that direction is how Corbyn-supporting Jews have themselves been treated.

◆ ◆ ◆

On 7 November, Lila Rose sat in the BBC Question Time audience as just another ordinary member of the British public. Lila and her whole family are Jewish. She stated, quite correctly, that Corbyn is not an anti-Semite. For the crime of telling the truth, she was stalked and harassed online, had personal information leaked out about her, and told her family would be tracked down. She received tweets like this. And this. And this. And this. And this.

Lila is far from alone. The same thing, as she explains in this powerful, shocking thread, has happened to Nadine Batchelor-Hunt, who even had to call in the police. It's also happened, among many others, to Charlotte Nichols, Labour's candidate in Warrington North; and Miriam Mirwitch, the Chair of Young Labour UK.

That is what happens to Jews who speak out in support of Corbyn. Any coverage of that in the media, including the JC? Of course not. To the Fourth Estate, all these good, gentle, caring people are an irrelevance; and their appalling lived experiences are to be treated as such. Nothing must be allowed to get in the way of a narrative which chills the blood and sells papers.

Indeed, I've had plenty of abuse myself: including being called a 'kapo' (meaning a prisoner in a Nazi concentration camp assigned by SS guards to supervise forced labour or carry out administrative tasks: the term is often used against left-wing Jews, and should be criminalised as hate speech) and told my grandmother would be ashamed of me... and believe me, that's very much the lightest stuff.

Even the so-called liberal media has, in its own way, been in on the act too. In July 2018, the New Statesman published far and away the most risible piece of nonsense I've ever seen from a usually sensible publication. Entitled 'Contemporary Anti-Semitism 101', after correctly stating that antisemitism is a conspiracy theory, David Bennun claimed the following:

On the left, this conspiracy theory manifests largely as part of what is known as 'anti-Imperialism'. The most obvious manifestation of this conspiracy theory on the left is in the fervent loathing of Israel.

This goes to the heart of the Labour Party taking it upon itself to rewrite unilaterally the International Holocaust Remembrance Alliance's definition of anti-Semitism...

... Jews are not unanimous on anti-Semitism, but those who differ are very few.

Let's break this down. According to Bennun's thesis, anti-imperialism - being opposed to the rich world's domination and exploitation of the poor - is somehow 'antisemitic'. That is to say: wanting a fair, just world, in which nobody exploits anyone, is 'antisemitic'.

Also according to Bennun, the left doesn't oppose the Israeli government because of its illegal occupation, the monstrous injustice which the Palestinians face every day, or the simple fact that left wingers support the weak, the vulnerable, the voiceless, the poor all over the world. Oh no. Its 'fervent loathing of Israel' is because the left is antisemitic!

The article repeated the complete falsehood that Labour had rewritten the IHRA definition, which it had in fact endorsed. As for Bennun's claims of near-Jewish unanimity on what constitutes antisemitism: first, he provided zero evidence; and second, it rather begs the question of why so many British Jews voted for the left for so long. Especially prior to Labour's dramatic shift rightwards under Blair.

The piece does three appalling things. It conflates antisemitism with anti-Zionism, an utter nonsense. It suggests that any Jews who differ with the author on what antisemitism is provide cover for anti-Semites (offensive, dangerous, self-regarding drivel). And as we've noted, it all but states that if you're opposed to rampant inequality, to the rich getting ever richer with all its pernicious consequences for the world, you are an anti-Semite.

I will never know how a publication on the centre-left saw fit to print such execrable rot. But in its defence, I have long suspected we'd reach the point whereby anyone opposing neoliberal globalisation would be denounced as antisemitic. It is, after all, dangerously close to a 'classic antisemitic trope' to believe that the rich have far too much influence on the world; regardless of the reality that they very obviously do.

◆ ◆ ◆

There is, though, one thing I want to re-emphasise. When I state, with categorical conviction (and, I would argue, proof) that the question of antisemitism on the left has been blown up out of all proportion, I am certainly not saying it doesn't exist. When I state, with equal conviction, that many of those cited as proof of the extent of the problem were either bots, or internet troublemakers and trolls with precisely nothing to do with either Corbyn or the Labour Party, I am not saying that antisemitism in Labour doesn't exist. There have been a few hundred cases in a membership of about 500,000: less than 0.1%. Any such cases must always be dealt with through speed and urgency. In this article, Formby explains how that's being done.

A personal view is that there's been a tendency to overlook antisemitism from all sections of society at times because, for want of a better phrase, most of us Jews 'blend in'. The problem is how so many of us, unconsciously or otherwise, feel we *have* to. The difference in how members of the public might respond to liberal Jews like me going about our daily business, compared with orthodox Jews who identify themselves as Jewish through their clothing, must surely be significant. That is awful, and something for everyone to reflect on.

And while there isn't, contrary to popular belief, a serious problem with antisemitism on the left, it is certainly the case that anti-Zionism is a lot more prevalent than on the right. Which is precisely why Labour focus on it in their code of conduct; but also, unhappily, why the likes of Bennun seek to conflate it with antisemitism. Without question, the language used against Israel is frequently far too strong; and the entire Israeli people being held responsible for the actions of their wretched government also occurs too often and is quite outrageous. When Jews, whether in Israel, Britain or anywhere else, are too... well, that is antisemitism, plain and simple.

More pertinent to this whole discussion, though, is the whole question of Zionism. I identify as a left-wing Zionist because of the desperate need, taught to all Jews throughout our tragic history, of a Jewish homeland and safe haven. But we cannot ignore the contemporary context: illegal settlers, an illegal occupying army, and far-right religious zealots doing the most horrific things on a daily basis.

For the Palestinians, on a good day, the reality of Zionism is something like this: On a worse day, it's something like this (the link is shocking, but should probably be viewed). And on an awful day, it's something like this (*warning*: graphic, horrifying, heartbreaking. Absolutely not for the faint of heart).

Almost all of us on the left are so because we stand with the weak against the strong; with the oppressed against oppression. The idea that we're all supposed to just turn our heads and say nothing about the Palestinians' plight isn't just grotesque. It's inhuman. And while no doubt, the conflict is enormously complex, with the disgusting Hamas (every bit as much of a nightmare for the Palestinian people as the Israeli government. Hamas aren't freedom fighters; they're monsters) doing nothing but making it worse, Israeli politics are unrecognisable from even 20 years ago, let alone forty or fifty.

So much so that Netanyahu, despite police recommendations to indict him for corruption, is still, somehow, prime minister. So much so that Israel passed the openly racist nation-state law, before Naftali Bennett and Ayelet Shaked quit the racist Jewish Home party... because it wasn't right-wing enough for them.

Bennett, the Israeli Minister of Defence, believes in unilaterally annexing the West Bank and openly opposes a Palestinian state ever occurring. Shaked is the former Minister of Justice, a huge fan of the nation-state law, and in 2014, shared the following post on Facebook.

In our war, it is even more true that the enemy soldiers are hiding in the population and only because of their support can they fight. Behind each terrorist stand dozens of men and women, without whom he could not sabotage. Participating in the fighting that incite the mosques, the authors of the murderous curricula, the shelter providers, the vehicle suppliers, and all those who give honour and moral support. All of them are enemy fighters and everyone is bleeding in their heads.

Now it also includes the mothers of the Shahids, who send them to hell with flowers and kisses. They have to follow their sons, there is nothing more just than that. They should go, and the physical house where they raised the snake. Otherwise other little snakes will grow up there'.

Netanyahu, Bennett and Shaked are not reasonable people. They make me feel ashamed. Israel was a beautiful dream for all Jews not so long ago. Now, it's little more than a nightmare for far, far too many people. The idea that the left should say nothing about attitudes such as that posted above... well, there are no words for that.

Nor, though, am I in any way trying to downplay antisemitism itself. What so angers me is how this evil scourge, with all its horrific consequences which people like me and my family know only too well, is being openly manipulated and twisted for political reasons by those who, when it doesn't occur on the left (i.e. the vast majority of the time), couldn't care less. This isn't Kafka, this isn't Orwell; this is actually happening in Britain in 2019.

I really cannot emphasise this strongly enough. British Jews are in *no danger whatsoever* from a Corbyn government. We couldn't be less so. Nor in any way is it the fault of the UK Jewish community that so much of it believes what it's been told. It's the fault of those charged with protecting them, who instead have played naked politics with as sensitive an issue as it's possible to imagine.

Thanks to which, there's a problem: the potential for which frightens me enormously. Just as it stands to reason that support for Israel will inevitably decline across the world unless its government drastically changes course, there's a very profound danger for Jews everywhere too. The more antisemitism is weaponised, the longer these ridiculous smears go on, the more it will sound like the Boy Who Cried Wolf. If, heaven forbid, British Jews were ever in the same kind of peril which European Jews found themselves in during the 1930s, we might find ourselves seriously lacking support and help.

That might partly be because of the actions of the Israeli government alienating and appalling so many. But it might well also be because, except in cases of actual danger, much of the public simply tires of the constant drumbeat around antisemitism. In fact, as Kriss has highlighted quite brilliantly, if the Tories get back in, there's even a mounting danger of the Jewish community being blamed:

> Are you not even a little bit worried that telling millions of voters who've never met a Jewish person in their lives that they can't have a living wage or a working NHS or any hope for their children's futures because 'it's not fair to the Jews' might create a misleading impression of the role of Jewish people in society and actually severely exacerbate antisemitism rather than getting rid of it?

Yet in that, please God, never to occur scenario, you know who'll be manning the barricades, fighting with us? Only pretty much all of those on the left who are being defamed and impugned right now. That is how disgusting this has been: the most shameless, dystopian, grotesque spectacle I've ever seen in public life. Those who conduct mass, McCarthyite pile-ons against good, caring people; who defame Holocaust survivors; and who when confronted with antisemitism or racism from anywhere other than on the left, turn a blind eye or even defend it, should hang their heads in shame.

As he was taken to his death in Riga in 1941, the great Jewish historian, Simon Dubnow, had a clear, simple message. 'Yidn, shreibt un ferschreibt' ('Jews, write and record'). That is what my grandmother did when she recorded over five hours of testimony for Steven Spielberg's Shoah Foundation Video Archive. Her experiences are on record for posterity.

Yet just as it is incumbent on all of us everywhere to ensure that the Holocaust is never forgotten; that each successive generation is taught its hideous lessons about mankind's capacity for unimaginable cruelty, so it is also beholden on us to scrutinise fairly and report objectively about current events too. When it comes to the question of antisemitism and the Labour Party, all too many have failed in that basic task.

7: APOCALYPSE INDEFINITELY DELAYED: BRITISH POLITICS, 2016-19

'Brexit means Brexit!' - Theresa May

24 June 2016. The morning after the night before, the majority of MPs found themselves in an almighty, unprecedented quandary. Essentially, they knew the British public had got it wrong. Horribly wrong. Disastrously wrong. But how could they now ignore its expressly declared democratic instructions?

More generally, Parliament was split. Into right-wing Tories desperate to take full political advantage, filling their own pockets and selling the country down the river; some on the left who believed in Brexit for perfectly principled reasons, so viewed it as a real opportunity; and a huge mass in the middle, most of whom, however reluctantly, were willing to carry out the public's orders, but were desperate to ensure as little long-term cost as possible.

After David Cameron stepped down and Theresa May replaced him, there was a very real chance to heed the lessons of the referendum and reach out across the aisle. Any serious prime minister at all interested in the common good would have done so. Instead, just as the referendum had been all about the Conservative Party, so now the whole of British politics and the country's future would be held to ransom by… the Conservative Party. All May was ever interested in was holding it together.

Worse: her very peculiar obsession with immigration (sometimes, I've been left with the hideous sense that May doesn't even view immigrants as actual human beings; her famous words on the steps of Downing Street about 'burning injustices' translated as, I'll always believe, 'too many immigrants taking your jobs') meant that the UK's negotiating position was already fatally compromised. Because controlling immigration meant no freedom of movement… which would mean leaving the single market. Despite a whole succession of Leave politicians, including even Nigel Farage and Arron Banks, having either insisted or effectively insisted there'd be no chance of it happening.

What's so extraordinary about the last three-and-a-half years is its sheer stasis was guaranteed right from the very start. Incomprehensibly, May even wedded herself to leaving the customs union too; despite the vast amount of voters probably not having a clue what a customs union even was. So she set a series of impossible to realise 'red lines'; compounding this with the utter folly of triggering Article 50, meaning the clock was already ticking on reaching a deal which her own position had rendered unobtainable.

In its official campaign literature, on page 11 here, Vote Leave had said this:

Taking back control is a careful change, not a sudden stop - we will negotiate the terms of a new deal before we start any legal process to leave.

Unlike so much else that passed for 'discussion' during the referendum campaign, this wasn't a lie. I'm quite sure Vote Leave wrote this in good faith; the idea that we wouldn't agree a comprehensive deal, with all the time that would inevitably take, *before* triggering the two-year exit clock, was unthinkable. No country could possibly be so stupid, could it? But with the right-wing press demanding we exit immediately and describing anyone of integrity or conscience as 'enemies of the people', 'traitors' or 'saboteurs', Britain, now apparently governed by the Daily Mail and Daily Express, was.

As for those 'red lines': these included a soft border in Ireland, frictionless trade *and* an end to freedom of movement. Utterly ridiculous. Because:

Frictionless trade would require us to remain in the single market… and hence, retain freedom of movement.

Maintaining a soft border in Ireland would involve either the whole UK, or Northern Ireland, remaining in the customs union.

Preventing a border in the Irish Sea, with all its massive ramifications for the Union itself, would require us to remain in the single market.

How would a mature country have gone about leaving? It wouldn't have conducted a referendum on the most important issue facing the UK since the war based on lies and emotion, but on facts and reason. And afterwards, its politicians would've *told the truth* about the reality: that we could end freedom of movement, but this would mean tariffs on trade; we could remain in the single market and maintain frictionless trade, but unless we brought in electorally unpalatable ID cards, this would mean freedom of movement continuing; we could leave the customs union, but this would mean a hard border in Ireland, a catastrophe for the peace process; and far and away the most sensible option (entirely in tune with a 52-48 outcome) would be to leave the political institutions and stay in the single market for reasons of trade and the economy; and the customs union, to protect the Good Friday Agreement.

But of course, none of these realities had been mentioned during the campaign, and they still weren't being mentioned now. Europe and 'Remoaners' (i.e. half the country!) were blamed instead by 'leaders' (sic) and 'journalists' (sic) no longer interested in reality at all.

Instead, a rather chilling cult of personality developed around May. And at the Tory Party Conference, she blundered: uttering words no British prime minister should ever say. Words which will be remembered by all those who heard them forever.

> If you believe you're a citizen of the world, you're a citizen of nowhere.

This was the racist, closed-minded, insular, angry, xenophobic beyond belief reality of Tory Brexit laid bare. This was not - has never been - what the British people stand for. And these words would come back to haunt May in a manner experienced by few other prime ministers in our history.

She called a snap general election to crush Labour for good and usher the hardest of hard Brexits through. Instead, Corbyn's extraordinary campaign, in which 13 million people united around commonly shared values of openness, tolerance and compassion, forced a hitherto unimaginable hung Parliament: which May knew would kill hard Brexit stone dead. From now on, it was a case of kicking the can down the road and hoping for a miracle.

Labour, of course, spent much of the time during the referendum campaign and a good 10 months afterwards in a state of open warfare. And a myth developed: swallowed by all and sundry, parroted by liars only interested in power and personal gain. This myth had it that Corbyn had only campaigned reluctantly for Remain; even that he'd barely campaigned at all. What was the reality? In fact, he made 123 appearances throughout the country... and the only Remainers who campaigned more (with disastrous effect) were Cameron and George Osborne.

Only weeks before she'd make a quite laughable, abortive attempt to oust Corbyn, Angela Eagle had said this:

> Jeremy [Corbyn] is up and down the country, pursuing an itinerary that would make a 25-year-old tired, he has not stopped. We are doing our best, but if we are not reported, it is very difficult.

'If we are not reported, it is very difficult'. That, you see, has always been the reality for Labour. The media chose to turn the whole thing into a Tory-on-Tory contest, and the media got its wish.

And as Britain is a place where reality no longer matters, the myth around Corbyn promptly grew arms and legs. He was a Leaver - despite voting and campaigning heavily for Remain. He was for Hard Brexit - despite having blocked it again and again in Parliament, bringing down May in the process. 'Corbyn will let the whole country go down the tubes just for a Labour government' (he did the exact opposite, by preventing Johnson forcing an election precisely in order to stop No Deal). He was for No Deal! Yes, even that disgraceful drivel was being spouted by many Remainers only this year. All of it utter, risible nonsense. Remain supporters, I'm afraid, are just as prone to believing and repeating fake news as Leavers.

All the way through, Labour's position has been as follows.

Its 2017 manifesto backed a soft, jobs first Brexit; and if you ask anyone who campaigned at that election, supporting Brexit and respecting the referendum was the only way anyone would listen to them on the doorsteps. A strategy which paid off handsomely.

Labour continued to respect the result (those arguing it shouldn't are effectively treating 17m Britons as irrelevant: the sheer, reckless arrogance of it is mindboggling), and at its 2018 Party Conference, its position was agreed, as follows:

Vote down May's deal (which it did)

Force a general election (which it couldn't, because it never had the parliamentary numbers to do so)

If forcing an election failed, to keep all options on the table. *All options*. Which naturally, included a second referendum.

As someone who follows British politics carefully, I knew this, so spelt it out on my Twitter feed here. That so little of the electorate ever did was because of deliberate, wilful misrepresentation and distortion by almost the entirety of the media; whose lies had done so much to precipitate Brexit in the first place, and whose response to the danger they had put the country in was... to treat it all as a game and keep lying. And keep lying. And keep lying some more. Playing ducks and drakes with the UK's whole future.

At this point, what we might call the 'continuity Remain' campaign seemed pretty clueless as well. Alastair Campbell, another of the many reasons why the country had grown so disgusted with its political system, went on TV to <u>talk down</u> to Leave voters. A campaign developed for a 'People's Vote' (PV): even its very title screaming of arrogance. We'd already had one of those; but presumably, the wrong people had voted then, the right people would now?

The PV campaign couldn't even explain what the question would be on the ballot paper. No Deal/May's deal/Remain would inevitably split the Leave vote and be illegitimate. With May's deal dismissed by Parliament, and Boris Johnson elected by the No Deal lunatics on the right of his party, the same would apply to a three-way ballot between No Deal, his deal and Remain; while a choice between No Deal and Remain would practically amount to the electorate playing Russian roulette.

Throughout all this, Corbyn, lampooned to high heaven by so many across the political spectrum and media, remained steadfast. In the absence of the Tories giving any ground at all, Labour ultimately confirmed what 'all options' meant by <u>committing</u> to a second referendum in summer 2019: not, again, that you'd know it given how much of the media barely reported this huge step forward at all.

Then, at party conference, it agreed the following:

If elected, it would seek a deal on its terms
It would immediately call a special conference to decide its position on that deal
It would put that deal, together with an option to Remain, to the country.

Why has it taken such an approach? There's two main reasons. First, yet again, FPTP: Labour Remainers are piled up in safe, metropolitan seats. The seats it needs to win from the Tories, however, are <u>full of Leavers</u>. Choosing either side would mean alienating far too many voters among a very broad electoral coalition of very differing interests and attitudes.

And second: because at this time of profound national crisis, ignoring half the country is a recipe for disaster. Corbyn, a cautious, reluctant Remainer (like me, as it happens) rightly believes the people should have the chance to start the long healing process… and that any fair referendum should be fought with both sides able to campaign as they wish. This isn't far off what Harold Wilson did in 1975, as he abandoned collective Cabinet responsibility: following which, there was no poison, no division.

Quite why there's been this mad demand for Corbyn to pick a side is completely beyond me. Why does the public need to be told how it must vote on an issue of such profound importance? Is it really so lacking in self-confidence in its ability to forge its own destiny?

As for Labour's chances of getting a deal... while the media cheer-led Johnson's recent monstrosity (which is not only a lot worse than May's, but sets the table for a highly likely No Deal at the end of 2020, because Britain can walk away from trade negotiations if no deal has been agreed by then; and it's impossible to do so by then) to the rafters, it has repeatedly ridiculed Corbyn's argument that he can renegotiate it.

But of course he can. A new government means a new (and crucially, good faith, friendly) approach. Not only that, but how many reading this know the following? In February, European Council president, Donald Tusk, described Corbyn's proposal as 'a promising way out of the impasse'; while instead of ruling it out, the Irish foreign minister, Simon Coveney, merely stated that 'a delay to Brexit' would be required if the UK submit an entirely new offer.

That's the head of the EU negotiating team and the foreign minister of a country directly impacted in all aspects by Brexit showing that in fact, it's not impossible at all. Very far from it. And in practice, the EU want an end to all this just as much as the UK does. If, under a Corbyn government, Britain stops demanding Narnia on thin air and blaming everyone else when it isn't forthcoming, the goodwill this will build will likely do the rest.

So that's Brexit. Never in human history was so much time spent by so many for so little outcome... but a Labour government can and will change that. Don't let the media, and campaigns of unprecedented levels of bad faith by both the Tories and Lib Dems, convince you otherwise.

And by getting Brexit sorted in a grown-up, mature, inclusive way, if elected, Labour can then move on to dealing with the UK's *real* burning injustices: housing, healthcare, education, poverty, inequality, the disgusting 'hostile environment', rebalancing the economy, and making it fit for a future dominated by climate change.

Sadly, instead of getting behind its leader, considerable portions of the Parliamentary Party have learnt nothing from 2015-17 at all. Instead, they've smeared him through an absurd, grotesque campaign of lies, as we noted in the previous chapter; contributed greatly to the nonsense narrative around him and even their own party on Brexit (proving themselves even more politically illiterate than I'd ever previously imagined); and some of them have even left altogether. It's to a number of these individuals I now turn.

◆ ◆ ◆

In February, eight Labour MPs broke away and, together with three hugely disenchanted Tories, formed 'The Independent Group', later rebranded as 'Change UK'. Naturally, the media, most of whom have understood precisely nothing about British politics for well over three years now, lapped it up. Was this the great new centrist hope for Britain?

Well, no. As anyone with half a brain (i.e. not most journalists) knew all along. But what was so revealing, so instructive, was the backgrounds of the egregious eight. To begin with, Chuka Umunna: once regarded as a future Labour leader, who was left rudderless when Corbyn ascended to the position instead. Labour's rediscovery of its true values, its soul, left Umunna flailing around in all directions. His very obvious personal ambitions could no longer be realised.

To borrow from Mhairi Black for a moment: 'Tony Benn once said that in politics, there are weathercocks and signposts. Weathercocks will spin in whatever direction the wind of public opinion may blow them, no matter what principle they have to compromise. And then there are signposts. Signposts which stand true, and tall, and principled. And they point in a direction and they say, "this is the way to a better society and it is my job to convince you why. Tony Benn was right when he said the only people worth remembering in politics [are] signposts'.

Corbyn is and has always been a signpost par excellence. By contrast, Umunna is the ultimate weathercock. In 2016, he sat on the Home Affairs Select Committee: which recommended 'clarifications' to the International Holocaust Remembrance Alliance (IHRA)'s working definition on antisemitism:

We broadly accept the IHRA definition, but propose two additional clarifications to ensure that freedom of speech is maintained in the context of discourse about Israel and Palestine, without allowing antisemitism to permeate any debate. The definition should include the following statements:

It is not antisemitic to criticise the Government of Israel, without additional evidence to suggest antisemitic intent.

It is not antisemitic to hold the Israeli Government to the same standards as other liberal democracies, or to take a particular interest in the Israeli Government's policies or actions, without additional evidence to suggest antisemitic intent.

The Committee found 'no reliable, empirical evidence to support the notion that that there is a higher prevalence of antisemitic attitudes within the Labour Party than any other political party'. Umunna sat on this

Committee… yet went on to slam the Chakrabarti Report's findings on antisemitism in Labour regardless; fulminate against the Labour Party's code of conduct on antisemitism (which provided the very clarifications his Committee had called for); and refer to Labour as 'institutionally racist'. Evidence-based, Umunna is most certainly not.

In December 2016, he urged Remain campaigners to abandon calls for a second referendum or risk being seen as a metropolitan elite 'who think they know best'. Three months earlier, he had also said, 'if continuation of the free movement we have is the price of single market membership then clearly we couldn't remain in the single market'.

On the basis that, whenever Umunna says something on an important issue, you can rest assured he'll say the opposite a couple of years later, he went on to become a leading campaigner first for a second referendum; then, through the Liberal Democrats, to revoke Article 50 altogether. These are his principles. But don't worry. If you don't like them, he has others.

Then, there was Chris Leslie. A man so unknown to the British people, he probably isn't even a household name in his own household, in 2005, he somehow managed to lose his seat to Philip Davies, one of the most reactionary men in Britain.

Leslie returned to Parliament: moving his way up the Shadow Treasury bench at a time Labour were pro-austerity. He briefly became Shadow Chancellor while the leadership was vacant; but immediately resigned from the Shadow Cabinet when Corbyn won a landslide victory. Party democracy is just for the little people, you see.

In June 2018, Leslie published a pamphlet for the centre-right Social Market Foundation, entitled 'Centre Ground: Six Values of Mainstream Britain'. That this pamphlet amounted to a manifesto for a centre party told its own story. In September, he lost a vote of no confidence tabled by his local party. Once more putting his true democratic values on show, this man - who was pleading for a second referendum, displaying zero respect whatever for the result of the first - didn't turn up for the vote.

Another of those breaking away was Angela Smith. In 2007, she voted unsuccessfully to keep her expense details secret. She'd been claiming for four beds in a one bedroom flat in London. For her senior parliamentary researcher, Smith employs… her husband. In 2016, the couple were repeatedly taken to football and dinner by Whitehouse Construction, a sub-contractor to Anglian Water and member of the 'Future Water Association':

an industry group led by private water firms, which also fund the All-Party Water Group.

Let the record show that, obviously by some unfathomable coincidence, Smith opposes Labour's plans to renationalise the water industry. She's cited a Social Market Foundation (they get everywhere, don't they?) report - commissioned by the water industry - in support of her argument. In fact, she believes that renationalisation 'could make us the sick man of Europe again'. British consumers, beset with ever-increasing bills and no choice, while shareholders carve off massive profits, must be thrilled at such comments.

On the very day of the Independent Group's launch, Smith went on the BBC... where she referred to the BAME community as 'funny tinged'. And this *after* leaving the Labour Party because of supposed racism! As I've said, truth in British politics is far stranger than fiction. Though as the Lord moves in mysterious ways, it more than amused me to read her recent, bitter complaints of 'discrimination' about losing a £ 22,000 parliamentary pay-out as a result of quitting her seat and standing elsewhere.

And Mike Gapes: who voted for the Iraq war, for which he never apologised; consistently voted against any inquiry into what had happened; and was incandescent over Corbyn having talked to Hamas when, in 2007, Gapes called for Tony Blair to... talk to Hamas.

In 2001 and 2005, Muslim groups, including the Muslim Public Affairs Committee (UK), accused Gapes of being 'anti-Muslim'. His response was to loudly and publicly support the hideous regime in Saudi Arabia and go on trips paid for by it; and even when, following Jamal Khashoggi's appalling murder, he finally spoke out against the Saudi government, his statement... mysteriously vanished from his website.

At this very election campaign, displaying the exact sort of integrity he's modelled to the country throughout his time as an MP, Gapes has tried to deliberately mislead his constituents into believing that he's still the Labour representative. Extraordinary. It's not illegal; but it certainly should be.

Among the more non-descript members of the new group were Ann Coffey and Gavin Shuker. The former has publicly advocated for scrapping trial by jury in cases of rape; and her expenses included claiming £1000 per month for mortgage interest; £160 per month for a cleaner. The latter opposed same sex marriage and even signed a letter to the Advertising Standards Authority, asking it to reverse its decision to stop the Christian group, 'Healing on the Streets of Bath' from claiming that prayer can heal.

At length, we come to Joan Ryan. Whose record of quite staggering awfulness is almost unparalleled. In May 2007, she too voted for her expense details to be kept secret. Hardly surprising given that in 2005/6, she ran up the second highest bill of any MP in London; and topped the charts the following year, claiming for the sum of £173,691. In fact, she'd spent £4,500 of this on her 'second home' - in her constituency - before 'flipping' it with her main home in south London. Thomas Legg's report of audited expenses claims, published in February 2010, found she owed some £5121.74 in mortgage interest.

Not only did Ryan see no need to apologise to her constituents; but at least 10 attempts from the parliamentary estate, and a further 20 from Enfield North, were made to remove any mention of her expenses from her Wikipedia page. Ryan dismissed the media's coverage of this as 'a politically motivated smear campaign'. But then, you'd know all about that, wouldn't you Joan?

As chair of Labour Friends of Israel, Ryan was filmed being told by Shai Masot, the soon-to-be disgraced Israeli Embassy official, that he had £1m to fund trips to Israel; and having a prolonged discussion about the Israeli/Palestinian conflict with Labour Party member, Jean Fitzpatrick. The latter asked her about how a two-state solution could realistically come about, and what Ryan's ideas were regarding this. To which, Ryan went on to make an absurd, outrageous formal complaint of 'antisemitism' about Fitzpatrick, which was rightly dismissed. If you ever wanted to know what these sorts of complaints (which the media constantly report as proof of guilt) are often founded upon, all you need to do is watch this video here.

In her letter to her constituents ahead of the 2017 general election, Ryan considered that they much preferred May to Corbyn as prime minister, and actually predicted May would increase her majority. Not surprisingly, before departing the party, she also lost a vote of no confidence among her constituency association; and blamed her defeat on 'Trots, Stalinists and Communists'. She declared: 'I am Labour through and through and I will continue to fight and stand up for Labour values'. But as I hope I've demonstrated with all this: she's not, she never has, and she never will either.

Disgraceful as Ryan's record is, though, she doesn't even hold a candle to one Ian Austin. A man so universally loathed across the House of Commons that he didn't even join Change UK; but remained an independent instead. And there are good reasons for his unparalleled unpopularity.

In 2009, Austin was reported to have attempted to split a claim for stamp duty on buying his second home in London into two payments, before claiming the cost back over two financial years. This allowed him to reclaim the majority of the money, along with his legal fees. He went on to 'flip' his second home designation weeks before buying a £270,000 London flat, for which he claimed £2,800 for furnishing it; while also claiming taxpayers' money to fund beds, stereos, sofas, duvets and even vacuum cleaners for his constituency home.

In 2012, he was forced to apologise after claiming, entirely falsely, that the Palestinian human rights group, Friends of al-Asqa, were 'Holocaust deniers'. In October 2014, and again in December 2016, he called for greater action to limit immigration: including tighter border controls, fingerprinting immigrants, charging foreigners for using the NHS, putting immigrants at the bottom of the housing ladder and measures even to discourage their employment.

Austin joined many of his colleagues in abstaining over the disastrous 2015 Welfare Reform Bill; and voted against an inquiry into the Iraq war on no fewer than nine separate occasions. After the Chilcott Report, which he'd opposed so often, was finally published, Austin yelled 'shut up and sit down' and 'you're a disgrace' at his own leader as Corbyn castigated the UK's role in that illegal war.

In 2017, Corbyn tabled a motion to suspend UK arms sales to Saudi Arabia, which was using them to slaughter thousands of innocents in Yemen. Austin, again along with many of his 'moderate' colleagues, abstained. In 2018, he was seen shouting in Ian Lavery MP's face that he was a 'wanker' and 'total bastard'. In January of this year, he even voted against Yvette Cooper's amendment designed to protect Britain from a No Deal Brexit. And in August, he took to Twitter to exclaim 'what planet are these loonies on?' in reference to the entirely accurate description of austerity as 'social murder': suggesting, to be frank, he clearly doesn't bother with meeting any of his constituents. Certainly not the poor and vulnerable ones, at least.

Yet despite all this - the record of a racist on the make, on the take, with principles which would make Al Capone blanch - when Austin popped up early in this election campaign to decry Labour 'antisemitism' and Corbyn as 'unfit to lead', he was all over the airwaves all day long. Nobody bothered questioning his record, or his non-existent objectivity; what he said was simply swallowed whole by a mass media desperate to parrot it for all it was worth. Laura Kuenssberg of the BBC, more of whom later, thought it was 'quite something'.

But what's really quite something is this. What on Earth have people of this little integrity, this much greed, and who are this right-wing been doing as Labour MPs for so long? These are the people Corbyn's had to deal with; these are the individuals who've left the public assuming the party was hopelessly split because of supposedly weak leadership. The wonder is that Corbyn himself didn't kick them out before they left; and that he didn't is, again, a sign of his humanity and extraordinary grace under fire from agents of the most colossal, disgusting bad faith.

Here's a glimpse of Austin in action. Shouting and hectoring at Michael Rosen for the crime of Rosen knowing his British and Jewish history, and Austin not having the first clue. A shabbier, more revolting individual, it's awfully hard to conceive of. In British politics, at least.

I write all this, incidentally, not to be nasty or even unpleasant. I'm doing so to highlight just how appalling the so-called 'moderate' alternative to Corbynism truly is. Unprincipled and vacillating; grotesque expense claims; nepotism, bought and paid for by the water industry, racism on national TV; voting for an illegal, catastrophic war and against any inquiry, while going on paid-for trips to Saudi Arabia; abuse of colleagues, abuse of his own leader, support for No Deal Brexit, support for the racist Conservatives, support for benefit cuts, support for the hostile environment. Between them, this shower truly have it covered. And the media refers to them as 'moderates'?!

Owen Jones[5], who correctly describes the UK political media as a 'cult' - cossetted, insulated, drawn mostly from the same privileged backgrounds and universities, trapped in a self-aggrandising world of bubble-think in which lifelong columnists become totally detached from reality and no longer even encounter anyone poor or vulnerable - knew that said media would love Change UK. If journalists ever formed a political party, that's exactly what it would look like. No substance, no detail, no clue; just 'we're centrist, so we're nice!' Very quickly, and entirely predictably, it collapsed... but not before the pollsters had tried doing their bit too.

◆ ◆ ◆

Go back to that Hitchens quote from Chapter 3. 'Opinion polls are a device for influencing public opinion, not a device for measuring it'. So it was that according to ComRes, Change UK hit 6%; the media splashed with this as though it posed some huge threat to Labour; and no-one bothered to ask the blindingly obvious question. Change UK only had 11 MPs (in fact, only 11 members, period). How could it possibly be on 6% if it was only standing in 11 constituencies? Were the 6% of the entire country somehow all living in those constituencies? 'Oh yes, I'd definitely vote for them; I'd do it by magic, even though they don't have an MP in my constituency or 633 others'.

That is the kind of utter nonsense which drives polls in the UK now. Nonsense which includes James Endersby, the CEO of Opinium, writing supposedly objective articles in The Guardian right before those Labour MPs broke away. Endersby, incidentally, is also on the advisory board of 'Progressive Centre UK'. If that name draws blank looks, fair enough; it's just that it's the think tank of none other than Umunna. For which he, the great 'progressive' hero, is paid £452 an hour.

Nonsense which involves Survation actually getting it right on the eve of the 2015 election; then not publishing their findings, because they were so out of kilter with all the other companies. Nonsense which sees Damian Lyons Lowe, the owner of Survation, selling private, secret data to Nigel Farage on referendum night: enabling the latter to short the markets. And as this article explains in detail, he wasn't the only one from the industry up to all sorts of murky business; very far from it. The number of individuals mentioned is astonishing. The Financial Conduct Authority is investigating the secret relationships between pollsters and hedge funds.

Nonsense which entails YouGov, the dominant polling firm in the UK, being set up by Stephan Shakespeare and Nadhim Zahawi, both Tories. The latter would go on to become an MP: and claim close to £6,000 for *heating his riding school stables*. He was most recently seen suggesting that a Corbyn government would, quite literally, shoot rich people.

In early January, YouGov released a poll whose headline figures suggested Labour would be doomed if it backed Brexit. James Morris, Ed Miliband's private pollster and former adviser, and no lover of Corbyn nor Brexit, quickly called it out as the nonsense it clearly was:

It's a priming problem. Brexit Brexit Brexit. Brexit. Now, who are you voting for? Obviously makes respondents think more about Brexit when answering. Real voting intention is affected by so much more that this method tries to get people to artificially ignore.

Almost comically, Shakespeare even admitted it was all about priming. Yet this didn't stop the newspapers and broadcasters churning out headlines based on a quite laughable poll: which in practice, measured nothing. And if you want to know how dominant YouGov truly are, Deltapoll, who published constituency polls last weekend which were extraordinarily favourable for the Liberal Democrats, but failed to disclose who funded them, have three directors. One of them is Joe Twyman: who after leaving YouGov, helped set them up. He's also mentioned in the articles about hedge funds I referred to above. Curiouser and curiouser.

When I talk about priming, what do I mean? Watch this timeless sketch from *Yes Minister*. It's funny because it's true; *this* is what so many polling companies do. More latterly, the industry has been financialised; it's about making a profit. So they ask questions designed to obtain a particular outcome.

Yet despite having been completely wrong in 2015, completely wrong in 2016 (in both the UK and US) and completely wrong in 2017, unbelievably, opinion polls are still allowed to drive political debate in Britain now. So many people take their cues from them; very few look any deeper. Instead of hearing about policies - what the parties are offering to make our lives better, or at least bearable - or the latest appalling scandal involving the Tories, it's polls this, polls that. In any other world, this would be called out for what it is. Corrupt.

Here's a video by the brilliant Mona Chalabi. She explains the whole problem far better than I can. And in the spirit of broken clocks showing the correct time twice a day, even when the pollsters get it right, it's because of this:

> By reporting on polling predictions, we help to make them come true. Each time we say who's ahead, the media sends a signal to the public that their vote won't be wasted if they just stick with the frontrunner. That boosts them even further in the polls. And if a [party] is falling behind, that seems to give the media a free pass to ignore them and their policies, so voters never hear about them. Sometimes polls are nothing more than a self-fulfilling prophecy. That's bad for democracy.

Now do you see what Hitchens was getting at? Yet the truth is: we have no idea how people will vote on any particular day. All sorts of things motivate voters; things which maybe haven't even happened yet, so cannot be predicted. Nowadays, opinion polls are about as reliable and altruistic as scamming soothsayers; any country which hadn't lost the plot would've long since stopped taking them seriously.

So at this election, as you see the media - whose relationship with polling companies is one of mutual, almost incestuous levels of dependence -

headlining yet again with big Tory leads, please remember. Opinion polls don't actually matter; and in an industry which attracts the likes of Zahawi, Ashcroft, or hedge funds, should never be trusted. The only thing which does is your vote on 12 December.

◆ ◆ ◆

There has, though, been one other particularly disturbing development in British politics in recent years; something which has helped the Tories destroy the country more than very little else. The ongoing, ever-accelerating corruption of the BBC. Once a beloved national institution on which so many could depend; but now, it's barely even trying to hide the reality that it's become a fully-fledged Tory propaganda unit.

During the referendum campaign, the BBC - obsessed not with policy, but personality, gossip, tittle-tattle, and myriad other examples of mindless drivel - failed quite miserably to carry out its publicly funded responsibility of educating the British people on the complexity of the decision they were about to take. And during the 2014 Scottish referendum, the BBC's bias towards a 'No' vote was so egregious, 'Yes' campaigners ended up protesting about it, with very good reason. When 'No' won, Nick Robinson, then BBC News' Political Editor, and a former President of Oxford University's Conservative Association, could barely get the smirk off his face all night long.

In 2018, Marcus Moore, who used to write for the BBC, posted this on Facebook.

A number of changes made during the last seven years or so, spearheaded by David Cameron, have led to the corporation's news and politics departments becoming little more than ventriloquists' dummies. Of particular note are the following:

Important posts at the BBC being filled by pro-government figures from the private sector (Rona Fairhead, David Clementi, James Harding, Robbie Gibb etc).

Direct links with the manipulative tabloid press being strengthened by Downing Street giving important positions to dubious characters like Andy Coulson and Craig Oliver.

The subsequent recruitment of people like Alison Fuller Pedley (of Mentorn Media), who is responsible for choosing who gets to be in the Question Time audience, and Sarah Sands (formerly of The Telegraph, Mail and Evening Standard) who now edits Radio 4's Today programme.

All of the above follows Cameron's appointment, in June 2010, of John Browne (Baron Browne of Madingley) to the post of 'Lead Non-Executive Director' for Downing Street, his role being that of 'recruiting business leaders to reformed departmental boards' - Browne's questionable history at BP notwithstanding.

How all of this quiet, underhand activity has been largely unreported, but has given the current Conservative government immense power within fashionable and influential circles.

This means they can not only dictate which information is made available to the public, but also the manner in which it is presented. You don't need to read many pages of that book by George Orwell to grasp how easy it is to control the populace once you have control of the means of communication.

Moreover, in 2016, a Cardiff University study found that the BBC has a 'high dependency' on the Conservative Party for statistics: almost three-quarters of those it receives (and rather importantly, presents to the public) from political sources. The study highlighted '"many instances" where quotes and statistics given to the broadcaster from the Conservative government were simply reported with a complete failure to fact-check and scrutinise the information or even question and challenge it on "any fundamental level". The Conservatives are effectively handing the BBC a script to read from'.

As Moore notes:

Many BBC journalists have Conservative party connections and most of its panellists are from the neoliberal centre right. They not only fail to comprehend and appreciate Jeremy Corbyn's anti-neoliberalism and promise of policies that provide long overdue priority and support for ordinary citizens, they seem to loathe and fear it.

The BBC's political output has long had more than its fair share of Conservatives in prominent roles - none more so than Andrew Neil, who previously worked for the Conservative's Research Department and who now chairs the holding company that owns the Daily Telegraph and the Spectator. It is unusual for any broadcaster, whether left or right wing, to dominate political coverage as much as Neil does on the BBC, who fronts the weekday Daily Politics show and presents his own programmes on Sunday mornings and Thursday evenings.

There's more, much more, on Moore's (pun not intended) website here. It makes for a profoundly disturbing read.

In practice, what has all this led to? We've already noted the BBC's appallingly biased, distorted coverage of the 2017 election, and its extraordinary decision to ignore its own Trust's condemnation of a disgraceful piece by Kuenssberg. On Twitter, she has often borne the brunt of much of the left's righteous fury over what's been going on: naturally so, as you'll see.

Here's a selection of her views, mostly drawn from the tweets of the most influential individual in British political broadcasting. In December 2018, she chimed in with Andrea Leadsom's criticisms of John Bercow: 'Leadsom articulating what lots of Cabinet ministers say in private and what they discussed at their meeting last week - questioning whether Bercow is impartial on all of this and whether his views on Brexit are part of making life difficult for the PM'.

This was the verdict of the BBC's Political Editor on the Speaker, thank heavens, being one of the precious few people remaining in Westminster doing his job with the utmost integrity. She preferred to repeat Tory gossip instead, and insinuate that not May, but the Speaker, was the problem.

In March, she considered that as Corbyn and May were 'shouting stats at each other, it seems appropriate to have a jammy dodger'. This was her perspective when people die in Britain every single day because of Tory austerity and savage cuts. Also in March, when Bercow correctly refused to allow a third meaningful vote unless it contained significant changes, Kuenssberg seemed not even to understand the slightest thing about parliamentary convention, let alone have read Erskine May.

Her response to Austin and Gapes being removed from the Foreign Affairs Committee because those positions are allocated to Labour MPs was the anything but impartial, 'if you are one of the people who was hoping The Independent Group might start to change the culture around here, you'll be depressed by this'. No facts, no explanation; just 'blame Labour'.

And when May made her latest pig's breakfast of Brexit, it was 'blame the EU' too. 'Another classic EU fudge?', inquired Kuenssberg, clearly trapped in some parallel universe right when the UK had Brussels granting its extension request to thank for not having already toppled over the cliff.

In September, we had a new low altogether. Confronting the new prime minister about the perilous state of the NHS, Omar Salem gave it to Johnson with both barrels. His seven-day-old daughter was seriously ill at the time. Kuenssberg's take on this wasn't even to mention the many appalling things which Salem had revealed... but to tweet 'turns out the man who challenged the PM is also a Labour activist'. Which triggered an absolutely disgusting pile-on and absurd conspiracy theories trumpeted by the right-wing press about a panicking father whose little daughter was gravely unwell. Britain, 2019.

Yet there was no censure for Kuenssberg for her conduct. None whatsoever. And in this campaign, it's somehow got even worse. When the Tories rebranded as a fake fact-checking account in order to pour out lies galore about Corbyn during his televised debate with Johnson, even Kuenssberg's BBC colleague, Emily Maitlis, had had enough. But not the former. Incomprehensibly, she described the coverage of the ruling party's attempts to wilfully mislead the public and commit electoral fraud as... a 'really daft row to pick'. That is how little she cares about facts, the truth, or journalism as we once knew it at all.

Elsewhere, we've had Maitlis being praised to high heaven across the media for the gross unprofessionalism of *rolling her eyes* at Barry Gardiner's truthful, entirely reasonable response on Labour's Brexit policy (only days following which, in positively Kafka-esque fashion, she was promoted); and serenading Anna Soubry with 'she's the opposition! That's the voice of opposition, isn't it?', while somehow failing to notice that Soubry wasn't even prepared to vote against the government in a vote of no confidence. We've had John Humphrys proudly displaying all the awareness on Brexit of a gnat, before confirming what we all already knew about him by, quite laughably, attacking the corporation for 'liberal bias' following his absurdly overdue retirement.

And we've had *Question Time* (QT) too. So long the BBC's flagship political programme: which I became an avid fan of even back when Sir Robin Day was presenting it. But in recent years, it hasn't merely declined; it's become a full-on right-wing propaganda vehicle. In his analysis, Moore highlighted the role of Mentorn Media; and in particular, Alison Fuller-Pedley. In 2016, she shared no fewer than five Facebook posts by the far-right group, Britain First, and 'liked' a page called 'British Patriotic Front'. Both pages contain extreme racist and white nationalist content.

Incomprehensibly, when this emerged, Fuller-Pedley wasn't fired. She was merely 'reminded' of the corporation's guidelines regarding social media use. Yet her job gives her the responsibility of choosing the QT audience; points which are intimately related to one another. Fairly often nowadays, QT doesn't feature a 'representative cross-section of the British public' at all. It features Tory plants.

In the edition on 21 November, the first *eight* speakers were all hostile to Labour. Next day, at the party leader's special, Corbyn was repeatedly harangued by someone in the audience making his fourth appearance; who just so happens to be a Tory activist. This followed a disgraceful episode in March: which featured fully five Conservative Party activists, all disguised as 'ordinary members of the public'. And it's precisely because the show is openly biased to the Tories, and has an audience selected by a far right sympathiser, that in January, Fiona Bruce sunk to the unthinkable low of actually whipping the audience up before the programme by making jokes about Diane Abbott's 'personal relationship' with Corbyn.

Abbott and Corbyn are former lovers. The inference here was that she'd only got onto the Shadow Cabinet because of this. Not only was this disgusting and outrageous - a wanton abuse of Bruce's position - but it was aimed towards someone who has received more abuse, both racist and sexist, than anyone else in British politics: by an absolute country mile.

Compounding this, during the programme itself, we had the perfect storm: of fake news spread by the BBC about polls, which the audience lapped up. On air, Isabel Oakeshott made the completely false statements (based on one poll by, you guessed it, YouGov), that Labour was 'way behind in the polls' and 'miles behind the Tories'. At the time, it was actually ahead in almost all of them. The audience, fed on a diet of BBC propaganda for years, clapped and cheered Oakeshott's comment. When Abbott responded by actually understating Labour's position - 'in the polls overall, we're level pegging' - Bruce interjected with the flat out lie, 'No, you're behind, Diane'. The audience hooted. The truth? Nowhere to be found.

In that edition, Abbott was interrupted more than twice the amount of times experienced by the Tory panellist, Rory Stewart. Even he looked embarrassed by what was going on. Watch this video here for a comprehensive analysis of the whole thing.

As chair, Bruce's job isn't just to encourage debate and discussion. Especially given all the country's been through thanks to the proliferation of fake news, it's also to fact check nonsense. Yet when someone in the audience made the hilarious claim that despite earning over £80,000 a year, he isn't even in the top 50% of earners in the UK (!), Bruce said nothing. That sum puts that individual firmly in the top 5% of earners; 43% of British people don't even earn enough (£12,500) to pay income tax at all.

And when an audience member rightly stated that Vote Leave is under police investigation, quite unbelievably, Bruce tried to suggest otherwise. In this, she either demonstrated such a profound lack of knowledge that it should instantly disqualify her from hosting such a programme; or she was trying to mislead the public. One or the other.

But QT doesn't just amplify fake news. It panders to the far right too. Nigel Farage has stood for election to the UK Parliament on seven separate occasions: failing each and every time. Despite this, he has appeared on the show a record thirty-three times. The very thing which turned this man - a failure at every parliamentary contest he's ever faced, denounced as a racist by the founder of the very party he stood for until very recently, who was behind the sickeningly racist poster during the EU referendum, and is an anti-Semite par excellence as well - into a figure of huge public prominence was QT itself.

Every now and then, we do get a balanced audience. The BBC can't afford to make what it's doing glaringly obvious to the public; even now, it's really only been called out by those who, like me, spend a lot of time monitoring British politics. But propaganda has always worked in more nuanced ways as well. Here's a good example: from a *Today* programme report by James Landale, yet another BBC journalist with a right-wing background; so much so that in 2015, May offered him the job of Downing Street Director of Communications, which he rejected.

The report was ostensibly about British foreign policy, and the divide between the two main parties on it. Which was put down almost entirely to... Jeremy Corbyn. Whose opposition to nuclear weapons and the use of force in most circumstances; views on NATO; and hostility towards many American governments was contrasted with the completely false statement of 'sympathy elsewhere' for Hamas and Hezbollah,

In practice, continued Landale, a Labour government would recognise the state of Palestine, allow the Chagos Islanders to return home, ban arms sales to Saudi Arabia, and conduct a wider review of UK weapons exports. All fine things if you ask me (and quite likely, a large proportion of the public); so how did Landale spin it? Naturally, by speaking to Tom Tugendhat, the most recent chair of the Commons Foreign Affairs Select Committee. That he's also a Tory MP went strangely undisclosed. This is what the very self-interested Tugendhat had to say:

I fail to understand what he wants other than the 1970s anti-imperialist, anti-US rally cry of the Vietnam War... that's irresponsible not just for any prime minister, but for anybody seeking high office in the United Kingdom.

But of course you fail to understand, Tom. You're a Tory. Instead, quite deliberately, Landale presented him as though he was some impartial foreign policy expert. This is not 'balanced reporting', least of all during an election campaign when purdah laws are supposed to apply. It's biased reporting, however subtle.

At the time of publishing this book, the report is still available on the BBC iplayer. It begins at 45:57 here. And remember: it was broadcast at a time when the UK's reputation around the world has never been more diminished; when it has continually alienated EU partners and allies through the behaviour not of Labour, but of the Tory government. The chances of Landale singling it out for similar treatment? Null and void.

This sort of thing happens on *Today* every morning. Most people won't notice and just instinctively accept what they're hearing. Which, of course, is precisely how the whole thing works. Control the means of communication; control the populace.

Over the last couple of years, this has taken on deeply sinister undertones. The magnificent barrister, Jo Maugham QC, a national hero for everything he's done to help prevent not only No Deal Brexit, but Johnson's attempts to circumvent parliamentary scrutiny altogether, is nobody's idea of a conspiracy theorist, and no fan of Corbyn in any way. In fact, he's been a persistent, often implacably hostile critic. In March of last year, he revealed what he'd been told by a senior figure at the BBC: namely, that it 'codes' negative messages about Corbyn into its imagery.

Remember that disgraceful image from the 2017 campaign, in which the BBC summarised Corbyn's views alongside a picture of Osama bin Laden? This is the sort of thing Maugham was referring to. Over the last year or so, you've probably seen footage of Corbyn apparently looking tired, stressed, even ill; which is likely a result of lighting. Deliberate work by cameramen to make him look unwell when he isn't.

During this election campaign, with purdah laws applying to all broadcasters, the BBC 'mistakenly' used three-year-old footage of Johnson laying a wreath at the Cenotaph. The reason this caused such controversy was because this year, at the ceremony the BBC was supposedly reporting on, he was so careless that he laid his wreath *the wrong way up*. Then after the QT debate between the four leaders, where Johnson was laughed at by the audience, BBC News *edited out* the laughter; and has since claimed this was another 'mistake'. How curious, then, that these continual 'mistakes' always favour the Tories; and never, ever favour Labour.

You'd also think, wouldn't you, that the BBC would encourage as many people as possible to register to vote. What could be better for democracy and more in line with its Royal Charter than that? Instead, a succession of radio discussions have run with the idea of voter apathy; that 'no-one's interested'. This publicly funded broadcaster appears to be trying to talk voter turnout down. Its website featured no information or links about registering.

Then there's the vexed question of newspaper reviews: in which panellists discuss the latest editions. Except, of course, that the UK print media is dominated by right-wing papers owned by offshore oligarchs: so all the reviews do is repeat their talking points, so often based on lies and nonsense.

In recent days, things have somehow got even worse than ever. First,

Corbyn agreed to an interview with Andrew Neil because the BBC told Labour that Johnson had consented too. Except he hadn't. The Leader of the Opposition, Labour sources are saying at least, was lied to and interviewed under false pretences by a supposedly 'impartial' broadcaster. Then, with less than 0.1% of Labour members having been guilty of antisemitism, he was relentlessly harangued about racism by someone whose media group's titles include the perennially racist Spectator. Racism which Neil personally profits from. We are completely through the looking glass here.

And second: in perhaps the most farcical moment of the entire decade, and the final nail in the coffin for anyone who thinks this has all been some accident, on the very day that Labour revealed documents which prove that the NHS will be up for sale in any trade negotiations with the US, this is what the BBC ran with.

I can imagine you laughing at that link. But much as I'd like to as well, I can't. It isn't funny. It's disgusting. Johnson wants to sell the NHS to private American companies. That's the only way a 'free trade deal' - in which we, with a population of 66.5m, give everything; and they, with a population of 327m, take everything - with the US is done.

And his plans - for a No Deal Brexit at the end of 2020, as he inevitably walks away from trade talks with the EU which would otherwise drag on for very many years, to his and his party's political cost - are precisely why the Tory right are so enthusiastic about his 'deal'. Quite deliberately, it's a road to nowhere; quite deliberately, the section from May's deal which protected against any possibility of the UK walking away after a year of negotiations was removed. In other words: if you think Britain right now is in a bad way, if the Tories get back in, you ain't seen nothing yet.

No Deal would be a catastrophe the like of which Britain hasn't experienced since 1940, which would devastate the country for generations to come. As for selling the NHS to the US: goodbye free healthcare, hello American-style premiums, co-payments and bankruptcy for anyone who becomes seriously ill.

The bottom line where the BBC are concerned is this. The way this organisation - whose News and Politics division have some very serious explaining to do - has behaved for a number of years now literally destroys lives. Many of them. 34 million Americans know someone who died because of being unable to afford healthcare. If the Tories win, that is the UK's future too.

Happily, some people have begun waking up to just what's going on here. In an extensive report published in October, Peter Oborne revealed how, under Johnson (and crucially, his senior advisor, Cummings), journalists across the right-wing press, and the BBC too, have simply parroted Tory smear campaigns against Remain-supporting MPs. Even when these campaigns were based entirely on fake news. He also noted how Guido Fawkes' website, home to some of the worst racists and cranks anywhere on the internet, had - just like Breitbart did for Donald Trump - become the 'provisional wing of Boris Johnson's Conservative Party press office'.

Quite correctly, Oborne concluded the following:

> The British media are not just failing to hold him to account. They are not even trying. They are behaving as cheerleaders to the government. They are allowing the prime minister to get away with lies and dishonesty.

Given that, what does it tell you that this brilliant campaigning journalist, who has held truth to power for decades on all sorts of issues, found it incredibly difficult to get his report into print? What does it also tell you that when invited onto *Channel 4 News* to discuss his findings, Krishnan Guru-Murthy (generally the best news anchor in Britain, to give him his due) tried to stop Oborne naming names?

In a subsequent piece for The Guardian, which highlighted Johnson's never-ending lies, and the immense damage being done to democracy by indulging them, Oborne provided a quite staggering revelation:

> I have talked to senior BBC executives, and they tell me they personally think it's wrong to expose lies told by a British prime minister because it undermines trust in British politics.

And there we have it. Right there, in black and white. The BBC openly admitting that it makes the deliberate choice not to hold Johnson to account: at the very time he's being investigated by the Independent Office of Police Conduct for the criminal offence of misconduct in public office; has refused to publish the report on Russian interference into British politics (which includes the EU referendum) while massive donations from Russians keep rolling into the Tory coffers; and when, even during this campaign itself, Tory fake news has been ratcheted up to such gargantuan levels that it makes the lie about £350m for the NHS look like a tea party (if you search for Labour's manifesto on Google, that link appears much higher than the real thing. Terrifying).

♦ ♦ ♦

As for Johnson: what does it tell you about not only Britain, but neoliberalism itself, that a complete fraud born into immense privilege; who has never known a moment's adversity in his life; lies practically every time he opens his mouth; tried to have a journalist beaten up; whose disgraceful, false public statements are a considerable part of why Nazanin Zaghari-Ratcliffe is still locked up in an Iranian jail cell; who turned from Remain to Leave purely and solely to further his own career, throughout which, he has treated women like dirt; said that 'seeing a bunch of black kids out and about set off alarm bells in his head'; said it was 'feeble' for a man to not 'take control his woman'; described working class men as 'likely to be drunk, criminal, aimless, feckless and hopeless'; branded the children of single mothers 'ill-raised, ignorant, aggressive and illegitimate'; said 'fuck the families' of the 7 July 2005 London terrorist attack victims; tried to break the law and misled the Queen in order to force Brexit through; whose own sister thinks his support for No Deal is because of hedge funds backing him; and who thinks Churchill fought Nazism not for moral, just, humane reasons, but purely to further his own career as well, is now prime minister?

Boris Johnson is what happens when the cult of the individual is allowed to dominate and crush everything in its path not merely for the last decade, but the last four decades. The cult of greed, selfishness, entitlement; the cult of not giving a damn and being admired, celebrated, for not giving a damn. A cult he grew up in, was indulged in, and benefited from. Read this brilliant expose by Simon Kuper into his time at Oxford for a look at the only world Johnson has ever known. It'll horrify you.

This cult has become so pervasive that pretty much the entirety of Britain's governing party, the Liberal Democrat leader too, and enormous chunks of the media believe that politics is just a game. They, like Johnson, don't give a damn either. Why would they? The world's rewarded them for not doing so. A world which rewards the ultimate bullshitter, the ultimate conman, with the highest office in the land on *both* sides of the Atlantic is one which has lost any semblance of reason, dignity or basic decency.

In June, during the Tory leadership election, the police were called to a loud altercation at the home of Johnson and his partner, Carrie Symonds. His neighbour had heard screaming, shouting and banging. At one point, Symonds could be heard telling Johnson to 'get off me' and 'get out of my flat'. Naturally concerned, the neighbour went to the flat, knocked on the door three times, but received no response. He called 999; wouldn't you do so in similar circumstances? Two police cars and a van arrived within minutes.

This was a concerned citizen trying to protect someone amid a potential incident of domestic violence. Yet the following day, the police initially denied any record of any incident at the address; and only came clean when given the case number, reference number and identification numbers of the vehicles called out by The Guardian. Meanwhile, quite unbelievably, the right-wing press was concerned not with potential domestic violence perpetrated by the soon-to-be prime minister... but identifying the neighbour.

Alison Pearson of The Telegraph went onto the BBC's airwaves to demand this - so we could discover the politics and Brexit stance of the man in question. The Times got in on the act too. Ben Wallace, the security minister no less, attacked the 'lefty neighbours' for alerting the police. And when public figures make comments like this, what happens in Britain in 2019? These poor individuals are forced into hiding... for the crime of being good, neighbourly citizens.

That is the kind of country which the Tories and their media lackeys have created. In which black is white; wrong is right. In which the PM is a possible criminal; while his opponent, whose decency runs through his very core, is treated like one, and both he and his supporters are hounded by a baying media mob. Remember what happened to Omar Salem too? Do you want to live in a country like this?

During the election campaign, Johnson has taken to visiting hospitals to show how much he cares about the NHS. Below is a full, detailed account of what that involves.

I am an NHS doctor and Boris Johnson visited my hospital recently.

We were only told on the day for security reasons. They painted the ward I work on. We were asked to hide dirty laundry. Cleaners were sent out into the car park, on a rainy, cold day, picking leaves off the ground. We were told he was going to use our acute area as a 'meet and greet'.

Then we were asked if we wanted to meet him. Every doctor in the hospital said no. They could not find a single consultant who was willing to meet him. The consultant who was on the rota for the day was not there and the rumour on the ground was that he had said he would not let Johnson onto the ward. Instead, the on-call consultant was replaced with another consultant, one high up in management. He was also trying to do a ward round and see newly admitted, acutely unwell patients. There were more management and executives than I'd ever seen. There were young men in expensive suits, looking around themselves at us like tourists on safari.

In the end, a handful of people agreed to meet him. One allied healthcare professional was so angry at his presence, she could not stop shaking, but wanted to let him know how unhappy she was. There was also a nurse who didn't follow politics and didn't really understand what the fuss was about. There was one healthcare assistant who was very excited he was there because she had seen his dad on I'm A

Celebrity Get Me Out Of Here. She didn't know exactly who he was, but she loved his dad and wanted a selfie. There was a photo of that which made the papers. Hers was the sole smile I saw that day.

The atmosphere was tense and unpleasant. Furious and sullen. Myself and two nurses were trying to see patients whilst hiding in rooms so we wouldn't meet him by accident. I could feel my ability to safely see extremely unwell patients was slipping - both by the physical space invaded, the wet painted walls, his enormous entourage, but also at the stress of our hospital being visited by the very people who had caused us such damage.

It was like being visited at home by your abusive boyfriend, asking 'what can I do to help?'

A number of people, staff and patients, were hanging around the entrance to see him arrive, but he was brought in quietly through a side door. He did not meet anyone other than people who had been seen by his team first.

There were some boos, and some people turned their backs. One member of staff dropped her glasses on the floor to avoid shaking his hand. Every patient I saw that day told me to keep him away from them. 'I'd give him a slap'. 'Kick him out the hospital!' Showing me texts from their relatives, after they'd told them he was here: 'Tell him he's a c***'.

This is a northern Leave town.

Then there were staged photos. Someone prepared some tea, and it sat there until it was cold. Then Johnson pretended to make it and poured it out for the staff who were obliged to drink cold tea while they took photos of Johnson serving them.

There were two very large men in scrubs who no-one had seen before, standing around cross-armed. One of the nurses asked who they were. 'We are anaesthetists'. I don't know. Maybe they were anaesthetists we'd never met before. I'd have asked for an ID badge if I'd seen them.

The hospital has been asking for funding to move one ward to a better location for over 5 years. This has been constantly refused by the Conservative government. On this day, it was granted. More photos.

It was a busy shift. A&E ran out of beds, as usual, and I dash past sick 90-year-olds waiting on trolleys in corridors on my way to resus to see the sickest. It's not yet winter, but in the NHS, it's always winter now.

He left eventually, with all his suited sycophants, and we tried to pick up the pieces of the shift. Some staff almost too angry to work. I recall the impotent shaking fury of a friend of mine, a nurse, with white paint on his arm where he'd accidentally knocked a freshly painted wall. Sick patients hadn't properly been reviewed with the distraction, and the numbers from A&E were piling in. I had a blinding headache and felt rattled. It was probably midday the next day before flow calmed a bit. I worked 12 hours that day and the next and the next. A nearby hospital went on divert on one of those days - too overwhelmed to be able to take new patients, so they sent them to us. Again the rammed corridors of the sick and the old, left in corridors when we don't even have bed space to see them in. The queueing ambulances outside waiting for someone free to hand over to. Hospitals on divert has happened with terrible frequency over recent years in the winter and is always very unsafe. It is not typical for November.

The chief executive apologised to me for how hard the day had been and acknowledged our fury but said the important thing was they'd been allowed their funding, after all this time. I said, 'thankyou for the crumbs'. He said, 'that's electioneering'.

There was some talk of voting afterwards and making sure everyone was registered to vote. What else can we do?

I have been a doctor for 9 years. Almost every doctor I know has an exit plan. So many have already gone. Without hope that things are going to change, I don't know how many more NHS winters I've got left in me.

Just in case you were wondering, the reason the account is anonymous is this. Remember those gagging orders on charities who work with the disabled and the poor I mentioned in the first chapter? Now NHS staff, of all people, are being gagged too. Chilling, authoritarian stuff straight out of a Banana Republic.

Beyond that: where in the mainstream media have you seen an account like that? Which lays bare the reality faced by doctors, nurses, staff and patients in a chronically under-funded, overwhelmed NHS: already at breaking point before we've even reached winter? Whose disgracefully, dangerously over-worked staff are treated as props by a prime minister who couldn't care less about the reality of their lives; only for a photo op? Every journalist and photographer who saw what was going on but played Johnson's pathetic game instead is complicit. *Do you want to live in a country like this?*

Nor is the above even an isolated case. Watch this video for the story of Johnson's visit to a different hospital. Would that the UK's journalists had the courage, integrity and compassion of this brilliant young woman. She has more of it in one fingernail than the prime minister does in his whole body.

Let's return, finally, to that contemptible BBC explanation which Oborne exposed. What is it that actually undermines trust in British politics? It's not just when politicians lie to the public on a continual basis; but when journalists, whose job is to expose these lies, become government propagandists instead. This results in an almost entirely ill-informed electorate voting against their own interests, to make themselves poorer and wreck Britain's global reputation... all because of the lies they are told day after day after day. Lies which, in many cases, *kill* ordinary people for the crime of their being sick, disabled, unemployed, poor, or a refugee.

The corporate-owned (print and social) media; the public (in practice, state) media; the economic system; the electoral system; the opinion pollsters; corrupt, self-serving MPs; the Conservative Party. All in it together; all out to screw the people of the UK for every last thing they have. And that, dear reader, is how Britain lost the plot.

CONCLUSION: CAN BRITAIN BE SAVED?
YES - BUT ONLY WITH YOUR HELP

'They're going to tell you that everything in this manifesto is impossible. That it's too much for you. Because they do not want real change in this country. Why would they? The system is working just fine for them. It's rigged *in their favour' - Jeremy Corbyn*

Any Jew speaking up in support of Corbyn and Labour is, to put it mildly, going to be criticised in the current lunatic climate. So: what are my motives in writing this book? I'm not some neutral bystander here. I'd like to hope I'm objective, but I'm a very long way from neutral.

In Britain, right now, while the narrative is all about Corbyn this, Corbyn that, a racist government led by a racist prime minister (whose predecessor was also a racist prime minister) continues to do the most horrendous things. When Afghan refugees, with no support, no help, are deported back to a place they've barely even known - where they are shunned by the locals, kidnapped by the Taliban, raped and/or murdered, that is racism of the most abhorrent form. When Nigerian refugee girls, with no support, no help, are deported back to a place many of them have barely even known - where they are also shunned by the locals, and many are forced into sex trafficking, that is also racism of the most abhorrent form.

When EU citizens living in Britain are treated not as people, but as pawns, by the British government, that is racist. When British-born nurses with no criminal record are deported, that is racist. When British subjects - British subjects! - are deported, and the government doesn't even acknowledge it until exposed by the press, that is profoundly, horrendously racist.

The minister responsible for that disgrace? You might have heard of her. Goes by the name of May. Her punishment was to be promoted to 10 Downing Street. The minister responsible when that disgrace was exposed? First, she tried to hide how many had been affected, then misled Parliament; then, after resigning, was promoted straight back to Cabinet only months later, to the sound of rejoicing by those wonderful centrists I referred to earlier. And lest we forget, she's both a tax dodger, and gets her own electoral opponent censored at hustings.

As for May, PM until only very recently: this was the woman behind the Go Home vans which disgraced the UK. This was the woman who gave one of the darkest, most racially charged speeches ever heard by a British politician, at the 2015 Conservative Party Conference. This was the woman who called 48% of the population 'citizens of nowhere'. And this was the woman who, after the country split 52-48 (which in practice means, 'we don't know'), with Leavers voting for all sorts of reasons, decided that only one thing mattered: freedom of movement.

It is not racist to support freedom of movement ending. There are many understandable, legitimate reasons for doing so. But it surely is racist to obsess with this one issue to such an extraordinary extent that it has imperilled Britain's entire future. All the UK's difficulties in getting a good deal have been based around red lines rendered wholly undeliverable by that obsession, and its government's continued intransigence.

Tell me: what exactly has Jeremy Corbyn ever said or done which compares in any way with any of the above? Who, exactly, have died as a result of his decisions? Yet *he*'s the danger to Britain?!

Not only that: but the very thing which led to Windrush was the 2014 Immigration Bill. Corbyn, John McDonnell and Diane Abbott were among just eighteen MPs who opposed it. Most didn't give it the remotest thought; while Yvette Cooper, for example, thought the Bill contained 'some sensible ideas'.

This wretched Tory government, moreover, isn't just racist. It isn't just cruel. It is wicked and pernicious. At least 130,000 people have died because of austerity. Homelessness is at such horrendous levels, even the US media has remarked on it on shock. Child poverty is set to reach a disgusting 37% by 2022: a figure which should shame us all. Foodbanks aren't just proliferating at an incredible rate. They're even found in schools. And in Britain, one of the richest countries in the world, baby foodbanks are opening as well. *Baby foodbanks*; just think about that for a moment and ask yourself what kind of dystopia this country has become.

74% of PIP and 72% of ESA cases are won on appeal; in other words, the government, condemned by the UN for both austerity and its treatment of the disabled, is denying untold numbers their basic human rights. As those appeals take so long to be heard, many die before they are. Wages haven't merely stagnated for over a decade; they're still below 2008 levels: with the average worker earning fully a third less than 11 years ago. Starving schoolchildren scavenge through bins for food, while young women sleep in them.

Corbyn? He wants to change all of this (watch this video: it will appal you). If he wins the election, he *will* change all of this, and give the UK its dignity, its heart, its compassion, its basic decency back. Yet *he's* the danger?! Are these people living on the same planet? If this campaign works, the suffering of so many millions will get far worse than it already is. Horrendous numbers of people can barely feed themselves or their kids right now. Must they suffer even more based on an almost entirely fabricated witch hunt?

A witch hunt which has been so malicious, so hysterical, so continually based on lies, that it's inevitably left me questioning the motives of those behind it. Nobody anywhere lies so relentlessly and so recklessly without there being some reason. What do these people have to hide?

Corbyn's such a humane man that if elected, I doubt he'll even bother to find out. But consider this. In 2016, the planet's leading expert on the mafia, no less, described Britain as 'the most corrupt country in the world'. Through its offshore territories (including the British Virgin Islands, Cayman Islands, Bermuda and Montserrat), Jersey, and the City of London, Britain is the de facto global leader in tax avoidance. So when someone comes along who'll clean this cesspit up with soap, water (state-owned, of course) and a wire brush, the heavy artillery is deployed against him like never before. How many of those involved in smearing him daily might be caught up in such schemes?

When a publicly funded broadcaster systematically refuses to discuss or engage with potential criminality surrounding a referendum, the consequences of which were generational; has even denied Vote Leave broke electoral law, when it's been found guilty of doing just that; and instead trumpets a prime minister who refuses to public a report on Russian interference in our democracy, there's something wrong here. Very wrong.

When a brilliant journalist writes a comprehensive report detailing the corruption of the media, yet almost no-one will even publish it, there's something very wrong there too. As, of course, there's been with everything else I've detailed in this book: from austerity to antisemitism to the BBC to Brexit. To say that something doesn't smell right here is the understatement of the century.

Corbyn, meanwhile, has been scapegoated and assailed in a manner I have never seen in any democracy anywhere. Scapegoated on Brexit. Scapegoated for MPs opposed to him from the very start of his leadership having left. I must've missed John Major encountering similar treatment when rebel Tories held his government to ransom. They, not him, were deservedly blamed most of the time.

Scapegoated for not waving a magic wand and changing the parliamentary arithmetic out of nothing. Scapegoated for not having a 'credible plan' for Brexit, despite Donald Tusk himself saying the EU could work with it. For the best part of two years, he was scapegoated for there not having been a second EU referendum; then when Labour guaranteed it, scapegoated again for not going even further and descending into narrow partisanship, rather than high-minded statesmanship.

Scapegoated for not having won the 2017 election... despite having inherited a bankrupt party without a clue, which had lost all sense of anything it stood for; then spending the next 21 months being constantly undermined by his Parliamentary Party, which had been completely wrong in all its analysis: above all, its ridiculous belief that under Ed Miliband, Labour had become 'too left-wing'. Scapegoated, for that matter, for not having won an election which Labour started 20 points behind, which May called for the express purpose of crushing Labour and Remain forever; yet ended in a hung Parliament.

Scapegoated for not having made greater inroads in Scotland; despite all the damage there having been done by New Labour's arrogance and complacency. Labour's image remains dirt to many Scots. It'll take a generation to undo that.

Scapegoated for opening up party democracy. Scapegoated, too, by political illiterates who don't understand our archaic voting system, so think he can afford to throw working class Leave voters under a bus... when they voted Leave precisely because the system had abandoned them for decades.

Scapegoated for being a 'Marxist', 'Leninist', 'Trotskyist' or 'Stalinist' (what? All of them?!), by people in such a bubble that they cannot see the world changing all around them and do not care about skyrocketing poverty, inequality, homelessness, rent or house prices. Scapegoated for not being an autocrat then scapegoated for being one (even though he's the exact opposite of one). Scapegoated for being a 'terrible economic danger' despite standing on a platform of mainstream European social democracy.

Scapegoated as a 'liar' on Brexit despite the very manifesto he stood on in

2017 supporting Brexit. Scapegoated for 'not getting his message across' when virtually the entire media is implacably opposed to him; and even the public broadcaster is wilfully, deliberately biased in its treatment of him and his party.

Scapegoated for random trolls anywhere in the world on the internet, who he apparently has the unique power to just magic away. Scapegoated for antisemitism despite his party taking more steps to combat it than any other party in British political history.

His policies haven't been scrutinised. They've been caricatured, by a media whose only interest lies in ridiculing and excoriating him and his supporters. A media which could not care less about the cause of his rise: the sheer perniciousness of neoliberalism and austerity. The failure of our entire economic system.

Even his personality and appearance are scapegoated. His raincoat. His glasses. His beard. His mild manner. His refusal to speak in soundbites and clichés at Prime Minister's Questions.

All this, at a time the public is sick to the back teeth of oily, slick-haired chancers who speak with forked tongue, then sell them all down the river the moment they get into power. 'Power', please note; not 'office'. I could hardly blame you if you've forgotten; but our leaders are supposed to be our democratic *servants*.

Corbyn is. Corbyn understands that perfectly. That's why his expense claims were so low, at a time so many of his parliamentary colleagues were bringing Westminster into disrepute. The true test of someone's character is what they do when no-one's watching; Corbyn passes that test with flying colours. It's also why he's taken a neutral position on Brexit: he will serve the people and do as they decide.

The bottom line is this. He cannot be both 'useless' and magically able to solve all our ills - or else - at the same time. Yet the truth is: he's inflicted more defeats on the government than the opposition to Major, Blair, Brown and Cameron combined. The truth is: he oversaw the largest rise in Labour's share of the vote since 1945: despite standing on a platform which the media and even his own Parliamentary Party insisted would destroy Labour forever.

The truth is: he saved Labour from a quite hideous post-2015 fate: bankrupt, bereft, clueless, hemmed in from all sides. The truth is: he, personally, has given so much hope to so many millions who were ignored, shut out and walked all over for decades on end.

Here's the thing about much of the left. Many of us have known the kind of adversity which our political opponents never have. That adversity, that - in many of our cases, trauma - is why we reach out and empathise with those who've experienced similarly awful things. It's why we see symptoms, not causes; and why so many of us are in caring professions, while some on the right disappear off to enrich themselves and give so little back (including, in many cases, even taxes: which they dodge via their accountants and offshore havens).

And it's also why, when we see someone under such sustained, never-ending attack, all just for the crime of representing us, we stand by them. The more abuse Corbyn's received, the more steadfast our resolve has become. He's an underdog, like us; he wants to help others, like us. And more than that: the unprecedented nature of this onslaught can mean only one thing. Much of the British establishment is up to its neck in cronyism, corruption and who knows what else, and is terrified of what might emerge under a government led by him.

That doesn't make us a 'cult'. Thanks to Corbyn, Labour is the largest mass movement in Western Europe: which 13 million people voted for in 2017. Are they all part of a 'cult' too? It merely makes us people who are appalled by what's become of the country we all love; and want everyone to have the chance to fulfil their potential and lead enriched, happy, even joyful lives. Because that's something that everyone deserves.

◆ ◆ ◆

Yet I'm not just writing this to preach to the converted. Far from it. I've written about working class Tory voters before; I entirely understand (and in many ways, completely agree with) the sense of alienation which so many felt for so long towards a smug London elite which talked at and down to them, always acted like it knew better; yet had no idea whatsoever about the often grim reality of their lives. Probably the biggest reason I voted for Corbyn to become Labour leader in the first place was because I was desperate for someone to reach out and listen to those many millions of lost voters, cast aside by a rotten to the core political, economic and electoral system.

Many of those voters, and enormous numbers of others besides, have had it banged into their heads from morning 'til night each and every day since 1979 that 'socialism doesn't work' or 'there'll be bin bags and coffins in the street again like in the Winter of Discontent'. Those constant messages are incredibly effective: mind-blowingly so at times. So much so that it takes a real act of faith to step outside and see it for what it is. Drivel.

The doctor you see or the hospital you rely on? That's socialism. The school you send your kids to, which equips them with the academic and life skills needed for their futures? That's socialism. The police who keep you safe, the paramedics who tend to you in an emergency, the fire services who risk their lives to save others? That's socialism. The roads you drive on or walk across every day, which enable goods to be moved, shops to open, and keep the economy running? That's socialism too.

Yet despite all this - despite nobody being able to achieve a damn thing without socialism - the idea that 'it doesn't work' is incredibly pervasive. How do I know that? Because it's what I used to believe too.

When my best friend complained to me about Blair's government during his time, I replied: 'This is the best government you'll ever know. The reason is the electoral system'. I decried those who wanted Blair out and Gordon Brown in; I knew the latter would be a disastrous prime minister. Then I despaired when Ed, not David, became Labour leader... because I just didn't think the electorate would accept him. Which it didn't.

Throughout this time - almost, but not quite entirely because of FPTP - my perspective was always, 'we have to accept the least bad option, because the alternative is horrendous'. Those on the left who refused to vote Labour drove me crazy: because it handed the UK to the Tories on a plate. Hence my complete disdain for Russell Brand when, in 2015, he advised young people not to vote. This would only make things worse; far worse. But then came the 2015 Labour leadership election.

I started out in that election thinking 'anyone but Kendall'. I finished it voting for Corbyn, the only grown-up in the room. But I didn't do so without a sea of doubts. I couldn't see the Parliamentary Party wearing it for a moment (which indeed it didn't); I doubted the effectiveness of what Corbyn was offering too. I was still trapped in the old ways of thinking: 'This won't work. This *can't* work. Young people won't vote. New voters won't vote'.

So much so that I spent a huge chunk of 2016 and early 2017 among many millions of others wondering who on Earth I'd be voting for at the next election. 'I'd rather be rogered to death with a red hot poker than ever vote Tory; I'll never forgive the Lib Dems for austerity...'. But Labour, miles behind an appalling government, seemed like such a shambles. Until, that is,

May 2017.

That was when I completed a very slow, very gradual, piecemeal process. When I finally crossed the rubicon and made that leap of faith. Politically, I've never felt more at home since. That campaign inspired me like I'd never been inspired before. Even though I'd always voted anti-Tory, always known who the political enemy were, never with a genuine leftie had I made the emotional leap to 'yes, he can! Yes, we can!' until then.

The brainwashing I mentioned above had affected me too, in other words. So much that is wrong in society owes to conditioning. Men conditioned to behave in a certain way and women likewise. Women conditioned to expect men to behave in a certain way and men likewise. This is true in politics too; massively so, in fact. The last 40 years have conditioned so many to expect:

'Strong leadership' and 'charisma' (meaning, in practice, horribly divisive leadership, ruinous policy and bullshit dressed up as soundbites).

Nothing radical to ever really change for the better.

Economically, that There Is No Alternative.

But of course there's an alternative; a very clear one. And unlike in the past, when just about enough people were doing just about well enough for the status quo to obtain, that's not remotely the case now. The radical option is the only sensible one.

Even the Financial Times has been quite warm towards Corbyn for a while now, and there's a reason for that. Tory Brexit is terrible for business, let alone anyone else; it's economic illiteracy on steroids. Then there's the climate catastrophe, which demands immediate, drastic action. The looming timebomb of a whole generation reaching retirement with no assets, meaning they'd all need housing benefit just to survive. The whole supply side of the economy having been wrecked by Slasher Osborne. The NHS heading towards meltdown. And a whole country which had been failed so much by everyone for decades, it voted itself poorer in the ultimate cry for help.

Cries for help aren't responded to effectively with 'there there, we'll just tinker with a few things around the edges, that'll make everything fine'. Quite the reverse: for there are no 'moderate' or 'centrist' solutions to challenges of this scope and magnitude. None whatsoever. In fact, to put it another way: the only genuinely moderate solution is offered by Corbyn. If you want to know where the mythical 'centre ground' really is, he's standing on it. With mainstream solutions which only seem 'radical' to Britons because of the last four decades of mostly the same old thing.

The Tories, by contrast, once renowned for supposed economic competence, are extremists. Vandals. Happy to wreck the whole country just so a few at the very top can get even richer, while everyone else suffers even more.

When the public got to know Corbyn during the 2017 campaign, they liked what they saw. They were really surprised. They'd been led to believe he was some dangerous, terrifying demagogue. They discovered he's a good, gentle, kind man. As soon as purdah was over and the mass media coverage resumed as before, back came the brainwashing day after day, so Labour's position fell back. But with your help, that can change very quickly.

In the televised debates he's been involved in so far, Corbyn has been calm, unruffled, statesmanlike, and positively brimming with ideas and vision. This is likely to have confused the heck out of plenty of viewers: some old bearded bloke in odd-looking specs who makes his own jam, tends to an allotment and wants to bring back socialism becoming PM? *Really?* The more they see of him over the next week or so, the more their assumptions will be challenged. Just like last time.

But then comes that vital leap of faith inside the polling booth. Then comes the chance to vote for real change. So many people have such difficulty letting go of the past; so many stick with the tried and failed. I understand those doubts completely: because that was me too. I've been there.

So let me show you a graph: which lays bare what neoliberalism is and what it does. A graph which proves beyond all doubt that the system is, as Corbyn says, rigged. Notice how the great reversal started under Thatcher and Reagan; and has reached preposterous proportions now. Growth has long been decoupled from living standards; the Tories are quite astonishingly bad at capitalism. That is why neither they or the Lib Dems will ever deliver anything meaningful for you, your family or your community. That is why we have the national disgrace of 43% of people not even earning £12,500/year, and therefore paying no income tax.

Britain is one of the richest countries in the world. If you ever wanted to know how Brexit happened, that statistic is why. Close to half the workforce earn less than about 1K a month. It's absurd, it's grotesque, it's shameful… and is why real change is so desperately

◆ ◆ ◆

Regarding that change: imagine someone came along with a prospectus which provided real solutions to many of the horrendous problems discussed in this book. That prospectus is called the Labour manifesto. Let's move through how it deals with plenty of the themes I've raised; themes which have brought an entire country to its' knees over a whole decade.

Brexit

Only Labour will give the people a final say via a second referendum with its deal and Remain on the ballot. The former will protect the NHS, jobs, workers' rights, environmental protections, manufacturing industry, consumers, farmers and fishing; and avoid a hard border in Ireland, thereby guaranteeing the Good Friday Agreement. It will immediately protect the rights of all EU citizens living in the UK (thereby ensuring reciprocal arrangements across the EU), and not treat immigration like some political football.

The referendum will be held within six months of Labour coming to power and be legally binding. The government will carry out what the people decide. Should Britain decide to Remain, Labour will pursue the correct approach of Remain and Reform within the EU. Back home, its stance is the only one which can enable the UK finally to begin to heal and move on.

Austerity

This would be a government which wouldn't just end austerity; it would rebuild Britain in a pretty similar way to how the greatest government in its history, the post-war Labour government, did. Meaning it would end the war on the most vulnerable. Given everything I set out in Chapter 1, Labour have come up with the ideal response. The DWP will be replaced with a Department for Social Security: there to help and support people, not punish, police and, in many cases, kill them. The catastrophic universal credit will be axed, and benefit sanctions suspended. The bedroom tax will be scrapped; the Local Housing Allowance increased so it's back in line with reality; and doesn't push anyone needing housing benefit into destitution.

Labour will ensure that disabled people will have the genuine chance to live fulfilling, independent lives. The work capability and PIP assessments, which dehumanise and even demonise claimants, will end; all assessments will be performed in-house, by proper professionals.

A humane immigration policy will be established, ending the hideous 'hostile environment'. The 2014 Immigration Act, which led directly to

Windrush, will be scrapped. As will the Tories' absurd minimum income requirements which have separated so many families from their loved ones. Under Labour, the UK will finally meet its international obligations on refugees and asylum too.

Public services

After a decade of scandalous neglect, these will be fully and properly prioritised. Public servants will receive an immediate 5% pay increase, followed by year-on-year rises above inflation. This follows a near decade-long pay freeze which has destroyed morale and left Britain's vital services at crisis levels.

There are 100,000 staff vacancies in NHS England, including a shortage of 43,000 nurses; and 15,000 fewer hospital beds in 2010. So expenditure across the NHS will be increased by 4.3% a year: which over time, will merely take health spending back up to the European average, where it was when Labour were last in power.

Any form of privatisation in the NHS will be reversed. Prescriptions will be free for all; as will annual dental check-ups. The Tories' appalling Health and Social Care Act, which has had disastrous consequences, will be repealed, and replaced with a comprehensive National Care Service, including free personal care for older people. Mental health funding will receive an enormous boost.

Sure Start centres, a thousand of which have been lost since 2010, will re-open. Paid maternity leave will be extended to 12 months; and within five years, all two, three and four-year-olds will be entitled to 30 hours' free pre-school education each week. Schools will have maximum class sizes of 30; and be funded by a fair formula which does not penalise poorer areas in any way.

Academies and free schools will be taken back into local authority ownership, ending the alarming marketisation of education. Curricula will be broadened to allow all children access to modern languages, arts and music, technical and engineering courses. Ofsted will be replaced; there will be free school meals for all primary school children. And lifelong learning will become far more accessible and affordable too.

At university level, tuition fees - which the vast majority of students are unable to repay at any point in their lives; yet saddle them with impossible levels of debt throughout - will be abolished, and maintenance grants restored.

At least 5,000 new firefighters will be recruited: heeding the lessons of Grenfell. Neighbourhood policing will be re-established, with thousands of frontline officers recruited. Youth services will be rebuilt, as will community outreach: with the police working hand in hand with mental health services, schools, drug rehabilitation programmes and other agencies.

A Royal Commission on substance misuse will also be established: which focuses on reducing harm, not criminalisation. There will be closer counter-terrorism coordination between the police and the security services. Prison officer numbers will be restored to 2010 levels. A long overdue public inquiry into Orgreave will finally happen.

The railways will, hallelujah, be renationalised after the disaster of privatisation: which has resulted in astronomically rising costs for commuters crammed into pathetically small trains, while shareholders have carved off gargantuan profits and even foreign governments have profiteered. Watch fares come down and roads become less congested as people return to using trains at last.

A National Refuge Fund will ensure the financial stability of rape crisis centres; a Commissioner for Violence against Women and Girls will be appointed. Royal Mail, a natural monopoly, will be brought back into public ownership. Local, community and youth services will be properly supported.

Housing

A £1bn Fire Safety Fund will do what the Tories have been entirely unwilling to: fit sprinklers and other fire safety measures in *all* high-rise council and housing association tower blocks; and enforce the replacement of Grenfell-style cladding on all high-rise homes and buildings. Mandatory building standards and guidance, inspected and enforced by fully trained Fire and Rescue safety officers, will be brought in too.

A new English Sovereign Land Trust will be given powers to buy land more cheaply for low cost housing. Developers will face 'use it or lose it' taxes on stalled developments. Brownfield sites will be prioritised, with the green belt protected. Tens of millions of existing homes will be upgraded to make them energy efficient; new homes will all be expected to be carbon neutral.

More than a million new homes will be built, with social housing at its heart. The right to buy social housing will end; but many low-cost homes will be reserved for first time buyers in every area. Overseas companies buying housing will face a levy. Rents will capped by inflation. Open-ended tenancies will stop unfair evictions. Every property will be required to meet minimum standards; landlords will no longer be able to discriminate based on someone's immigration status or if they're in receipt of housing benefit.

£1bn a year will be earmarked for local councils' homelessness services; hostels will be expanded and upgraded; 8,000 additional homes for people with a history of rough sleeping will be made available. There will be a national levy on second homes used as holiday homes: so those who've done well from the housing market pay a bit more to help those with no home at all. Given this, Labour believes it will end rough sleeping within 5 years.

Green New Deal

This, the central theme running throughout the manifesto, is how this can all be paid for. At last, at last: a major political party in the developed world has pledged a green industrial revolution: almost 250 years since Britain led the world in transforming itself into an enormously strong economy. There are only 11 years remaining to prevent catastrophic climate change: so Labour, with the vision and the boldness to re-imagine the whole economy, will create a million jobs which will transform energy, industry, transport, agriculture and buildings.

This is not just the right thing to do - the urgent, *this must happen now, or else* thing to do - if the planet itself is to be saved; it will lead the world in finally giving our young people a real future, and completely revitalise all those communities which remain devastated by the demise of heavy industry. As with so many things in the manifesto, in other words, it combines the head and the heart. This is what's truly needed to provide sustainable, long-term growth.

Every penny spent by the Treasury will be compatible with the government's climate and environmental targets. A National Investment Bank, National and Green Transformation Funds will all be set up; with a key goal being to truly rebalance the economy across the whole country. Britain's energy and water utilities will be brought fully into public ownership, with an emphasis on democratic control.

Nearly 90% of electricity and 50% of heat will be delivered by renewable, low carbon sources by 2030. 7,000 offshore and 2,000 onshore wind turbines will be built, along with enough solar panels to cover 22,000 football pitches.

Taxes, wages, workers' rights, business, pensions

Tory cuts to corporation tax will be reversed; yet it will still be below 2010 levels and most countries in the Western world. The biggest crackdown on tax avoidance and evasion ever seen will stop offshore havens carving off the billions which should be spent on creating a thriving, prosperous Britain. Nobody earning £80,000 or below will pay a penny more in income tax - but the top 5% will, finally, pay their fair share. And quite rightly, there will be a windfall tax on oil companies.

Meanwhile, a *real* living wage of £10 per hour, not the Tories' fake 'living wage' (which was just the minimum wage with added marketing blurb to conceal its harshness), will be implemented for all workers aged 16 or over.

Workers will be given a stake in the companies they work for and the profits they help generate by requiring up to 10% of large companies to be owned collectively by employees.

Minimum standards on pay and hours will be established. Zero hours contracts will be banned; all workers will be given the right to flexible hours.

Paternity leave will rise from two to four weeks; bereavement leave, guaranteeing workers time off to grieve the loss of close family members or following a miscarriage, will be introduced. Unpaid internships will be banned; employers will be fined if the gender pay gap is not eradicated.

Companies will be expected and incentivised to prioritise long-term growth. Late payers, who cause misery to small businesses especially, will be banned from public procurement. Pension funds will be protected.

Free, full fibre broadband will be delivered to all by 2030. Very few initiatives could be better equipped to help close the North/South divide than this; because in an ever-changing, ever more competitive digital economy, businesses will not set up in the many areas of the UK, especially the more rural ones, where the internet isn't reliable. This will change that completely.

For the record, Uruguay has state-owned fibreoptic broadband. It's very fast, very reliable (much more so than I ever experienced in Britain) and very affordable. It also has 95% green energy: and since that was brought in, electricity bills have plummeted. If this small, middle-income country can do it, why in the world can't the UK?

A whole generation of women born in the 1950s, who have pursued the 'Back to 60' campaign because their pension ages were changed arbitrarily without proper notification, will be recompensed. Labour will legislate to ensure that accrued rights to the state pension can never be changed again.

Constitutional and political reform

The voting age will be reduced to 16: finally giving young people a proper say over their futures and their lives. Full voting rights will be given to all UK residents (including EU citizens outrageously denied the vote at the 2016 referendum). Automatic voter registration, the very opposite of the Tories' constant attempts to emulate the Republicans and suppress turnout, will be introduced; which can only be excellent news for democracy itself.

Labour will call a constitutional convention, led by a citizens' assembly. This will look at how power is distributed in the UK, how nations and regions can best relate to each other, and how a Labour government can best put power in the hands of everyone. Decision-making will be decentralised, and local government empowered. The goal is a fully devolved UK, in line with reality as we head into the 2020s; not an absurdly over-centralised system fit for the 1820s, but hardly now.

Other than a few very limited exemptions, MPs will be prevented from taking paid second jobs. Donations from tax avoiders or evaders will be banned. The rules governing corporate lobbying will be overhauled; and the Electoral Commission given real teeth. Freedom of information will be extended. Northern Ireland, Wales and Scotland will all receive desperately needed investment; in the latter case, £100bn over a decade.

Foreign policy

Human rights, international law and tackling climate change will be foundation stones. Every single recommendation from the Chilcot Report into the Iraq war will be implemented in full; while a War Powers Act will ensure that no prime minister will be able to bypass Parliament in committing military action ever again.

Arms sales to Saudi Arabia for use in Yemen, or to Israel for use against the Palestinians, will be immediately suspended. Britain's entire arms export regime will be subject to root and branch reform, with arms export controls implemented to the very highest, most exacting standards.

The people of the Chagos Islands and their descendants will be given the right to return to their home: from where, they were forcibly removed by the UK.

Labour will pursue a fully multilateral approach across all international organisations. Conflict resolution and peacebuilding will be its priority; the very opposite of that of so many British governments of recent decades.

Defence

Funding for UN peacekeeping operations will be increased. Contrary to what the media might have led you to believe, Britain's commitment to NATO and its European partners will be maintained. Trident will be renewed.

At least 2% of UK GDP will be spent on defence. Decent housing, good-quality schools for their children and proper pay will be ensured for all Britain's armed forces. Veterans - neglected and abandoned by the Tories, frequently to homelessness and mental illness - will have access to lifelong learning and training, housing, mental and physical health services. A lump sum of 50,000 will be paid to each surviving British nuclear test veteran, for the horrendous health problems they have suffered through radiation exposure.

Internationalism

Labour will properly utilise Britain's influence within the World Bank, International Monetary Fund and World Trade Organisation to transform the rules of the global economy. The Department for International Development (DFiD)'s aid budget will be at least 0.7% of UK GDP; a green investment bank will be established. Relationships with countries in the Global South will be reset, based on principles of redistribution and equality: including reducing poverty and inequality, and ensuring gender equality.

Fairer international tax rules which do not penalise poorer countries will be fought for. The Global South will be given help in building progressive tax systems, social safety nets and public services.

All aid spending and UK Finance Export support for fossil fuel production overseas will be stopped. Any trade deals conflicting with Labour's climate principles will be rejected. An aid-funded Food Sovereignty Fund will help small-scale farmers in the Global South gain access to land, seeds and finance; uphold indigenous peoples' rights to their land; and support sustainable local food and agriculture markets.

And all this is just a snapshot. There's more; lots more. Take a look yourself! You can find it here; along with a grey book which provides fully detailed costings of the entire programme; and a further document which explains Labour's review of corporate tax relief.

Taken together, this is the most holistic, fully joined-up programme for radical, positive, sustainable change I've ever seen from any major political party in the Western world. What's so impressive is the whole thing is so integrated: positive change in one area will beget positive change in another; growing the economy in one sector will mean the opportunity to do the same in another; and the interests of the people, both domestically and even around the world, are prioritised throughout.

If Labour are elected, will this manifesto solve all Britain's ills? No. But it'd make a gigantic leap towards doing so. This is a programme full of hope and aspiration, for a country in desperate need of both. And it also provides a timely reminder: this election is not a reality TV show. It's not the X-Factor or I'm a Celebrity. The people are supposed to vote for *policies* which can make their lives better... and Labour are brim full of those. So if you don't like Corbyn (and goodness knows, most people don't), why cut your nose off to spite your face and plunge your family, your country, into disaster just because of that?

The complete absence of governments and politicians who truly cared about the British public, and were only out for themselves instead, landed the UK in this gigantic mess to begin with. This manifesto represents comprehensive recognition of that; and not only provides a truly democratic solution to Brexit but tackles the *causes* of the Brexit vote: poverty, inequality, injustice, division, austerity and disgraceful lack of investment into so many communities up and down the country.

The opportunity for you and your family to transform your lives is right here. In my view, you'd be mad not to take it. Alternatively, you could vote Lib Dem to prop up the Tories (leading to more misery, more despair, and in all likelihood, a hard or No Deal Brexit); or in spite of everything you've read in this book, somehow convince yourself that Boris Johnson cares one iota about anyone other than himself, and vote both for No Deal and the NHS to be sold off to US profiteers.

There has never been a greater crossroads faced by Britain since the war. Real hope and a country at ease with itself again lies in one direction; ever-worsening division, poison, hatred and the most profound social and economic injustice lies down the other. On 12 December, that decision is yours.

You might be shocked having read what I've revealed in this book. You might think I'm crazy; you might well go into denial, a perfectly natural human reaction. That's why I've provided so many links and so many sources; unlike almost the entirety of our God-forsaken media, I believe in this really annoying thing called *evidence*. Besides, I was still in denial five years or so myself. A great pal of mine woke up to all this long before I did; and to my eternal embarrassment, I berated her for it! Lee, if you're reading this: you were right. You always are.

As we stand on the verge of the 2020s, my earnest hope is for this book merely to mark a historical record of the disastrous path taken by the United Kingdom over the last decade; and for the election to mark the End of an Error. My great fear is its many warnings will be ignored, and that things get worse. Far worse; unimaginably worse. And if you think that's hysterical: while self-praise is no praise, despite living thousands of miles away, I've been right far more often than not over recent years. Much though I wish it'd been otherwise.

Please don't let me end up being right again.

------

[1] For the definitive account of the Grenfell fire, see: A. O'Hagan (2018). The Tower. *London Review of Books*, 7 June. Online, available at: https://www.lrb.co.uk/v40/n11/andrew-ohagan/the-tower

[2] J. Chait (2007). *The Big Con: The true story of how Washington got hoodwinked and hijacked by crackpot economics*. Houghton Mifflin Harcourt. Quoted in: J. Hari (2009). Why are we silent as Cameron preaches voodoo economics? *The Independent*, 27 May. Online, archived at: https://web.archive.org/web/20090528220922/http://www.independent.co.uk/opinion/commentators/joh hari/johann-hari-why-are-we-silent-as-cameron-preaches-voodoo-economics-1691107.html

[3] Her recent work on the financialisation of the global economy is highly recommended. G. Blakeley (2019). *Stolen: How to save the world from financialisation*. Repeater Books.

[4] His recent work is a fascinating, visionary view of a totally different, hugely exciting future. A. Bastani (2019). *Fully Automated Luxury Communism: A manifesto*. Verso Books.

[5] Jones' *The Establishment - and how they get away with it* (Allen Lane, 2014) was probably the greatest political book of the decade. There is no finer campaigning journalist anywhere on the British left.